More Praise for
Social Change Anytime Everywhere

"The pervasive nature of the Internet makes action a possibility anywhere, from the streets and homes in your nearest city to the tractors and woods of rural life. *Social Change Anytime Everywhere* authors Allyson Kapin ~~and Amy Sample~~ Ward offer a needed new look at how mobility and social tools ~~...~~ ness of change."

—Geoff Livingston, author, public speak~~...~~

"People are more impatient, busy, and distracted than ever, but they still want to help causes like yours—and they will, if you follow the advice Amy and Allyson are handing you in this book. No more excuses about how hard it is to get people's attention these days. You have the manual now. Read it, and go for it!"

—Kivi Leroux Miller, president, NonprofitMarketingGuide.com; author,
*The Nonprofit Marketing Guide: High-Impact,
Low-Cost Ways to Build Support for Your Good Cause*

"Social technologies change not just how we market our programs and services, but how we manage and lead our organizations, and how we build our communities and create movements. Understanding the multichannel landscape is more important than ever before, as the pace of change is growing exponentially. Pay attention to the lessons in this book and build the long term capacity for harnessing these powerful forces for *your* social good efforts."

—Maddie Grant, social strategist; coauthor,
Open Community and *Humanize: How People-Centric
Organizations Succeed in a Social World*

"It's time to move from using social media 'because everyone else is' to defining a strategy that ties social media to your organization's goals. *Social Change Anytime Everywhere* will help organizations use social media smarter and in a more customer-centric fashion, regardless of their size or resource constraints."

—Carie Lewis, director of Emerging Media,
Humane Society of the United States

SOCIAL CHANGE ANYTIME EVERYWHERE

How to Implement Online Multichannel Strategies to Spark Advocacy, Raise Money, and Engage Your Community

SOCIAL CHANGE ANYTIME EVERY WHERE

Allyson Kapin
Amy Sample Ward

JOSSEY-BASS
A Wiley Imprint
www.josseybass.com

S

Cover image: ©Stockbyte/Getty

Cover design: Jeff Puda

Library of Congress Cataloging-in-Publication Data

Kapin, Allyson, 1974–
    Social change anytime everywhere: how to implement online multichannel strategies to spark advocacy, raise money, and engage your community / Allyson Kapin, Amy Sample Ward.
        p.   cm.
    Includes bibliographical references and index.
    ISBN 978-1-118-28833-7 (pbk.); ISBN 978-1-118-33379-2 (ebk.); ISBN 978-1-118-33157-6 (ebk.); ISBN 978-1-118-33491-1 (ebk.)
        1. Nonprofit organizations.   2. Social media.   3. Social change.   I. Ward, Amy Sample, 1982–
II. Title.
    HD62.6.K37   2013
    659.2'8802854678—dc23

                                                                                            2012039944

Printed in the United States of America

FIRST EDITION
PB Printing   10 9 8 7 6 5 4 3 2 1

CONTENTS

FIGURES AND TABLES

FIGURES

TABLES

FOREWORD

Folks, the Internet and social media are a really big deal for nonprofits. I'm constantly communicating and working with organizations and people who are doing real important work online.

Problem is that many nonprofits don't spend enough time using social media, online channels, and mobile to connect with their supporters (and other organizations) and engage them wherever they are online. That's why this book, *Social Change Anytime Everywhere*, is a big deal. Allyson Kapin and Amy Sample Ward have been working with nonprofits on their online strategy for over 10 years—they're the real deal.

My own contribution to the Internet was based on an idea about giving back, and then listening to feedback, and doing something about it. It's based on software I wrote for craigslist between 1995 and 1999, though the team has taken it far beyond that. It worked out okay, and has helped maybe a hundred million people, or more, mostly Americans.

These days, I spend my time running craigconnects, the initiative started in 2011 designed to use tech to give the voiceless a real voice, and the powerless real power. My team (which includes Allyson) and I work with good organizations registering folks to vote, community building, fact-checking, fighting for open and accountable government, using technology for social good, and working on military families' and veterans' issues.

We work with these orgs to really help promote their social media and make sure they're working with people who have the same mission. Social media can really help make those connections, and this book is a great guide to start opening those lines of communication and do some good work with advocacy and fundraising.

You'll also find me communicating with folks frequently across platforms and devices. I use my smartphone and tablet, and other tools like Hootsuite, to post updates to Facebook, Twitter, Instagram, and Pinterest. Add a camera, and I'm frequently updating social media with the wildlife that surrounds my home.

The deal is, while I'm really just a regular guy who thinks that the Internet, good customer service, and doing good stuff is really important, I've learned a lot launching craigconnects and craigslist. At craigconnects we make sure to follow up when folks ask for our help and ensure that our content's easily shareable on the channels folks prefer. It really is important for social change to be able to happen anytime, everywhere.

Nonprofits, like you, can use platforms like Facebook to exert influence by building a network and getting your supporters to share your nonprofit issue via your social networks. Allyson, Amy, and I are really talking about your "social graph," that is, your organization's friends, followers or subscribers, and then, their friends and subscribers.

That means that we put news and announcements and other links, into bite-sized pieces that are easily shared across different sites, or we put information into easy-to-understand graphics (like infographics) that organizations and individuals can reuse and repost. That often means sharing links to posts right into Facebook, Twitter, Google+, and/or LinkedIn.

In terms of my coverage, you'll see me either pushing the good work of people who get stuff done, or indulging my sense of humor. (Note to self: I'm not as funny as I think I am.)

I'm excited to see *Social Change Anytime Everywhere* come out now, as social media and good customer service is such a big deal. I've seen the difference that strategy makes in an organization when an executive director, a communications manager, and a community organizer truly get social media, and the fact that it takes all channels to make real, lasting changes.

Change is one thing that inspired me to launch craigconnects, and I know that *Social Change Anytime Everywhere* will help organizations, regardless of size or issue, engage people across multiple channels.

A nerd's gotta do what a nerd's gotta do.

Craig Newmark
Founder of craigslist and craigconnects.org

Just 35 seconds after the 2010 earthquake in Haiti began, 316,000 people were dead, 300,000 more were injured, and more than one million were displaced. As we witnessed one of the worst natural disasters in modern times, nonprofits such as Doctors Without Borders, Oxfam, American Jewish World Service, and the American Red Cross rushed to the aid of people in Haiti and began coordinating large-scale advocacy, fundraising, and community response through multichannel campaigns.

The U.S. Fund for UNICEF raised $3 million from donors within the first hour after the earthquake struck.[1] In that same time, the American Red Cross raised more than $3 million just through mobile donations.[2] Apple helped by creating a page in its iTunes Store that asked people to donate up to $50. Altogether, organizations raised $4.6 billion in the days following the disaster, according to the United Nations.[3]

Nonprofits raised more than $50 million of this sum through mobile fundraising for the first time in the United States by $5 and $10 donations made via text message.[4] And it was the third time in history (after Hurricane Katrina and the South Asian Tsunami) that the nonprofit community used integrated messaging and multichannel strategies to engage people on a massive scale, not just to raise record-breaking funds, but also to share personal stories, messages, photos, and videos from the ground and to coordinate relief efforts.

How did they engage people so quickly and raise so much money? First responders, nonprofit staff, and the media already on the ground in Haiti weren't taking photos or writing updates about Haiti's toppled buildings, torn-up streets, affected families, only for the benefit of staff back in the office. They were capturing all of these stories to engage with people watching in disbelief from around the world. The content they produced was easily shared by the organizations and then reshared by supporters via email, social media, texting, and word of mouth.

Several nonprofit bloggers, social media influencers, and celebrities who had large followings also pitched in to direct people to Haiti relief campaigns online, especially ones raising money for critical supplies such as food, bottled water, blankets, tents, and antibiotics. Some nonprofits and supporters posted the latest resources and news on their blogs and websites—how to locate family members, updates on damage, etc. Others pushed that information out to their networks.

These efforts required that nonprofits do a considerable amount of work and coordination, both internally and externally. Wendy Harman, director of social engagement for the American Red Cross (ARC) during the earthquake, knew that to make a real impact on the relief efforts she had to coordinate with different departments across the organization, including the communications, fundraising, and mobile team. She also recognized the importance of rallying the ARC community on social media to ensure that updates were posted and cross-posted frequently. She and the rest of the ARC social media team personally engaged in social media efforts to ensure that the right text-to-donate numbers, links to resources and assistance, and answers to common questions were answered promptly and correctly. Harman found every minute of those first 24 hours crucial to engaging the Red Cross community.

These multichannel strategies were successful because they focused on four key organizing principals:

- Share the emotional story about what's happening on the ground in real time.

- Identify and tell prospective donors and volunteers what is needed and how they can help immediately.

- Tell (or better, show) donors and volunteers the real impact that their money and time will have on the ground.

- Bring people together through the shared experience and the mission of the organization.

As we mentioned earlier, relief organizations used a mix of online channels to get the word out about the disaster and to mobilize prospective donors and volunteers. They used email and texting for fundraising appeals; social media to share the latest news, information, and how to donate money; blogs to share stories of people impacted by the disaster; and their own websites to pull the content together. They used these channels to ask for money, build community, and spur action by:

- Reporting on devastating conditions in Haiti after the earthquake
- Asking people in Haiti and around the world to share their personal stories, video footage, and photos
- Providing supporters with multiple ways to donate—online, mobile texting (Short Message Service, SMS), calling, and sending checks by snail mail
- Informing donors about how their dollars would be spent—on medical supplies, fixing broken water systems, providing nonperishable food, creating temporary housing, distributing hygiene kits, etc.
- Recruiting emergency aid volunteers
- Asking technologists to collaborate on building web and mobile applications that would map the relief efforts and quickly spread vital information to relief workers and first responders
- Sharing information about support services and news syndicates, and about Haiti and organizations working there before and after the earthquake
- Documenting the state of communities and infrastructure after the earthquake on photo-sharing sites such as Flickr and video-sharing sites such as YouTube and Vimeo

It's these moments when we realize that the Internet, social media, and mobile technology have evolved into some of the most effective tools to facilitate social change that the world has ever seen. Prior to their prominence, nonprofits faced a difficult challenge: time. Can you imagine how long it would have taken for the news of the Haiti earthquake—the true scale of it—to reach the rest of the world if it had happened even just 20 years earlier? It would have cost organizations so much more time, resources, and money to connect directly with people, gather and share stories and resources, mobilize action, and reach people anytime, everywhere.

The world witnessed powerful movements—civil rights, anti-apartheid, anti-nuclear proliferation, and others—effectively advancing social and political change long before the Internet. But the nature and immediacy of technology have changed how organizations operate and how they structure campaigns—and not just during natural disasters. Every nonprofit and social change maker now has the power to use multiple online and mobile channels to amplify their message, foster a community, support activism, and cultivate donations 24 hours a day.

But the power of these tools goes even further. Their real power comes from organizations using them to craft and implement multichannel strategies— that is, integrating messages and actions across platforms. These messages and actions reinforce each other and fuel both online and offline peer-to-peer connections that can power social change anytime, everywhere. That's how real change happens, and it is what inspired us to write this book.

WHO SHOULD READ THIS BOOK

Do your communications, fundraising, and grassroots teams work in silos? For example, when a critical campaign opportunity arises and you need to act on it immediately, is there a power struggle between departments about which email list an online fundraising appeal or an action alert goes to first? Is there a lack of coordination between departments during these important campaign moments, when time is of the essence and you must ensure that key messaging across multiple channels is succinct and optimized for each channel? Is it like pulling teeth to get a consensus between the web, outreach, and social media staff about what should be posted to your website, blog, Facebook page, or Twitter account, and when? And by the time all the internal politics have been worked out, do you miss major fundraising or advocacy opportunities across all of these channels, or both?

If you answered yes, you are not alone. We have worked with hundreds of organizations over the past decade and have witnessed these problems time and again at organizations large and small, experienced and inexperienced.

Social Change Anytime Everywhere is a practitioner's guide for nonprofit communications, marketing, fundraising, and social media staff who struggle with departmental politics and silos. It is for those who recognize that they need to be more nimble with their approach to building and mobilizing their communities—through multifaceted campaigns and by integrating online channels with offline tactics—if they want to be successful and make an impact on the ground. If you're ready for your organization to develop a shared vision and a plan to integrate multichannel strategies for communications, advocacy, fundraising, and outreach—to connect with constituents and engage new supporters online—then this book is for you.

Inside you will also find sections focused on tactics that drill down into how to achieve measureable results across multiple channels. Whether you're a communications manager, social media campaigner, development director, advocacy or community organizer, or web strategist, this book will provide you with all the tools you need to launch successful online multichannel campaigns to help you change the world.

WHAT DOES *ONLINE MULTICHANNEL* MEAN?

Social Change Anytime Everywhere is based on our personal experiences and research over a decade of working with and for many nonprofit organizations and social movements. Our work has involved using multichannel campaigns to deepen connections with constituents, move supporters up the ladder of engagement, and empower communities to take action both online and on the ground. But what exactly does *online multichannel* mean?

You may have heard the term *multichannel* in the context of advertising or fundraising, usually in reference to uniting an online channel (email, websites, social media, etc.) with an offline channel (direct mail, TV, telemarketing, etc.). An advertiser might use *multichannel* to refer to a coordinated campaign that integrates both TV and direct mail to promote a product. Or a fundraiser might use *multichannel* to refer to a campaign that syncs up a direct mail appeal with an email message or series. But in our work and in this book, *online multichannel* refers to strategies that operate across several online channels—namely email, websites, social media, and mobile.

Today, it's essential that nonprofits use multichannel strategies to integrate their communications and outreach efforts throughout their organization to reach goals and create greater impact. In this book, we focus on three core categories of communications and outreach: advocacy, fundraising, and community building. From your website to social media, email to mobile messages, online to offline, multichannel strategies require coordination and creative thinking across teams and departments, and a focus on the core of your work beyond any one specific call to action.

In the following chapters, we show you how you can create online multichannel strategies to meet your mission and campaign goals, and how other organizations are successfully integrating multichannel efforts into their work.

WHAT'S AHEAD IN THE BOOK

In Chapter One, we give you an overview of the multichannel technology landscape as it impacts organizations and your constituents. This includes a comprehensive data overview that we hope will serve as a resource for you and your staff—especially if you need to sell the importance of investing in these strategies to others in your organization.

Chapter Two outlines the five principles of operating in an anytime, everywhere world. These essential principles start with differentiating your community from the crowd and build toward creating a movement. We cover how to approach your work, as well as how you actually do it—both in strategic planning meetings and in your everyday work.

Chapters Three, Four, and Five address the planning and implementation of online multichannel strategies for advocacy, fundraising, and community building, respectively. These chapters constitute the meat (or for vegans, the protein) of the book. They provide examples and case studies to illustrate these strategies in action, and they cover both the specific techniques and the big picture directions for success.

Chapter Six gets down to what integrated multichannel campaigns look like in action with a close look at case studies from the National Wildlife Federation, Surfrider Foundation, and the Iraq and Afghanistan Veterans of America.

By Chapter Seven, you're ready to get started! We explain how to equip your organization and staff so that they're ready for anytime, everywhere advocacy, fundraising, and community building. Changing aspects of your organizational culture or staffing model may seem daunting, but we provide the guidance for getting started immediately.

And just in case some of your colleagues are resistant or nervous, or just aren't as excited and ready as you are about the enormous potential of these tools and strategies for your organization, Chapter Eight offers practical advice for easing the transition from being a reactive organization to a proactive one.

In the Conclusion of the book, we invite you to enter the next era of change making. We discuss disrupting the nonprofit sector and the importance of taking chances, learning from failure, iterating, and not giving up. We also share trends on the horizon so that you can prepare to seize forthcoming opportunities.

We hope that when you finish this book you will join us online at www.social changeanytime.com to continue learning, ask your questions, and share your own stories and examples of multichannel strategies that are helping your cause and your organization achieve real impact.

READING THIS BOOK

The book is filled with a lot of strategies and tactics for creating social change anytime, everywhere that you can utilize for your upcoming campaigns and across different online channels. If you are a small organization, pick two or three strategies to test from each chapter. Then analyze the results. If you are a mid-size or large organization you may be utilizing a few of these already, and we encourage you to test at least three new strategies listed in each chapter to see if it increases your ability to spark advocacy, raise money, and engage your community.

As you read the book, you will notice that some sections are highlighted in gray. These special resource sections include how-to notes, additional background or case study information, and tips for using the tools discussed in the chapter. If you initially want to bypass these sections and come back to them later, that's fine. We designed them so that they are easy to find, in case, for example, you need to find a passage during a meeting to share something important with your teammates!

We've also included many notes throughout the book. Sources for data or research, links to organizations or online tools, and even resources available for further reading and support are all documented in the Notes section. These additional resources are also available on the book's companion website at www.socialchange.com.

CONTINUING THE DISCUSSION—WHILE YOU'RE READING THE BOOK, AND LATER ON

We couldn't write a book about multichannel strategies without employing multiple channels for continuing the conversation and inviting you to connect and learn beyond the book that you're holding now. Please visit http://www.socialchangeanytime.com, where you'll find updated data and resources, as well as opportunities to engage and ask questions. We've designed the website to complement the material in the book and to help you put into practice the lessons and suggestions you're about to read.

ACKNOWLEDGMENTS

We are so thankful for our families and our husbands, Jared and Max, who supported us, made us dinner, listened to our brainstorms, and sometimes let us sleep in while we worked on this book. We couldn't have done it without them.

We also want to thank Jenifer Morgan, Ted Fickes, Clint Obrien, Avi Kaplan, Justyn Hintz, Holly Ross, Brian Reich, and Danielle Brigida for all of their insight and thoughtful feedback. Special thanks as well to our designer Spence Nelson for designing several of the graphics and infographics used in the book.

We would also like to thank the many inspiring nonprofit campaigners we interviewed for the book, as well as our peers in the community who provided incredible support throughout the process, including Frank Barry, Jill Foster, John Haydon, Wendy Harman, Kristin Johnson, Beth Kanter, Josh Kittner, Carie Lewis, Geoff Livingston, Alia Mckee, Stacey Monk, and PVSM.

Finally, we want to thank Google for inventing GChat—the only tool that kept us connected and writing away into the wee hours of the morning.

THE AUTHORS

Allyson Kapin has been named one of the Most Influential Women In Tech by Fast Company, one of the "Top Tech Titans" by the *Washingtonian*, and one of the top 30 women entrepreneurs to follow on Twitter by Forbes for her leadership role in nonprofit technology, online advocacy, fundraising, and social media.

As founding partner of the web agency Rad Campaign, she leads the firm's online strategy division. For over 15 years, Allyson has helped nonprofit organizations and political campaigns create dynamic and award-winning websites and online marketing and recruitment campaigns.

Allyson is an expert in the latest trends in mobile, social networking, blogging, online video, and other online tools and strategies and advises nonprofits on how to cost-effectively incorporate them into their Internet plans and online campaigns. Her campaigns have been recognized with several prestigious web awards and featured on several top media networks ranging from CNN to NPR and the Daily Show with Jon Stewart.

She has also been a featured speaker on web design, Internet marketing, and social media at national conferences such as the American Marketing Association's Nonprofit Marketing Conference, NTC, Personal Democracy Forum, SXSW, Vocus Users Conference, and more.

In 2007 Allyson founded Women Who Tech: A Telesummit for Women in Technology, working in the nonprofit and political campaign worlds. As the founder of Women Who Tech she champions women who are inspiring change and transforming technology. She also serves as an expert for news reporters who are writing about technology and social change.

Allyson sits on several Advisory Boards, including the Anita Borg Institute, the Green It Consortium, and the Planning Committee for NTEN's NTC conference.

Allyson also blogs for Fast Company and is the Blogger-in-Chief for one of the top-ranked nonprofit communications blogs: Care2's Frogloop. In 2010 she cofounded the Nonprofit 2.0 Unconference.

Amy Sample Ward is an author, speaker, and trainer who has spoken at conferences and worked with groups all over the world to help changemakers use technology to build community and make real change.

Amy's nonprofit technology blog and presentations have been highly ranked by groups including Alltop, List of Change, Slideshare, and various other industry leaders. She has previously been a "most-read blogger" for Stanford Social Innovation Review's opinion blog, and named on the list of 100 Most Powerful Women on Twitter by TwitterGrader.

She is the coauthor of *Social by Social: A Practical Guide to Using New Technologies for Social Impact*, written in 2009. With her coauthors, David Wilcox and Andy Gibson, she has worked with various community groups, voluntary sector organizations, and local governments throughout the UK on creating engaging, community-driven strategies, applications, and online networks.

Now based in New York, community continues to be a focal point of her work as she co-organizes the 501TechNYC group, bringing together nonprofit staff, technologists, activists, and interested community members each month to learn and share collaboratively. Amy also manages the #CommBuild community, which holds a weekly online chat around community building best practices, examples, and resources.

In addition to her blog and regular contributions to the Stanford Social Innovation Review, Amy continues to speak regularly around the United States and beyond, presenting at events like SXSW Interactive and the Nonprofit Technology Conference. She is a frequent keynoter and university guest lecturer, as well as a trainer working directly with organizations and communities.

As a leading voice in the nonprofit technology sector and an active community organizer, she's also the Membership Director at NTEN: The Nonprofit Technology Network.

SOCIAL CHANGE ANYTIME EVERYWHERE

Why Are Online and Mobile Channels So Important to Nonprofits Today?

chapter
ONE

When it comes to using social and mobile technology, size does not matter. Your organization might be a large foundation, association, or advocacy group. It might be a five-person think-tank. Or maybe it's an all-volunteer, neighborhood group. Regardless, you need to build strong relationships with your constituents, and you need to reach them wherever they are and at a moment's notice. To truly cultivate these relationships and to mobilize your base, you will need to expand your outreach to include multiple online channels and tools such as social media, email, and mobile. All of these platforms are experiencing explosive growth and will continue to gain momentum. No organization can continue to thrive unless they use these channels strategically.

Today, more people are online than ever before. And that number is increasing every single day. In the United States, 78% of the population (or more than 245 million people) use the Internet, according to ITU, the United Nations agency for information and communications.[5]

Quantcast, one of the biggest analytics companies measuring websites and social networks such as Facebook, YouTube, and Twitter, shows that social networks dominate the top five websites ranked by U.S. traffic. And there are 5.2 billion mobile accounts, meaning there are now almost five times as many mobile phone subscriptions as there are personal computers or landline phones.[6]

It's no coincidence that both prominent organizations such as the Humane Society of the United States and small grassroots groups such as Epic Change, a volunteer-led organization that raises funds to support localized projects such as building classrooms in Tanzania, have experienced significant growth and success using online and mobile channels. One secret to their success is that they recognized early the enormous growth of online channels, and they utilized these channels in tandem. Instead of solely focusing their energy on one offline channel, such as direct mail, to connect to new supporters and generate action, these organizations also leveraged online social networks such as Facebook and Twitter and blogging platforms such as Tumblr, and they fully embraced email and mobile communications. They found ways to coordinate and integrate all of these channels effectively into their advocacy, communications and outreach, and fundraising campaigns.

THE GROWTH OF SOCIAL NETWORKS

Americans spend about 25% of their time online on social networks, according to the Nielsen report "State of the Media: The Social Media Report."[7] They spend a roughly equal amount of their time reading blogs, of which there are more than 156 million.[8] Facebook and other social networks are so popular that Americans are spending even more time on them than Google.

The infographics that follow, Figures 1.1 and 1.2, show a snapshot of year-to-year growth in social media use from 2011 to 2012. Keep in mind that although the online multichannel landscape will continue to evolve, these channels are here to stay and will be effective organizing and fundraising tools, as well as complementary to your offline engagement, into the future.

WHO IS USING MOBILE?

We live in a mobile-dependent world: 83% of U.S. adults own mobile phones and three-quarters of these adults send and receive text messages on their phones, according to the Pew Research Center's Internet and American Life Project.[9]

Mobile usage has grown so much over the last five years that it's now one of the main channels that people use to communicate with their friends, colleagues, businesses, and favorite organizations. People are also using mobile devices to make purchases, donate money to their favorite organizations, play video games, post updates to social networks, upload and share photos, record and post videos, track and share their location, take online actions such as signing petitions, and so on. In 2011, 20% of all emails opened were accessed via a mobile device, according to a report by Knotice.[10] And only 3% of emails opened on a mobile device were later opened on a desktop computer, thus suggesting people's

Figure 1.1
Year-to-Year Growth in Social Media Use from 2011 to 2012

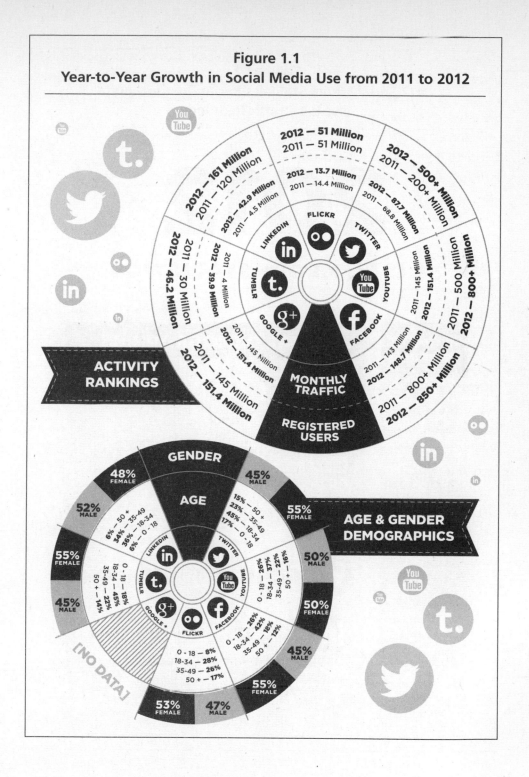

Figure 1.2
2012 Social Media Statistics Racial Demographics and U.S. Traffic Rankings

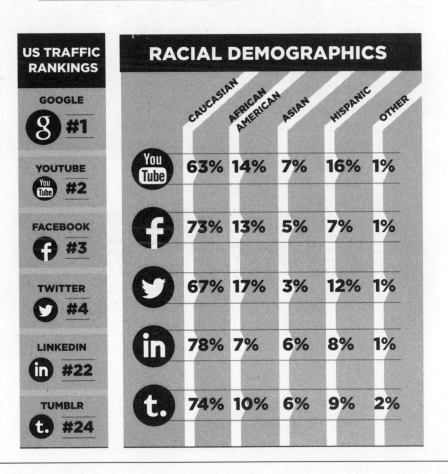

	CAUCASIAN	AFRICAN AMERICAN	ASIAN	HISPANIC	OTHER
YouTube	63%	14%	7%	16%	1%
Facebook	73%	13%	5%	7%	1%
Twitter	67%	17%	3%	12%	1%
LinkedIn	78%	7%	6%	8%	1%
Tumblr	74%	10%	6%	9%	2%

US TRAFFIC RANKINGS

GOOGLE	#1
YOUTUBE	#2
FACEBOOK	#3
TWITTER	#4
LINKEDIN	#22
TUMBLR	#24

Figure 1.3
2012 Mobile Use Statistics

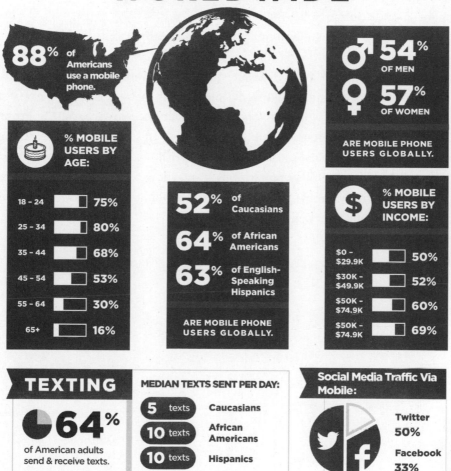

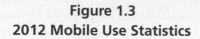

2012 MOBILE USE STATISTICS

THERE ARE
5.2 BILLION
MOBILE ACCOUNTS
WORLDWIDE

88% of Americans use a mobile phone.

♂ **54%** OF MEN

♀ **57%** OF WOMEN

ARE MOBILE PHONE USERS GLOBALLY.

% MOBILE USERS BY AGE:

18 – 24	75%
25 – 34	80%
35 – 44	68%
45 – 54	53%
55 – 64	30%
65+	16%

52% of Caucasians

64% of African Americans

63% of English-Speaking Hispanics

ARE MOBILE PHONE USERS GLOBALLY.

% MOBILE USERS BY INCOME:

$0 – $29.9K	50%
$30K – $49.9K	52%
$50K – $74.9K	60%
$50K – $74.9K	69%

TEXTING

64% of American adults send & receive texts.

MEDIAN TEXTS SENT PER DAY:

5 texts	Caucasians
10 texts	African Americans
10 texts	Hispanics

Social Media Traffic Via Mobile:

Twitter 50%

Facebook 33%

growing comfort level with mobile communication as an effective substitute for computer-based communications. Nonprofits can no longer afford *not* to have a mobile strategy. Check out the data in Figure 1.3 and you'll see why.

DON'T FORGET: OFFLINE COUNTS BIG TIME TOO!

A survey by Georgetown University's Center for Social Impact Communication and Ogilvy Public Relations Worldwide found that Generations Y and X think social networking sites such as Facebook "help increase visibility for causes and help them get the word out about causes more easily." The same study found that Generations X and Y also are "significantly more likely to report that they would support a cause online rather than offline."

Likewise, the same study found that 62% of Americans—nearly two-thirds of them—reported that being told *in person* is the way that they are typically informed of causes and social issues in which others want them to be involved.

The myriad technologies that we have now and that are emerging every day will never replace the work that organizations do face-to-face, on the ground. True multichannel strategies integrate online and offline opportunities to build community, raise financial support, and create real change. The following chapters are designed to highlight opportunities and showcase examples of successful multichannel strategies that leverage online and mobile strategies while continuing to build on offline action.

So let's begin!

chapter TWO

Guiding Principles for Anytime Everywhere

There are many ways to share your message with supporters, call a community to action, and ask for feedback or support that will ultimately help you spur social change. Organizational communications are increasingly personal and direct, thanks to social media platforms and the prevalence of public access points. Yet despite the increasing number of methods for reaching out to and communicating with your constituents, certain guiding principles remain the same. Like houses, there are many different architectural styles, but certain elements are critical to structure—no matter what, the walls must support the ceiling and the doors must align with their frames. Whether you have a modern brownstone, a farmhouse, or a large Colonial style home, there's a foundation under the floor, nails and screws joining pieces of wood, and insulation in the walls and ceiling.

The same is true for campaigns, appeals, and for building a movement. During our work with organizations of all sizes and missions, we've identified five principles as integral to a structurally sound campaign or movement. These five principles are the "make it or break it" checkpoints, regardless of whether you are a community group or enterprise-level organization, creating a political or advocacy campaign, or launching into short-term or year-round fundraising efforts.

1. Identify your community from the crowd

2. Focus on shared goals

3. Choose tools for discovery and distribution

4. Highlight personal stories

5. Build a movement

Keep these principles in mind as you develop your strategies and communications. In the preplanning stage, let these principles shape your decisions about audience, voice, and which platforms to use—they will help you and your colleagues navigate many conversations and add focus to your strategic planning.

You should also use these principles during the active phase of events, campaigns, and projects. As anyone who has ever sent out an email to more than one person or who has organized an event knows, your work only *increases* after you hit the send button. As the reach and traction of your message grows, you need to evaluate and evolve your work continually to ensure that you are still on target. You need to make changes to reflect any shifts in your community, goals, and accomplishments. These principles serve as reference points for that reevaluation of your work during the active phase, and also afterward.

Regardless of the channels you use or the goals you set, these five principles should influence the way you operate and contribute to the potential success of your endeavors. Let's look at each of the principles in detail.

PRINCIPLE 1. IDENTIFY YOUR COMMUNITY FROM THE CROWD

The words *community, network,* and *crowd* are often used interchangeably. They are not, however, interchangeable. These three words indicate very different segments of people, and you should use them to denote not just *whom* you engage and communicate with, but also *how* and *why*. You can see the three groups in Figure 2.1.

Your Community

The ring closest to your organization represents your community. This is made up of people you can contact directly. Their email addresses, phone numbers, or mailing addresses are in your database. They receive your email messages and appeals. Maybe they attend your offline events. There is nothing preventing you from communicating with them directly.

Your community members have opted in to engaging with you. That opt-in comes in various forms—for example, maybe they signed up on your website to receive email updates from you, "liked" your Facebook Page, or subscribed to your YouTube channel. If you buy a list (that is, you acquire new names and contact details from similar organizations or campaigns), those new "names" aren't part of your community until they confirm their participation or connection.

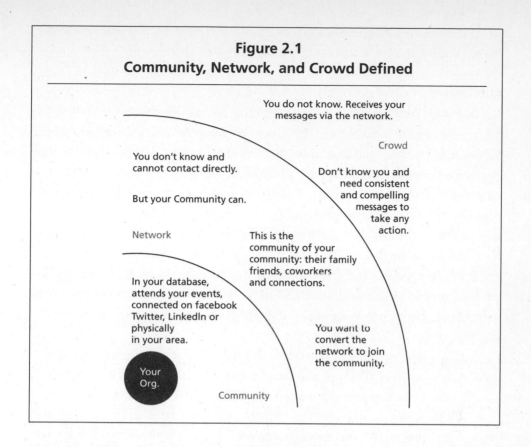

Figure 2.1
Community, Network, and Crowd Defined

You do not know. Receives your messages via the network.

Crowd

You don't know and cannot contact directly.

But your Community can.

Don't know you and need consistent and compelling messages to take any action.

Network

This is the community of your community: their family friends, coworkers and connections.

In your database, attends your events, connected on facebook Twitter, LinkedIn or physically in your area.

You want to convert the network to join the community.

Your Org.

Community

Your Network

The next ring represents the people who are just one step farther out from your organization: your network. You can make some educated guesses about the people in this category—they tend to be the family, friends, colleagues, and coworkers of the people in your community. Your messages, information, and updates reach your network through your community. Your community members are the messengers, not you. The community may share your links or posts via Facebook; they may let their friends and family know that they support you or donate to your campaigns. Maybe your organization creates and posts beautiful, compelling photographs that community members enjoy sharing across the web, or printing and posting in their office or home. Whatever the content or platform, your messages move through the community to the network. And when members in the network find a message interesting, exciting, or compelling enough to sign up for your email list, like it on Facebook, retweet it on Twitter, or subscribe to your organization's blog, they convert themselves from a member of the network to a member of your community.

The Crowd

The last ring, farthest out from your organization, represents the crowd. In the most general and literal sense, the crowd is everyone else—the whole world. However, in planning and evaluation, the crowd comprises all the people we hope to reach who aren't connected to us through the network. The way we communicate when we speak to the crowd is very different from the way we speak to the community—we can't be as personal and are guessing at how to make our message relevant. The crowd is the biggest segment, but that doesn't mean it is the most influential or most important of our multichannel strategies. Information about online networks and the web shows that you should focus on how to best tap the power of your community and network to spread your message, and not overestimate the chance of the crowd stumbling across your message and distributing it for you.

You'll notice that none of the words in Figure 2.1 are "audience" or "service area"; that's because all three sections (the community, network, and crowd) already may be part of your organization's audience or service area.

For example, if your organization were the *Northwest Indiana Times,* a regional newspaper, you would not actually engage with every member of your service area, since that could reasonably translate to every resident in northwest Indiana and even the southeast suburbs of Chicago—you don't know who they all are or what they all do. Your community is thus composed of the people who subscribe or buy papers, connect with your reporters or stories by following them online and commenting on posts to your website, and attend your offline events. Their friends, colleagues, coworkers, and family are the network—the people you reach through your community. The network knows about you but isn't yet directly connected. Maybe a friend of someone in your community told them about a story or a featured series they read recently, or they have family members who attend an annual event sponsored by the paper. The crowd is everyone else who lives and works in the neighborhoods in northwest Indiana; yes, they are part of your service area or audience, but you haven't reached them yet.

Ultimately, you should have a plan for each of these segments of your audience. Communicating with the crowd, network, and the community are very different but can be really valuable to the success of your campaign or call to action. Setting goals and defining your message for each group at the start of your process will help you effectively engage with each group.

The core elements in building relationships with the crowd, network, and community are time, action, and people. You can use these three elements to help you identify the various options for any given engagement.

Time

Is this a one-time or sustained engagement? Is it just an event, and do you have the capacity to maintain or support a community around it once the event is over? Recognize the limits or options within your organization—what capacity do you have to maintain the action you're considering?

Action

The action you want people to take—remember, even if your message or campaign doesn't have a "call your Congress person" or "sign this petition" action, you are still asking them to do *something*. Actions can be passive or active. An active call is more appealing to your community and less appealing to the crowd, because the community members already know you, trust you, and have opted in to support your work. This kind of action might include sharing a personal story or experience, recruiting a friend to join the campaign, or signing up as a volunteer.

Similarly, a passive action isn't very interesting to your supporters, considering that they are already taking passive action by following you on Twitter or signing up for your email list or campaigns. But a passive action can be attractive to the crowd if it is simple and provides value directly. For example, posting an infographic showing important facts about a piece of proposed legislation provides valuable information to someone whether or not they know about your organization; and it is an easy request to ask people to share it with their friends. These actions are usually things that the community may do as a way to show they are listening and connected but can be of more interest to the crowd because of a focus on a larger topic, news story, or even an interesting issue.

People

Who do you need to reach? Is it the crowd, community, or a hybrid? It is important to have a plan for each segment and an understanding of what your message

Table 2.1

Engagement Overview for the Community and Crowd

Designing for the Community	Designing for the Crowd
Customizable—let the community own your message and cause by personalizing their involvement or output.	Shareable—messages, content, and actions that are shareable can be picked up and pushed around the network and crowd easily.
Consistent/clear/compelling goal—your supporters have joined you because they care about your cause (sometimes, even if it doesn't seem like anyone could care any more about it than your organization, they do!) so provide clear and inspiring goals to meet together.	Consistent messaging—to ensure that this layer of people who do not know you are able to understand what you do and who you are, your messages need to be consistent.
Aggregate and promote—be sure you are pulling together all of the contributions from the community and promoting people in real time.	Compelling story—research continues to show that compelling stories are one of the most important triggers to donations and actions.

is for each group. You may run a campaign or promote a targeted call to action to your community that asks a lot of their time, energy, or support. During that same campaign, a message for the crowd would focus on sharing information or learning more about the focus of the campaign—things that require less commitment.

Table 2.1 is a quick reference guide for designing for each group.

Opportunities for your organization to build trust, catalyze action, and affect change exist at all levels of the human landscape. To be successful, however, it's crucial to recognize which group to target, how to communicate, and *what* to say. Some of the best metrics of success are the size and engagement level of the community ring. Is it growing? Are people taking on more responsibility and leadership? Are you increasing the number of people who are volunteering or stepping up as champions of your cause or superfans? It's important to achieve a balance between your goals for crowd-to-community conversion and your goals for leadership development within the community.

PRINCIPLE 2. FOCUS ON SHARED GOALS

Let's be realistic: your community—even your most die-hard fans—isn't interested in everything your organization does. (Okay, we all have that one volunteer that is, but that's another story for another book.) It's crucial to recognize that not everything your organization wants to do or achieve matches up exactly with all that your community wants to do, and vice versa. And that's okay!

Maybe your organization provides important local services that your community appreciates but doesn't want to be responsible for managing. Or maybe the community wants to create a new park or a new local government department, but your organization isn't interested because the project doesn't advance your mission. The good news is that there are programs, services, projects, and groups that both the community and your organization want to help fund, improve, and support. Figure 2.2 describes that sweet spot, where you can focus your calls to action and community engagement.

First, identify what your community wants to do. What are the issues that bring the community together? An event? An action? A movement? What are hot topics for them in the news, in community meetings, and during elections? What are the values and priorities not only of community leaders, but also of general members?

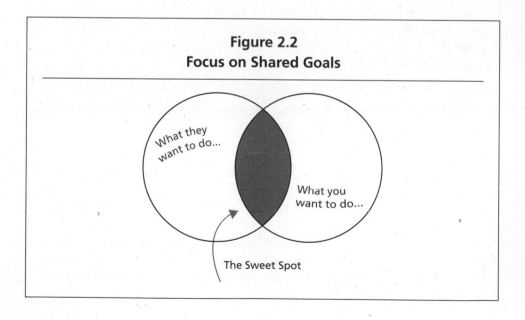

Figure 2.2
Focus on Shared Goals

What they want to do...

What you want to do...

The Sweet Spot

Next, identify what you want to do. What are your organizational goals? What outcomes have you identified in your strategic plan? What does success look like, and how will you know you're meeting your mission? What are you doing to gauge your impact?

The sweet spot in this case is where your organization's and your community's must-haves and wish lists overlap. That's the place where you can invest your time and your energy, knowing that you are all rooting for the same end. This means that instead of spending all your time, energy, and messaging recruiting supporters, you can focus on getting people to take action. Knowing the topics that both you and your community care about can transform individual campaigns, communication, and events into successful community-building work.

You may have a whole list of specific topics, proposals, and projects that bring you and the community together. Or you may have just one point of overlap. This visualization of goals is not intended to imply that the community never wants

---

FIND THE SWEET SPOT WITH YOUR COMMUNITY

Whether you conduct a survey online or organize an in-person focus group, use these questions to help identify what people are interested in and where their goals align with your organization.

1. How did you become aware of our work?

2. Which of our programs/services/campaigns are you most interested in?

3. Would you like more information about any of our work to share with your friends or family?

4. What aspects of our work are you least interested in?

5. What do you think we should focus on with you and the community?

The political organization MoveOn surveys its community every year and asks them to vote on which issues MoveOn should prioritize for the next twelve months. This helps give the MoveOn community members a voice and helps them understand that they are a valuable part of the organization, because they are helping to set the campaign agenda for the upcoming year.

---

to hear about the other work you do. It's great to include updates about services and programs that don't directly overlap in your communications or appeals, but focusing on the items in that sweet spot ensures that you have an engaged community working alongside you—online or offline, locally or globally.

Community Mapping

Principle #1 focused on identifying your community from the crowd. There are also subgroups within your community. Every email campaign you build isn't going to interest every person on your list. Recognizing the groups within your community and segmenting them by their goals (and your own) helps ensure that messages are well received and that people take action. It also positions you well for successful engagement across your community. We call the process of segmenting your community by type and goal "community mapping." First, identify the groups, and then identify your goals.

Identify the Groups

To start mapping your community, you need to identify the groups within it. There are big buckets of people such as volunteers, donors, and advocacy supporters. And within those, there are even more specific and narrowly defined groups—take volunteers. There are year-round volunteers, event volunteers, volunteer trainers, and youth/school volunteers, to name a few.

In our experience, the more diverse group you can get together in your organization to discuss and brainstorm the groups in your community, and work through this planning together, the more complete a picture you can draw of your community. When people who work in services, programs, grant writing, and fundraising, for example, get together to share their view of the groups that constitute the community, you can have rich discussions about the way different parts of your organization view and interact with the community.

Identify the Goals

The next step is identifying the goals associated with each segment. There are actually two sets of goals: The first are the goals of that specific segment—what do they want from you, why do they want to come to you, and what do they get out of it? The second are the goals your organization has for that group—what are you hoping they will do, how will they contribute, and what are you asking of them? For example, your event volunteers may be interested in free access to galas, speakers, or concerts you host, as well as including volunteer experience in a field they are passionate about on their résumé. Your organization's goals for that group may include the value of additional event support staff, as well as increased engagement of community champions that support your cause.

Again, this conversation can be really eye opening as a part of building the community map; it can also encourage dialogue within your organization and provide clarity around the organizational goals and how they play out in community engagement.

To use ourselves as an example, do you remember how you used to answer the question, "What do you want to be when you grow up?" When Amy was in elementary school, she said professional athlete! Allyson said an astronaut. Today we enjoy watching these professionals from a distance, but we've pursued wildly different paths. People change. Consider your community map, which identifies the segments and the associated goals, a living document and resource for your organization. When people change, the map should too! If a new group of supporters takes shape, add it to the list. Or if a group's interests change or evolve, reflect that in the document. As your goals for various groups change with your work, make sure you update the map.

There's one more step to the community mapping process, but we will talk about that in the next section.

PRINCIPLE 3. CHOOSE TOOLS FOR DISCOVERY AND DISTRIBUTION

You're online, reading a news site that has just published a list of the "Top Cities to Visit this Year." Your city is number one! You're excited and proud, and want to share the positive review with your friends and family; so what do you do? The news site has already included social sharing options within the article so you can easily post it to Facebook, Twitter, Google+, and many other platforms. You choose Facebook, and just ten minutes later, you see that three friends in other cities have commented on it and two friends have posted it to their Wall.

That's often how sharing happens. Good content appeals to our interests and offers easy ways for us to distribute it. We share it as individuals (or organizations), and then our friends (the network) pick it up. Understanding the best tools and platforms for sharing content and calls to action are crucial to the level of engagement and reach of your message. Said another way, your message will only get picked up or spread if you think strategically about access and distribution.

Although this book is intended to help you focus at the strategic level, we will still talk about tools and tactics throughout the various examples and case studies. What do we mean when we talk about access at the strategic level? What does distribution really mean with social and mobile technologies?

Align Tools with Groups of People

Just as different restaurants or neighborhoods see different people, the user base of each tool, application, and platform is slightly (sometimes dramatically) different. Part of this comes from the functionality that each offers, and the types of users who are interested in or attracted to those options. People often adopt or ignore tools based on cultural and social norms. Certain elements or requirements can also influence the types and numbers of users. Is the application free or does it come with a cost? Is it only available in English or are there various languages supported? Does it limit the amount you can upload or create or does it even limit how often you can use the tool? You can explore various divergences in user groups and data in the infographics provided in Chapter One of this book.

This is the last step in the community mapping process. Now that you have identified the groups and their corresponding goals, you need to couple those groups with the spaces, platforms, and applications where group members congregate and where you can communicate with them. Even though many of these will be online channels, don't forget about the offline spaces. Identifying the mechanisms you can use to communicate with each group may help you target your efforts, but in many cases, it illuminates areas where only one or a couple of groups use a certain platform while others use something else entirely—this fine-tuning helps you figure out which topics to promote when given the segments using those platforms, or the platforms in which there may be many different segments coming together.

Identifying Preferred Tools

How do you know which tools these groups use, especially if you aren't on those platforms yet? Remember that you have access to a great source of information: your community. Ask them! You can ask in myriad ways, via an online survey or a Facebook poll, for example. Include questions about preferred tools and platforms in other surveys or feedback mechanisms you have in place. Ask at offline events, and solicit information and suggestions in your communication subscription options or other sign-up forms on your website. You can also use Google Analytics and other tools to learn what platforms your community is using. Which social networks refer the most people? Are those networks where you already have a presence? It may be that your community members are sharing your blog posts or fundraising campaigns with their friends and family online via platforms that you don't even use!

Once you've investigated the tools your community and network prefer, dip your toes in and give them a try. You can't fully understand the potential of a tool or evaluate whether it is the best option for your organization without using it yourself. This does not mean that you need to set up a full organizational profile on every new social network and mobile application. You can create an account and try out functionality as an individual or as a team first. When experimenting with a new platform, set a few goals for yourself that are similar to the kind of engagement or functionality you would put in place if you were deploying the tool for the organization. Use those goals as guides to help evaluate whether it is worthwhile to spend additional time and energy on the new platform or to set up an official organizational presence.

Your messages and calls to action will fail to reach your community if you aren't sharing via the tools the community uses; similarly, the community will not share your messages on your behalf if doing so is difficult. When you evaluate tools to use as an organization or as part of a campaign, be sure to include a review of the content sharing options—for example, are there clear options to post to social networks built in? You also will want to spend some time on new platforms, observing how the tool is used by the community, looking especially at how sharing happens. Keep in mind that you shouldn't determine sharing practices based solely on which platforms users prefer—the type of content is also important. Images and videos are extremely popular media for creating and sharing from both the web and mobile devices.

Take Tumblr, a popular blogging platform, as an example: Users re-blog (post another user's content to their own page) the average Tumblr post 9 times (resulting in only about 10% original content throughout the platform as a whole).[11] It is critical that content you create for your community to share includes appropriate links or information for readers to find your organization.

A great example is the image-centric "Rise Above Plastics" campaign from the Surfrider Foundation.[12] The images are compelling and striking, but simple and direct messaging make them ripe for sharing and posting on social media. Just a couple days after launching, thousands of people had shared the images. Smart design ensures that the images contain all the information that is needed, including the call to action, the organization's name, and the campaign URL. This way, it does not matter whether it's community members, animal lovers, or even photographers who share the images without fully comprehending the campaign. When people share the image, they share a whole package, which helps the campaign reach many more people than it would if it relied on individual users to include the Surfrider Foundation information and credits every time.

After identifying the community, focusing on the shared goals, and matching groups to the tools they use, many organizations ask us next: What do we talk about? That's the next principle! (Also, in the Advocacy chapter, we discuss how to identify where your community hangs out online and provide examples of platforms popular with specific communities.)

PRINCIPLE 4. HIGHLIGHT PERSONAL STORIES

When presented with somber news, such as a famine in a foreign country and the magnitude of suffering that goes along with it, many people feel overwhelmed by the need. In contrast, when presented with the story of just one person impacted by the famine, people often feel like even a small donation or action really can make a difference.

Why is this the case? According to the psychology of giving, which we explore more in Chapter Four, "Fundraising Anytime, Everywhere," people are motivated to donate money when they can personally and emotionally identify with a single person in need. And as much as we desire a peaceful and just world, we also want to know that our giving has a real, positive effect.

Our community wants to help others, and the more directly we can achieve that, the better. Email, social and mobile technologies, and our own websites give us the opportunity to use storytelling to craft these clear appeals.

Technology allows members of our community to share stories in various ways, provides organizations diverse platforms for storytelling, and helps us reach more people and raise more money through the way it distributes those stories.

Individuals

Social publishing tools and the web make it easy for people to share their stories across a range of media. Whether it's photographs, videos, or text—or a mashup of media—your community members can share on social networks, local news sites, blogging and micro-blogging platforms, and even media-specific networks such as YouTube (video), Audioboo (audio), and Flickr (photographs).

The web is full of people posting their stories, updates about what they are doing, and even news that resonates with them. How do you get your community to share stories about your work or about the way your organization is impacting their lives? First, you have to ask! Most likely, you do not have many community members who, without prompting, will take the time to tell you how much they appreciated or learned from or benefited from the work you do. If you ask your community for their stories, you'll find people open to sharing.

Many organizations try to incorporate personal stories from their community—either from people who benefit from services and programs or those that support their work—in advocacy campaigns, fundraising appeals, and general operations updates. If you have the capacity to directly recruit and craft these stories, you probably have a standard structure for collecting information—maybe a set of questions you use for every interview you conduct with program or service participants or a format you like to use in an annual report.

That same structure can help you tap into the community to have individuals tell their story related to your services, program, or mission. Share a prompt for people to respond in a Mad Libs–like style: "Complete the sentence, 'I'm walking for Diabetes because ___, and I hope you will support me by ___.'" Post an example story from your staff or volunteers and ask for others to share their version, whether it is a written story, a photo, a video, or a combination. Ask an open-ended question using the medium or platform you want people to respond with; for example, pose the question in a quick video and ask viewers to create a short video response with their answer.

Regardless of the kind of content or where people post it, providing structure for what to create and how to share it gives the community a starting place to share their story for your organization. Similarly, be sure you are also the first to complete the prompt, or create a video, or upload a photo in the way you are asking your community to do. This is a great way to seed the space with content and provide an example that meets your criteria—your supporters can see what to do to participate. You don't want the same staff person always in the spotlight? Rotate in other staff (ask ahead of time) or tap your biggest supporters with a request and a sneak peak.

Organizations

It's exciting and inspiring to see your community members share their stories as part of your campaign or in support of your message, but as an organization, you have an equally important and inspiring role to play in storytelling. Storytelling is a two-way process. If the individuals that respond to your prompt or call to action have nowhere to share or no one to share with, the motivation for sharing and the potential number of participants are greatly diminished.

The web is a vast repository of pages, pictures, and information—stories are everywhere. When your community starts contributing their own stories, your organization must reciprocate by aggregating and showcasing the stories. By pulling together content, through tags (the use of keywords to identify content) on various platforms or by using a dedicated group on a specific application such as Flickr, you have the potential to transform a set of disparate stories into a pool of supporting voices for your work. Tools such as Tumblr, Flickr, YouTube, and Twitter are often utilized in campaigns as popular places for posting as well as sharing content. Similarly, tools such as Pinterest, Scoop.it, and Storify help organizations and community groups curate content in real time for aggregation and sharing.

Regardless of what content or platforms your community uses, you have many options for collecting their contributions, both within a platform and back on your website. Pulling together content on your organization's website or a campaign-specific microsite is important, as it places the stories and comments from your supporters where visitors can find out more about your work or get involved, thus showing the value you place on their voices. It also validates the contributions of individuals by giving them space in your organization's online property.

HOW PLANNED PARENTHOOD FEDERATION OF AMERICA'S STORYBANK HELPED IN CRISIS COMMUNICATIONS

Both during and outside of formal campaigns, Planned Parenthood Federation of America (PPFA) asks its supporters to share their story of how PPFA impacts them—direct health services at a local health center, educational information online, or anything in between. Collecting these stories helped PPFA identify influential stories and experiences from the community, and provided diverse and authentic perspectives to use in public outreach to encourage participation at online and offline events.

These stories also came in handy for the organization during the crisis campaign that launched after the announcement in early 2012 by Susan G. Komen for the Cure. The announcement was that PPFA would no longer be eligible for funding to conduct breast exams, which help detect breast cancer. The PPFA staff drew from its well of stories and rapidly provided real stories in support of their work around breast health and cancer.

As supporters started other channels and actions related to supporting PPFA and sharing their experiences with breast health issues and the services PPFA provides, previously collected stories mixed with new stories, all being shared in real time. This showcased the breadth of the issue. Sharing stories from a diverse audience—stories that spoke directly to the breast cancer screening services at risk of defunding that people and organizations could share immediately across several online channels—made a huge difference for PPFA's response. It ensured that the voice of the community, not just the voice of the organization, called people to action.

When you aggregate the stories, you also have an opportunity to spotlight contributors and community members. You might highlight a specific story in an email appeal, feature someone's story on the top of your blog or in the banner of your website, or even spotlight stories on your social media channels. New visitors are drawn to personal stories, while other community members are inspired to contribute and share the spotlight. This is a key leadership development component, and in campaigns or appeals like this, it serves as a mechanism for encouraging participation and identifying superactivists, donors, and fans.

Just as individuals in the community are sharing their personal stories, you can tell the bigger story by bringing together single voices, using data to create a story, and creating a space where the community comes together with your message. Data can tell stories too. As you aggregate contributions from your community, take advantage of any additional data you're collecting to help tell a larger story, like the locations where the most requests for help are generated or the distribution of ages of contributors. Whether you use a map (like Google Maps) to plot the locations of contributors or their stories and photos, or tools to count or visualize the numbers, words, or funds contributed, as an organization leading this storytelling effort you can pull the voices and the data together to support your mission.

If you're collecting or aggregating content and conversations created by your community on your own website or a campaign microsite, you are providing context and supplemental information within the actual space where the content is showcased. If you use tools for *curation* (an industry term meaning aggregation coupled with narrative or notation) that house the content on a third party platform (such as Pinterest, Scoop.it, or Storify), it's important that you add contextual information, links, and other general descriptions to the accounts and individual content pieces. Curation allows your organization to shape the larger story and add in a frame or lens for the community to see stories linked together or as evidence of a bigger picture. For example, as news is breaking about a piece of legislation important to your cause, you could use a tool like Storify to pull together tweets, news links, and blog posts along with your notations about what the decision and impact mean for your community.

Personal storytelling is an important building block of the Internet—it manifests in blogs, social networks, and niche topic forums. Tap into the natural inclination for humans to share by providing a clear prompt that your community can respond to and the network and crowd can share.

PRINCIPLE 5. BUILD A MOVEMENT

Just as the terms *community* and *network* are often, and incorrectly, used interchangeably, the term *movement* is often misused or vaguely defined. So what is a movement? Here are some parameters. Movements are larger than partnerships and coalitions. They are deeper than engagement, and longer than campaigns. A movement is inherently counter to branding and requires the participation of more than just a few inspired individuals.

As such, a movement is built on collaboration and encourages co-creation between individuals and organizations. It remains focused, even in the midst of specific events or campaigns, on the larger goal of lasting, real impact. To that end, movements that have unifying goals—goals that rally both individuals and entire communities—replace brands operating in a silo.

Branding

More than ten years ago, long before the namesake organization formed, "350ppm" (indicating 350 parts per million), used as a tag or category on blogs or a keyword on files and images, was a rallying point on the web. It helped bloggers find each other's content, facilitated photo and documentation sharing among environmentalists and nature lovers, and helped individuals find and share news about the impacts of or legislative actions related to climate change. Over time, as interest and the community grew, an organization took shape and based its name on this "call sign." It became 350.org. The community's process remains the same. People of all backgrounds, in all locations, and in all occupations use "350" or #350 on social networks, in signs, and in photographs, during global action days and every day in between, to indicate their affiliation with the climate change movement. As exemplified by 350.org, there are tremendous opportunities for starting and growing movements by focusing on a singular change or action.

Figure 2.3 is a Facebook Page where many organizations across the environmental, climate, and animal welfare sectors came together to share news, updates, action alerts, and much more after the BP Oil Spill. You can see it's focused on action. There's a petition built into the page and the page doesn't have an organization's name—it doesn't even have anything about BP in the name.

In recent years, some very large organizations have been in the public spotlight as they try to manage and control their branding via extensive lawsuits and legal battles. For example, Susan G. Komen for the Cure's efforts to maintain the exclusive use of pink ribbons, and even the color pink and the phrase "for the cure" by suing other nonprofits has landed them in the online and television media.[13]

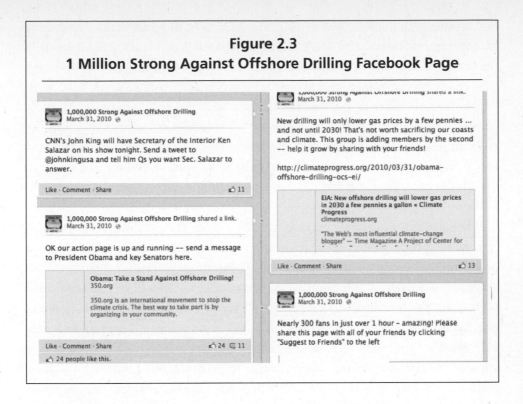

Figure 2.3
1 Million Strong Against Offshore Drilling Facebook Page

1,000,000 Strong Against Offshore Drilling shared a link.
March 31, 2010

1,000,000 Strong Against Offshore Drilling
March 31, 2010

CNN's John King will have Secretary of the Interior Ken Salazar on his show tonight. Send a tweet to @johnkingusa and tell him Qs you want Sec. Salazar to answer.

Like · Comment · Share   11

New drilling will only lower gas prices by a few pennies ... and not until 2030! That's not worth sacrificing our coasts and climate. This group is adding members by the second -- help it grow by sharing with your friends!

http://climateprogress.org/2010/03/31/obama-offshore-drilling-ocs-ei/

EIA: New offshore drilling will lower gas prices in 2030 a few pennies a gallon « Climate Progress
climateprogress.org

"The Web's most influential climate–change blogger" — Time Magazine A Project of Center for

1,000,000 Strong Against Offshore Drilling shared a link.
March 31, 2010

OK our action page is up and running -- send a message to President Obama and key Senators here.

Obama: Take a Stand Against Offshore Drilling!
350.org

350.org is an international movement to stop the climate crisis. The best way to take part is by organizing in your community.

Like · Comment · Share   24   11

24 people like this.

Like · Comment · Share   13

1,000,000 Strong Against Offshore Drilling
March 31, 2010

Nearly 300 fans in just over 1 hour - amazing! Please share this page with all of your friends by clicking "Suggest to Friends" to the left

Nonprofits, like all organizations, have the right to safeguard their trademarks, but many view the Komen example as just one illustration of an organization fighting to "own" a cause. Doing so diminishes your opportunities for true movement building and catalyzing impact. Why? Because if your organization seeks to own the idea of, say, a future without cancer, any organization working on that issue is off the list of potential collaborators and champions. Working in an anytime, everywhere world with our supporters and all those trying to create a better world will require that we reevaluate how we market and safeguard our brand.

Co-Creation

Actually creating social change anytime, everywhere relies on your organization's ability to let go of some of the more traditional ideas about social action, campaigning, and organizing—mainly, the idea that an organization is in control and orchestrating the community's every move. Certainly, there are some elements of an organization's work that the community probably isn't interested in (usually the boring stuff!), but communities around the world are getting used to playing a role, along with organizations and service providers, in creating change.

As we said earlier in this chapter, when evaluating your goals and the goals of your community, it's critical to identify the role of your organization and the roles of your community leaders, partners, and groups. Many organizations focus on including the community in their work only after they are ready to launch the campaign, announce the new program, or start registering new users. In an anytime, everywhere world, organizations that wait to bring the community in until this unveiling point are missing out on the potential for collaboration and support, as well as direct feedback and guidance that can make for a better and more valuable product, service, program, or platform.

We aren't suggesting that you do your planning work in huge public forums, with decisions by consensus. There are plenty of opportunities to invite interested community members to form an advisory committee, beta test and provide feedback, or post regular updates about new programs or plans in the works that the community can respond to. Working in tandem with your community—listening to needs, surfacing ideas, and sharing responsibility to move things forward—is really about empowering your community for co-creation, not just adoption.

HOW YOUTHNET HARNESSED VOLUNTEERS FOR A WEBSITE REDESIGN

YouthNet is the United Kingdom's first exclusively online charity, guiding and supporting young people in making informed decisions and participating in society to fulfill their goals. In 2010, it was investing in a complete overhaul of its main programmatic website: TheSite.org. The staff—mostly mid-20s and older—realized they were not the target audience. The community they worked with were primarily young people, aged 16 to 25. That meant that the aesthetic, style, and language they might pick might not have the same meaning or value to those they served.

YouthNet invited website users and other young people to play a very active part in the web design process by weighing in on features and voting on colors. The YouthNet staff admitted that many of the decisions they ultimately made did not include the features they previously envisioned or personally would have identified. The staff also learned that by including this group in a real way throughout the process, not just a one-time user group meeting, the participants on the advisory committee ended up just as invested in the success of the website as they were and became champions for it when it launched.

Co-Creation Cycle

Co-creation is one of those terms that, for many of us, gets our heads spinning. Many people have defined it in different ways, contingent on the context and product they were working with. For social impact in an anytime, everywhere world, co-creation is a process or cycle that helps you be responsive, iterative, and inclusive in the way you work with your community.

As you can see in Figure 2.4, there are three distinct components of the co-creation cycle: listening, engaging, and building. The first step is listening to the

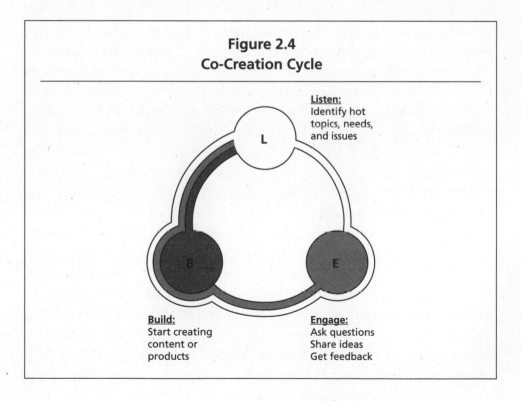

Figure 2.4
Co-Creation Cycle

Listen:
Identify hot topics, needs, and issues

Build:
Start creating content or products

Engage:
Ask questions
Share ideas
Get feedback

community—asking questions and gathering feedback. Next, you reach engagement. You don't stop listening, but now you are also sharing back what you hear, asking for clarification and really fleshing out ideas with the community. If you try to jump directly to this stage, without dedicating time to listening first, you can get frustrated with incomplete or ungrounded conversations. Community members can also get frustrated talking about topics or having conversations about issues that may not match their goals or interests.

The third segment of the cycle is building. Again, your previous elements do not cease when you reach this point; you want to continue to listen and engage with your community, but now you are building out the ideas directly—whether it's a website, a piece of content, or a whole campaign. This is where the cycle really becomes a continuous process: once you've done some of the building work, you should pause to focus just on listening to feedback and responses, then build up to engagement again, and then another round of building. This second or third (or 50th) turn around the cycle may have a shorter duration for each component, but it is important that the process includes a pause to gather feedback and engage your community so that you don't leave them behind as you build and launch something new.

The three elements of the co-creation cycle also lend themselves to different groups in your community and different numbers of participants. Many community members may share their feedback or ideas, but for most organizations there are far fewer community members with the interest or capacity to participate in the building phase. That's certainly okay, though, and very natural. Providing opportunities to engage at all levels helps increase the total number of community members involved and the feeling that they have influenced the end results.

Slacktivism or Micro-Action

Some critics of social media engagement call actions that don't take much effort "slacktivism" or "clicktivism," the terms used by many to mean a "slacker action," especially things akin to a "like" on Facebook or a "retweet" on Twitter. We think the conversation needs to start by talking about information. Regardless of the era (this isn't a new phenomena), the emphasis and effort spent on spreading information and raising awareness has always resulted in people doing what organizations ask, even if it's considered slacktivism. Previously, learning, spreading information, and raising awareness were very passive actions. With the rise of social media, we can further confuse the information stage of campaigning or change efforts with an active action.

Social media is a tool, not a tactic or a strategy. Whether you are urging supporters to make change or chronicling the revolution in your state, it is still a tool. But because social media allows people to engage and share personal information, it's very easy and common for organizations to be satisfied with asking for and measuring the information stage.

Let's take a step back for just a second and look at how our modern slacktivism came into this information-equals-activism dynamic. Just as social media was really taking off, people and organizations were caught up in new ways to gain brand recognition. Marketing strategies focused on the idea that nonprofits should recognize that they could be just like companies in messaging, recognition, and branding. Visibility and information sharing were the keys.

Here's a great example. How many of us had a plastic bracelet from one organization or another, or maybe we still do? How many of us worked for an organization that created bracelets for general marketing or a specific campaign? We did! And it was an organization with a staff of three and a board of twelve. Why'd we do it? To get into people's lives, to start increasing touch points toward fundraising asks, to be part of how people associated themselves. Most important, it was to build awareness of our work.

Now instead of rubber bracelets, we have Facebook Fan pages. There's nothing fundamentally wrong with a Fan page. But as organizations or campaigners, there *is* something wrong if we praise likes and count followers instead of understanding that our fans are primed for real action and that we should build opportunities for them to engage in something meaningful.

Metrics

Let's look at your organizational metrics for a minute. What do you measure every day, week, month, year? What do you point to when funders, donors, board members, and the community ask if you are making a difference? How do you evaluate your programs and services? Those metrics and accompanying goals are the best resources for identifying the focus of content and the calls to action for your campaigns and even daily messages across channels.

When you ask your Facebook fans to "like" a post, you're telling those fans that to support the organization, all they have to do is click "like." It's no wonder, then, that clicktivism and slacktivism are slapped on top of much of the engagement organizations have online. Liking a page, liking a post, and all the rest are not the actions and real impact you're looking for, ultimately, but those actions are important! Why? Because, through them, people are telling you that they want to hear about what you're doing and that they will do what you ask to support the cause. The opportunity is for you to hear that response and give them more than a post to like—give them something with more forward motion for your mission or campaign, like signing a petition, watching an informative video, making a pledge, or recruiting their friends.

What we are measuring obviously impacts what we focus on. When the only things we are tracking are the number of fans on a Facebook Page, or the number of email addresses in our database, we set ourselves up to feel satisfied with slacktivism alone—that those small signs of interest from the community are all that we need. Instead, look at your goals and build metrics that actually track your progress. Yes, the number of fans on Facebook still counts, but it is just one data point to help explore the full context of your engagement. For example, you could also track the number of community-generated posts to the Facebook Page wall versus staff posts, the number of comments from the community versus staff, the kinds of content that generate the most response, and the level of engagement (whether it's just likes, comments, or outside action).

Likes, retweets, and other simple actions are still valuable and a great way to support visibility and information sharing, just like the bracelets. When a supporter likes your post on Facebook, that content and action show up in the news feeds of their friends, helping move your messages out to the network. They are also valuable in that they keep your supporters feeling connected to your work and up-to-date on the latest news or information related to your cause or issue. We aren't suggesting that you discount these simple actions entirely, but ensure that they are tracked with the right context and in tandem with other actions tied to your goals.

If we consider slacktivism a micro-action, how do we move "likes" into real action?

We need to recognize the critical role we play as organizations. For all the negative talk about slacktivism, people are failing to recognize that it constitutes a huge community response. People are taking the actions we are asking them to take—we are the ones giving them slacker-actions! Instead of crafting a compelling message and asking people to like it, we should see all of our fans as community members who have raised their hand, saying, "Please give me something worthwhile to do for this cause!" and give them opportunities to start making real change—whether through advocacy, fundraising, or community-based calls to action, as we discuss in the following chapters. Recognize the role of those more passive engagements (the likes and the retweets) as small touch points, keeping people connected between the other calls to action.

We are so caught up in social and mobile technologies as a concept, a topic, causes in themselves, that we forget to move people up the engagement ladder. We forget to connect to people, period.

Impact

Your organization probably has an important mission and valuable programs or services. Your campaigns may have big goals and your messages may be filled with compelling stories that your community reads and shares. But your organization is just one piece in a network of individuals, organizations, government agencies, or businesses that are working toward or supporting some of the same ends. Even if you partner with other organizations on a project, that partnership is just the beginning of real movement building.

When those partnerships lead to sharing data so that more tracking, planning, and communicating supports real action, then you are one step closer to building a movement. Two organizations focused on climate change policy, 350.org and 1Sky, took this approach in 2010, sharing data and combining the strength of their communities for campaigns and petitions. In early 2011, they announced that they would fully merge to better tackle the issues around global climate change. Figure 2.5 is a screen shot from the announcement.

Shortly after the 350.org-1Sky announcement, David Foster, executive director of the BlueGreen Alliance (BGA), showed that he shared a similar vision for his organization and the sustainable energy organization Apollo Alliance:

> I believe that the decision to combine the BlueGreen Alliance and the Apollo Alliance is one of many important steps that all of us need to take to forge a stronger movement to demand the transition to a clean energy economy. But building a movement that can lead to a new direction in Washington, D.C. will not come easily, nor can it rely on sticking to old orthodoxies. We simply must be willing to build new partnerships and take risks on new organizational structures. The BGA-Apollo merge is done in that spirit.

Figure 2.5
350.org and 1Sky Website Announcement

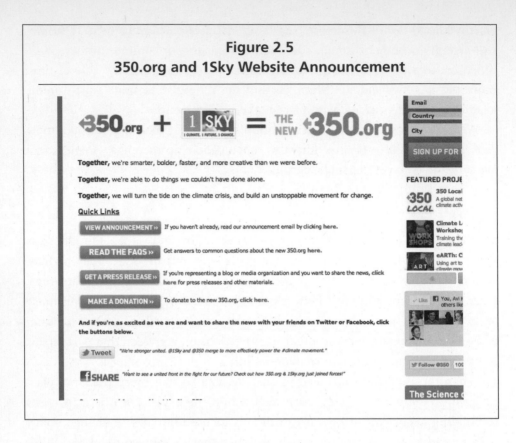

We don't share these examples of mergers to say that there are too many nonprofit organizations or that we believe more organizations should merge. Instead, they are examples of what it looks like when we truly double down on our focus to create change. And just as David Foster shared in the merger announcement, building a movement requires partnerships and risks.

Part of the structure that goes into building movements is the way we organize all those participating. Another component is the way we position organizations and communities to come together. Organizations may have the research or data, and the capacity and staff, to identify problems and opportunities and to build messages, calls to action, and campaigns. But the organization can't make the change alone. The community, partners, and government are all necessary to really make a change. Organizations need to let the community drive. That doesn't mean organizations sit back, relinquish all responsibility and control, and wait for the community to take action—quite the opposite! The organizations get to do everything but drive: You are the vehicle, the gas, the map, but if the community isn't in the driver's seat, you won't have the engagement or power to go anywhere.

Anytime, everywhere technology is an important tool for engaging your supporters. In the following chapters, we show you how social and mobile technologies help with advocacy, fundraising, and community building. The tools we cover provide communications options, collaboration spaces, and opportunities to make data usable and sharable. They can help you open up your data, employ a networked approach to collaborate and distribute actions, and work with your community and partners outside of formal campaigns to ramp up for the next push.

HOW TO MAMA WITH LOVE BUILDS A MOVEMENT

What does all this actually look like? Take a group like Epic Change and its To Mama With Love projects.[1] To Mama With Love is an online fundraising effort and co-creation campaign that supports women social entrepreneurs who care for and support communities of youth around the world. The co-creation campaign happens in the week leading up to Mother's Day, though over a hundred interested supporters connect via a private Facebook group ahead of time to help shape the campaign and plan (we explore this more later in the book).

To Mama With Love is hosted on a platform where anyone can build a "heartspace"—an online space with text, photographs, and videos that express individuals' love for their mother, another important woman in their life, or people that inspire them. Users create the actual content of the campaign; the more that people participate, the more content and stories appear on the map.

This effort is less about the number of people who retweet, like, or blog about it. It's about helping the women who receive the funds. The project doesn't focus on a dollar amount; it focuses on the women's stories and communicates all that they wish they could do. The more money raised, the bigger the impact they can make. There's no limit to either the funds raised or the impact they fund. Instead of saying in the middle of the campaign, "We need $X," the organization will share an interview with one of the beneficiaries or invite people to connect (via Twitter) with children in Tanzania who attend a school funded through the campaign. It instantly becomes less about numbers and more about impact. And that's hard to ignore.

To Mama With Love combines all of the elements of building a movement, including a focus on impact reinforced through metrics, calls to action that move people from liking a post to participating in the campaign and even donating, co-creation of the campaign concept and the content, and a focus on mothers instead of the organization.

PUT THESE PRINCIPLES INTO ACTION

In the simplest terms, social and mobile technologies allow organizations to work with—not for—the community, which includes other organizations. We need to let go of the idea that we are simply serving our constituents, and recognize the ways that we can work together to change their neighborhoods or lives. When we use the "with" instead of the "for" perspective, we can see skills and contributions the community can make, opportunities for growth outside of our programs or our walls. We can see that we are part of a solution and not responsible for engineering the entire fix. We can then use social media, email, and mobile technology to elevate conversations, connect all those working together, and scale our reach and impact.

The following chapters will guide you through the ways you can put social and mobile technologies to use to engage, empower, and catalyze social impact. We return to these five principles throughout the book to highlight the strategic decisions, opportunities, and guidelines they offer to any organization. There are many case studies in the chapters that illustrate these principles in action, demonstrating how others have recognized the role of their community, selected tools, and collaborated with the help of technology—all to make real impact on our world.

DISCUSSION QUESTIONS

Spark a conversation with your team or organization about these core principles with the following questions:

1. Who is in your community? How do you know? How do you communicate with them now?

2. What are some of the goals you share with your community? What operations or programmatic work does your community not share a passion for?

3. Which tools are your community members active on now? Are specific groups using different tools?

4. What mechanisms do you have for capturing stories from your community? What are the stories you wish you had from your supporters or donors?

5. Who are the partners or collaborators that would help you open up your next campaign to a focus on the larger movement instead of your organization? How will you approach the idea with them?

chapter THREE

Advocacy Anytime Everywhere

One of the biggest barriers nonprofits fighting for social change face is how to consistently and effectively mobilize their base to take action anytime and everywhere. To build a movement, every component of your advocacy campaign must explain to people why taking action could lead to plausible, real world change.

For example, when Scott Harrison, founder of charity: water, was inspired to start an organization dedicated to funding organizations that supply clean drinking water in developing countries, he had to do much more than raise money. Scott developed a theory of change (the steps that he needed to follow to create the change he wanted to see and that would ultimately guide the organization's strategic plan and evaluation) wherein a global grassroots movement solved a problem they had never personally experienced.

Harrison's theory of change depended on creating an organization that people could believe in, and he targeted people just like him: people in their 30s, cynical but still wanting to do good in the world.

He realized early on that many people are burned out by constant requests to do the same thing over and over again—take action, volunteer, and donate money. Harrison found that most people (even the cynical ones) could be inspired by stories and wanted to be part of creating change that really worked. People wanted their action, time, and money to have an impact they could see and track. That is what charity: water set out to do in 2008. For the past five years the organization has tested creative campaigns that focus on powerful storytelling, demonstrating impact, and communicating with supporters regardless of channel: website, email, social media, and mobile.

The results? Since 2008, charity: water has built a passionate community of hundreds of thousands of people in the United States and worldwide, raised $60 million dollars, and funded over 6,000 water projects in 20 countries. Today, many of the poorest villages in the world have safe drinking water as a result.

charity: water is considered one of the most innovative organizations in the nonprofit space, but it wasn't successful from day one. It spent over two years trying different organizing strategies, and experienced failures along the way. Harrison and his staff learned from their experiences. Even today, charity: water operates like a lean startup: it plans, tests, learns, and iterates on its campaigns.

In this chapter, we discuss building a movement (like charity: water did) by advocating for social change through multiple online channels. First, we highlight three core principles for organizing an effective advocacy campaign that empowers people to take action. Next, we move into the components of a multichannel advocacy plan that you can adapt for your own organization. We then dive into the different online channels you can use to engage people in your campaigns. The last sections of the chapter focus on evaluation and metrics that help you identify campaign successes and failures (we all have them and what matters is learning to change course along the way). Plus, if you are interested in global advocacy, we have a "Special Focus" section that explores strategies and tactics unique to working at that scale.

ADVOCATING FOR SOCIAL CHANGE: THREE PRINCIPLES TO LIVE BY

There are three guiding principles that we never lose sight of whenever we're creating an advocacy campaign. We find that using these as a lens through which to view our strategies and tactics helps us develop clearer, more compelling, and ultimately more effective campaigns that have a real world impact.

1. **Use multiple channels to engage people.**

   Don't think of an advocacy campaign as one event using one channel to connect with people. We touched upon this some in Chapter Two. Instead, craft multichannel advocacy plans that provide relevant and timely opportunities for people to engage with the organization on their own terms and in ways that meet their interests, needs, and desire to see their impact as part of the campaign.

2. **Tell stories that move people into action.**

   Time and again we find that people respond best to advocacy campaigns that tell stories and use calls to action that connect on a human level—basically, skip the jargon and talk to people like you were at a dinner party. Don't be afraid to get creative. Be funny, and use drama and emotion to inspire supporters to take an action no matter where they are—sitting at their desk reading emails on their computer, standing in line to grab coffee and reading a text message on their mobile phone, or checking Facebook updates from their iPad at the airport.

3. **Measure, learn, and iterate.**

   Your campaign is not a wind-up toy that you get ready, launch, and then watch until it's over. Campaigns are more like organisms: they evolve. Understand your campaign benchmarks, set realistic goals along the way, and be nimble enough to adjust based on failures (you'll have some, and it's okay—you'll learn valuable lessons from them) and successes. This will help you to fine-tune your messaging, outreach, and advocacy actions across online channels so you can continue to improve campaign response rates and better communicate with your supporters. The metrics will also allow your organization to assess the campaign's impact.

In today's world where people are online and connected 24/7, multichannel campaigns are key to reaching your constituents and mobilizing them to create social change. To rally them, you need to start with a solid advocacy plan.

CREATE A SUCCESSFUL MULTICHANNEL ADVOCACY PLAN

The best advocacy campaigns are partly planned and partly organic. As you begin to map out your multichannel advocacy plan, it's important that you treat it like a living document, one that you continue to review and refer back to, test, and iterate on, even during the campaign.

1. Identify Realistic Short-Term and Long-Term Goals and Objectives

Break down long-term goals into small chunks so that people inside and outside the organization feel motivated to join you and help achieve shared goals. Your constituents and even your staff may feel that large-scale goals such as ending world hunger are too big for them to really achieve. Instead of inspiring people, it can make them feel powerless and say to themselves, "What can I do about it? I'm just one person." This is especially important because we want people to feel inspired to take a meaningful action that they know is going to make a real difference when they are reading your email appeal or skimming a blog post.

Mobilizing your base to achieve small goals can lead to long-term change. Stacey Monk, cofounder of Epic Change, which mobilizes volunteers across the United States and abroad to raise money for building classrooms and computer labs in Tanzania and other projects around the world, says setting small goals gives the organization an opportunity to consistently demonstrate impact, and each success inspires its community to support future possibilities. "Once someone realizes whatever they have to offer is enough to build a classroom, they're more likely to believe that it's enough to build a school. Small goals, and small successes, allow us to constantly re-engage our base to remind them of their ability to create even more possibilities for the world." Epic Change does a great job of communicating these small goals and updating their community about when they achieve them through multiple online channels such as email and social media profiles such as Flickr, Facebook, and Twitter, which we highlight in Figures 3.1 and 3.2.

But what if you are part of a policy-focused organization with long-term goals such as fighting global warming or making sweeping changes to health care?

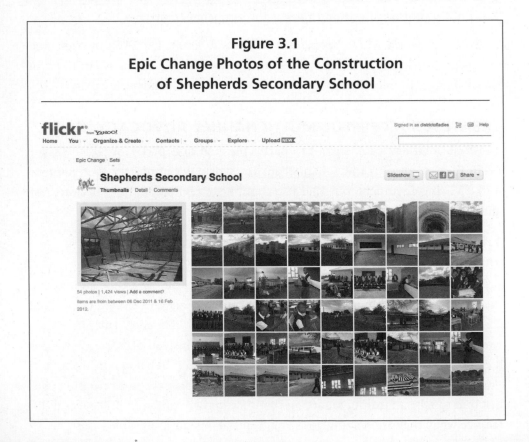

Figure 3.1
Epic Change Photos of the Construction of Shepherds Secondary School

Figure 3.2
Epic Change Blog Post Telling Supporters of the Opening of Shepherds Secondary School

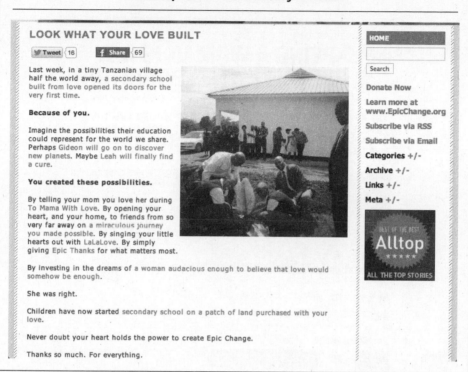

LOOK WHAT YOUR LOVE BUILT

Tweet 16   Share 69

Last week, in a tiny Tanzanian village half the world away, a secondary school built from love opened its doors for the very first time.

Because of you.

Imagine the possibilities their education could represent for the world we share. Perhaps Gideon will go on to discover new planets. Maybe Leah will finally find a cure.

You created these possibilities.

By telling your mom you love her during To Mama With Love. By opening your heart, and your home, to friends from so very far away on a miraculous journey you made possible. By singing your little hearts out with LaLaLove. By simply giving Epic Thanks for what matters most.

By investing in the dreams of a woman audacious enough to believe that love would somehow be enough.

She was right.

Children have now started secondary school on a patch of land purchased with your love.

Never doubt your heart holds the power to create Epic Change.

Thanks so much. For everything.

HOME

Search

Donate Now

Learn more at www.EpicChange.org

Subscribe via RSS

Subscribe via Email

Categories +/-

Archive +/-

Links +/-

Meta +/-

Alltop
ALL THE TOP STORIES

Frame the campaign around smaller goals with clear targets and ask people to take actions that you know will have tangible results. Finally, connect the smaller goals and actions to the big, long-term objectives so that staff and supporters see how their work today is connected to greater results. For example, the National Women's Law Center (NWLC) advocates for laws and policies on women's health care and reproductive rights. That's quite a large goal. During the health care debates in 2009, its members felt that members of Congress weren't doing enough to protect women's health care. In response, the organization launched a campaign around the core message that "Being a Woman Is Not a Pre-existing Condition" (as shown in Figure 3.3) to illustrate how the proposed health care bill would discriminate against women who were seeking health insurance.

Specifically, the campaign identified key loopholes in the bill, such as how women were being charged higher insurance premiums on average, and in eight

Figure 3.3
Microsite Campaign http://awomanisnotapreexistingcondition
.com/ by the National Women's Law Center

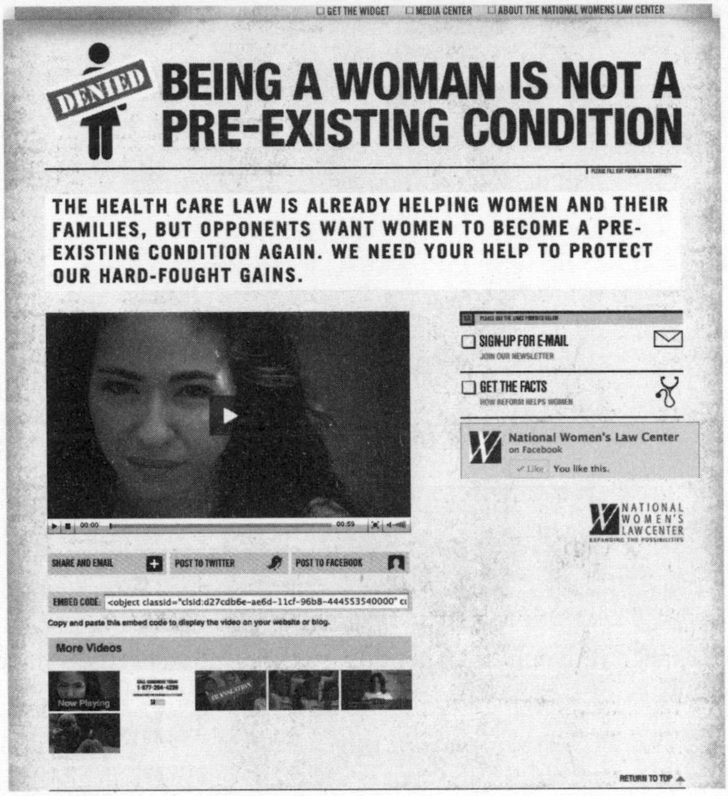

states and Washington, D.C., it was legal for insurance companies to deny health coverage to victims of domestic violence. The campaign mobilized tens of thousands of women across the United States to petition members of Congress to close these critical loopholes. By breaking down the campaign into smaller goals and actions (closing the loopholes in the health care bill), NWLC was able to connect the campaign to their overarching goal of incorporating policy reform to protect women's health.

2. Identify Advocacy Targets

Who are the people, branch of government, corporation, or other entity that have the power to affect direct and/or immediate change on the goals and objectives you laid out? Avoid generalities and be very specific about the people that need to be targeted. Who, exactly, has the power to make the change you want to see? Remember the change you seek must be plausible to your supporters, so it makes no sense to pick a target that is incapable of affecting that change.

3. Craft Your Core Message

After you identify your objectives, you will need to develop a core message for your campaign. If your audiences were only going to remember one thing about your advocacy campaign, what would it be? Focusing on this will help you get to the root of your core message.

4. Outline What Actions You Want People to Take

Determine what kinds of actions will make an impact on your targets. What will influence them? What will they respond to? For example, do you need constituents to call their members of Congress and encourage them to support a legislative bill that is coming up for a vote? Do you need people to sign a petition to get something on the ballot in your city?

Be sure to match the action to the size and seriousness of the problem, says Tracy Frauzel at Greenpeace International's Mobilisation Labs. "Can it be changed and is the solution plausible? We're not going to solve a big problem like climate change with one email petition, so the solution needs to match the size of the problem. And explain why this solution is the one that is going to make change happen, even if only a small step on the route to big change."[14]

And don't forget to follow up after people have taken action. It's essential to provide ongoing updates about the advocacy campaign and share the results (both the good and the bad).

5. Know Who Your Supporters Are

In advocacy work, we're usually dealing with two audiences. The first audience is the community we seek to mobilize to take action by calling their members of Congress, attending an event, donating to support program priorities, or any number of other actions. The second audience, as mentioned above, is the advocacy target and includes the people, legislators, or corporations with the power to create policy, dedicate funds to programs we want to see funded, or implement the change we are advocating. It's easy to focus our attention primarily on the advocacy targets, but it is just as important to think about the ultimate supporters you are trying to reach to take action.

WHO ARE YOUR PEOPLE?

- Where do your people like to hang out and get their information: TV, online newspapers, blogs, Twitter, public or talk radio, print newspapers, or with friends and colleagues?

- How old are they: Millennials? Baby Boomers? GenXers?

- Are they African Americans, Hispanics, Asian American, etc., or all of the above?

- Do they prefer to read the *New York Times*, *Gawker*, or *Ms Magazine*?

- What are they interested in: politics, education, fishing, vegetarianism, human rights, faith issues, health?

It's also important to think about the people who are influential within these niche audiences. Perhaps it's an established blogger who your target audiences turn to for information related to your issue, or the founder of an active Facebook or LinkedIn group. These community leaders and niche experts can be instrumental in helping to amplify the campaign.

6. Understand How Your Supporters Think

Once you identify your target audiences, you will want to research how familiar they are with your organization and cause (if you don't already know or track this). What are they saying about your cause in social communities like Facebook and Twitter? What about on blogs? If your organization is a service provider, what do people say about you on Yelp? Are there pain points around the issue, and if so, what are they? What kinds of actions or discussions motivate or inspire them? What's not resonating with them?

Have you done member or supporter surveys recently? Surveys (by mail, web, or phone) can be one great way to get a better sense of the language that your supporters respond to and use on different channels. You can also manually analyze sentiment (how supporters are feeling about the issue and organization) on social media channels or use social media analytics from channels like Facebook to understand the language that works best in different channels. Are responses positive, neutral, or negative? Note, the writing that motivates responses to your emails won't necessarily be what works for Twitter and Facebook users, so you will need to adapt messaging for each channel and audience.

7. Find Out What Makes Your Supporters Tick

Similar to #6, it's important to find out what aspect of your issue ticks off your audience. For example, when Allyson began organizing Women Who Tech[15] in 2007, an initiative to promote women breaking new ground in technology, she examined some of the community's pain points by using Twitter to talk to women currently working in the technology sector. Allyson learned that these women were upset because they were not feeling represented on panels at technology and social media conferences. Some women felt frustrated and alienated trying to break into what they saw as an "old boys network." These specific pain points became a focal point for short-term goals, which included:

- Using social media to lobby highly influential conference organizers, such as Tim O'Reilly of O'Reilly Media, to better market their call for panel submissions to women in technology networks and feature more women on panels at major conferences, like the Web 2.0 Summit

- Creating the Women Who Tech TeleSummit as an affordable online conference in which any woman in the world could participate as long as they had a phone line and/or Internet connection

- Showcasing the vibrant and thriving community of women in technology and social media, including Arianna Huffington, founder of Huffington Post; Rashmi Sinha, cofounder of SlideShare; and Rebecca Moore, a computer scientist who leads outreach for Google Earth

Finding out what makes your audiences tick around the issue you are working on is an important step, since advocacy goals should never be set without direct input from the target audiences you seek to mobilize. And a great way to assess this is by asking questions both in person and online; listening and gathering feedback through email, social networks, online media, and blogs; and even surveying your audiences through mobile texting if you have a sizable list.

8. Identify How Audiences Prefer to Get Information and Communicate

In Chapter One, we discussed the rise in social network and mobile use. When you create an advocacy and outreach plan, it's critical that it reach your target audiences across multiple channels.

If your audiences are composed of 65-year-olds, for example, direct mail and email may have more impact than trying to reach them on Twitter or mobile texting. But if your target audience is composed of Millennials (those born between 1980 and 2000), your plan might include video, texting, or engaging with them on Facebook.

However, don't assume that older people aren't online. Recent surveying has shown that 53% of seniors 65 and older are online and using social media to stay connected.[16] Planned Parenthood is an organization with both young and older supporters. To reach both audiences, it used both email and social media to launch its successful rapid response campaign and petition Susan B. Komen for the Cure to refund Planned Parenthood's breast cancer screening services.

9. Reach Your People in Online Communities

Just as television shows attract certain demographics, you can identify potential online communities based on the demographics of your target audiences. For instance:

Care2 If your target audiences are 40- to 50-year-old women interested in "green" and progressive issues, they may be surfing Care2.com, a popular network started in 1998 that focuses on social action. Care2 and its sister site, ThePetitionSite.com, supports a community of 20 million "do gooders," mostly women between the ages of 25 and 65, who take action online every day. Care2 members have signed online petitions more than 80 million times since the year 2000, and in 2011, Care2's members started more than 60,000 new petitions targeting Congress, local and federal government agencies, and political figures.

Change.org Change.org is another popular online community offering all organizations and individuals (regardless of their political affiliation) a platform to start both free and paid petitions around a variety of issues (the environment, women's rights, labor reform, human rights, education, etc.) that reaches millions of people monthly.

DailyKos Recognized as one of the most popular political blogs, DailyKos has built an active community of 350,000 political activists and bloggers who discuss politics and U.S current events from a liberal perspective. DailyKos also has a petition feature, and organizations that are looking to brand their campaigns can use their online advertising platform. Staffers from various advocacy organizations also blog on DailyKos, sharing their opinions, insights, and experience.

BlogHer If your target audience is GenX women (those born between 1960 and 1980), you may find them hanging out on BlogHer, one of the largest networks of women online that discusses topics ranging from politics to nutrition to technology. BlogHer also has a large advertising network that you can use for banner ad campaigns.

Once you have identified your advocacy campaign objectives, core message, target audiences, and what channels and devices they are using, you will need to implement and promote your campaign and calls to action across multiple channels.

USE MULTIPLE CHANNELS TO ENGAGE SUPPORTERS

We have found that if you build a good relationship with your supporters, share actions through stories, frame the problem as something people can realistically address, and tell them how their action will lead to success, your supporters will not only take action on your advocacy campaigns, but also use their own influence on channels such as Facebook, Twitter, blogs, and email to share your campaigns.

Paull Young of charity: water says it best: "The web is like a solar system. Every individual has his or her own sphere of influence online. While we tend to think about the big communities and channels like Facebook and email, our constituents are influential on different channels like Reddit or Yelp, and in different ways."

Young says, "Organizations think if they have a presence on Facebook and Twitter, 'We are good.' That is not how it works. Big things can happen if organizations can share their story and get supporters excited and inspired enough to re-share them with people in their communities. What organizations can influence in these communities is miniscule compared to what your community can spread on these channels due to their connections and influence in all of these different spaces."

Tailor Messages and Calls to Action to Channels and Audiences

When communicating with constituents on different channels such as email, mobile texting, or social networks, you need to adapt your messaging and conversations to each platform, as each one has a different tone, nomenclature, length consideration, and even social purpose. The key is to leverage the power of the channels collectively as part of a cohesive outreach and cultivation strategy to connect with people anytime, everywhere. We outline a few next.

Email Email is perhaps the most popular form of communication and is the cornerstone of most campaign communications. According to the Nonprofit Digital Teams Benchmark Report, "external research continues to show that email remains by far the largest, most engaged, must lucrative, and most active tool in the digital strategy toolkit."[17]

There are more than 188 billion emails sent every day, which means that 3.3 million emails are sent per second around the world. In 2011, mobile email use rose 28% in the United States, according to a comScore study.[18] That's an estimated 89.6 million mobile users who accessed email on their mobile device. In Europe, the mobile email user base increased by 55% and in Japan by 53% in 2010.[19] By 2015, it's estimated that there will be 4.1 billion email accounts worldwide—that's an average annual growth rate of 7% over the next four years, according to The Radicati Group.[20] To compete with all the other emails landing in your constituents' in-boxes and increase open, click through, and action rates, you need to do everything in your power to make your email alerts stand out and immediately capture people's attention.

TIPS FOR EMAIL SUCCESS

Do you like to read boring books, articles, or emails? No, of course not. So why would any of your constituents want to read a boring email from your organization that sounds like a wonky press release? Use these tips to craft compelling email alerts, and watch your online action rates soar.

- Captivate people by telling them a powerful story. As we mentioned earlier in the chapter, people love drama, humor, and personality. It makes no

---

difference if you are a women's organization focusing on equal pay or an association encouraging veterans to get into IT, emails should not be written too formally or like a press release. Consider framing your story in a fairy-tale structure. Who is the villain, who is the victim, who is the hero, what is the quest, what are the setbacks, what are the obstacles, what are your victories?

- Personalize your emails. First address people by their first name like "Hi Allyson." Follow that by telling them how the campaign action impacts their life or a policy or topic they care about.

- Have a clear call to action, similar to the email action alert from the National Wildlife Federation (NWF) in Figure 3.4, within the first two or three paragraphs. Make the action bold and hyperlinked so people clearly see it and understand how to take action.

- Use deadlines to create a sense of urgency.

- Don't intimidate people with data overload. Be strategic and use only relevant information that your audience needs to understand the campaign and the action you are asking them to take.

- Make emails scannable. People tend to skim emails, not read every single word. Use short paragraphs, bold headers and calls to action, bullet points or numbered lists. If you feel it's important that people have more information on an issue, link to more details so that those who want to learn more can do so at their leisure.

- Integrate social media sharing widgets so that people can spread your message far and wide.

- Test short subject lines (about 50 characters or less) to capture target audiences' attention (remember you are competing in the battle of the in-boxes).

- Segment based on target audience for the campaign. Don't send your entire community the same exact message. People joined your list or were recruited through different paths and at different times. For example, if you are running a state- or city-specific advocacy campaign you will want to segment by zip code. A good CRM (constituent relationship management system) allows you to do this type of segmenting.

Figure 3.4
Example of NWF Action Fund Email Alert

Dear Friend of Wildlife,

In Cánada, **plans to slaughter more than 6,000 wolves** over the next five years is coming closer to reality as escalating tar sands development transforms vital habitat into huge toxic wastelands.

But that's not stopping Big Oil and their allies in the U.S. Congress, who are once again pushing legislation to fast-track the Keystone XL pipeline--a project that would drive a rapid expansion of tar sands operations and put the lives of thousands of wolves at risk.

<u>Save wolves from dirty oil--urge your members of Congress to vote NO against the dangerous Keystone XL pipeline today.</u>

Stop the Senseless Killing of Wolves

Help Save Wolves from Dirty Oil

Widespread deforestation of habitat as a result of oil and gas development in Canada has pushed woodland caribou to the brink of regional extinction. But instead of protecting caribou habitat to ensure their survival, the Canadian government has made wolves the culprit--**shooting them from them air and poisoning them with strychnine.**

Over 500 wolves have already been killed, and this persecution is planned to expand because of tar sands development. Canada's Minister of Environment Peter Kent has said that 6,000 wolves will need to be killed to "rescue" caribou impacted by loss of habitat.

<u>Stop the senseless killing of wolves by urging Congress to stop the Keystone XL pipeline today.</u>

Stopping the massive Keystone XL pipeline--which would roughly double imports of dirty tar sands oil into the United States--is a critical step in protecting wolves from the dangerous expansion of tar sands. Earlier this year, the U.S. Senate rejected a bill that would have overruled President Obama's rejection of the Keystone XL pipeline and expedited its approval. Now, this dangerous legislation has resurfaced--and we may not win this time if we don't speak up.

Your members of Congress need to hear from you that boosting Big Oil's profits at the expense of wildlife is not acceptable. With your voice today, **we can help stop these cruel killings** and ensure wolves and many more wildlife can thrive for years to come.

<u>Keep up the fight for Canada's wolves by urging your members of Congress to stand up against the Keystone XL tar sands pipeline.</u>

Thanks for all you do to protect wildlife.

Sincerely,

Sue Brown
Executive Director, NWF Action Fund
info@nwa.org
Twitter: @wildlifeaction
Join us on Facebook

Mobile Texting (SMS)   Text messaging can be used to interact in real time with constituents and provide them with important resources and campaign updates quickly and efficiently. Text messages are short—they're limited to 160 characters or less.

Texting has been used all over the world by protestors and organizers to quickly disseminate information and coordinate logistics. It was used as early as 2001, when activists protested the halt of Philippine President Joseph Estrada's impeachment trial and used it to coordinate actions. "During several days of intense protests, text message traffic in the Philippines more than doubled from 30 million messages a day the month before to 70 million a day during the protests (in a country of 85 million). In the end, the intense protests caused the Supreme Court to declare Estrada's presidency void, and he was removed from office. Similar mobile phone–based organizing was used by supporters of the two main candidates in the 2004 Philippine elections," according to NP Action.[21]

Texting can be an important advocacy and education tool, particularly for reaching people in developing countries and communities who don't have a phone line, and it is a lot more accessible than computers, the Internet, and social networks. Since mobile phones are personal and portable devices, they often serve as lifelines to people.

In Africa, nonprofits such as Text to Change have used texting since 2007 to communicate with people in rural areas to educate them on a wide range of health issues such as AIDS and maternal health.

In the United States, texting started gaining more momentum during the 2008 presidential elections. The political parties and organizations used text messaging for GOTV (Get Out the Vote) drives, important announcements like vice presidential campaign picks, and to acquire more supporter information.

Although texting in the United States has certainly been widely adopted in people's personal lives (particularly among Millennials) and nonprofits are using it more than ever before, it's still in its infancy stage for advocacy purposes.

"New technologies emerge quickly—but the pace at which they are adopted takes time," said Doug Plank, CEO of MobileCause. Plank cautions that nonprofits in the United States need to be careful and look at mobile as an opportunity for engagement rather than focus on it as a quick way to raise money. "To view mobile technology as little more than a one-and-done text-to-give platform is to utterly miss the real opportunities mobile [is] offering nonprofits to engage with their supporters."[22]

There are a few main ways organizations can integrate texting into their advocacy campaigns if they have a sizable mobile list. Send short text alerts (up to

160 characters) to constituents informing them about breaking news and actions they can take. You can even use texting to follow up from an email alert that you sent them 24 hours earlier, reminding them to take action.

Texting is also a good way to survey a segment of constituents and gather data about their interests and preferences. The results will help improve your communications and lead to more meaningful engagements. The American Red Cross has experienced success using texting campaigns to survey and learn more about their members' and donors' preferences for receiving different types of content and how often they would like to be communicated with via mobile.

In addition, texting can be used to reach communities who are seeking information that will help them on a personal level. For example, Planned Parenthood in Orange and San Bernardino Counties has a texting program that allows people to text them seven days a week to connect with a certified health educator to learn about sexual and reproductive health, including questions about birth control, pregnancy, sexually transmitted infections, healthy relationships, and more.

Another great example of an advocacy appeal via text message comes from AARP. After hearing Senator Alan Simpson say that Social Security was like trying to "milk a cow," AARP sent a text message to 44,000 members urging them to call AARP and leave a voice mail about why Social Security mattered to them. AARP generated close to 1,000 voice mail messages from their members in the first 24 hours, which were delivered to certain members of Congress. This example also shows that mobile campaigning is not exclusively for "young" people.

If you decide to implement a texting program, make sure staff are properly trained on how to engage in conversations over texting, including how to deal with challenging personalities or constituents whose first language isn't English.

KNOW THE SPAM LAWS

There are many legal issues and carrier rules around texting, and they are ever-evolving, so it's important stay on top of them. One of the most important laws is the m-Spam Act of 2009 that was enacted to stop unsolicited text messages. You can contact people via text message only after they have provided you their mobile numbers and opted-in to your mobile list. You must also provide opportunities for them to opt-out.

MISSED CALLS AS AN ORGANIZING STRATEGY

Mobile phone use in campaigns is not just about text messaging. In much of the world, mobile phone networks are the only thing that connects cities and countries to the rest of the world. Landlines are rare, but inexpensive mobile phones are available widely. Cost structures are different and often text messaging is cheap while calls are expensive.

In India, for example, "missed calls" have become a campaign tool. Greenpeace India has used missed calls as a cheap and quick way to engage people and build lists. Instead of people sending a text message to sign up or get information, a caller dials a number on their phone, waits for the line to connect, and then hangs up. Nobody answers but the incoming number is saved.

In one campaign, citizens rallied to oppose widescale coal mining in central-eastern India's forests. Greenpeace India set up a call number through a mobile vendor and then promoted the campaign with a call to action—call this number to stop the coal mining in central-eastern India's forests. "Callers knew that dialing the number was a way to indicate their support for the campaign. For many in the West, 'missed calls' are a bit of a mystery but the practice has been around for years," says online strategist Ted Fickes.[23]

Organizers set a goal of 80,000 missed calls and generated 100,000. How did they get such a large response?

- They texted their lists (supporters and online activists with phones) to urge them to "sign" the "petition" to save forests from coal mining in the form of a missed call.

- They advertised (for free) on a popular "cricket game channel" with 2.5 million users during a big match, which directed traffic to the campaign.

QR Codes   Quick Response Codes (QR codes) are 2-D codes with black dots arranged in a square pattern on a white background (See Figure 3.5). Information encoded on them can include a text message, website address, locations, images, and other types of data. When someone scans the code with a QR scanner (such as with a smartphone app), they can access the data. You've probably seen dozens of QR codes on your way to work. They are used commonly on bus stop

billboards that advertise a movie or consumer product. You also may have seen them on pamphlets or flyers at sporting events or concerts. QR codes have been gaining popularity among marketers for their space efficiency in marketing materials and flexible use. Nonprofits can utilize QR codes as advocacy and educational vehicles, too.

For example, the Juvenile Diabetes Research Foundation used QR codes during their "Promise Campaign" on meeting request forms that they sent to legislators. On each form QR codes were linked to a video hosted on YouTube from a local volunteer who requested a meeting with their legislator. Meeting commitments increased at a faster-than-normal rate, said Mike Kondratick, former director of Grassroots Advocacy.[24]

"We had an interim goal of getting 250 meetings scheduled by December 31, 2011, which we beat with a total of 262. This was a lofty goal, as the last time we did this campaign, two years ago, we only had 200 done by the end of the calendar year. Our approach to scheduling, including use of QR codes, has certainly helped us. The more personal a request we can make for a meeting, the better."

The National Aquarium in Baltimore directly posts QR codes on exhibits throughout the Aquarium.[25] They often include short, catchy questions like, "Wonder how sharks spend their day?" The QR code directs visitors to videos that answer the questions and provides additional educational information about the sea creatures and their habitats.

Mobile Advertising

Mobile ads can be effective in promoting advocacy campaigns to your target audiences, since many people are constantly connected to their smartphone. Because of the GPS (Global Positioning System) features built into smartphones, mobile ads can be aimed at people based on their search queries, said Colin Delaney, in his Online Politics 101 Guide.[26] It is also possible to deliver ads and other content based on where a person is located, down to where they are standing.

And if your advocacy targets are members of Congress who do a lot of traveling, mobile advertising could be another way to reach them, especially if you know where they will be.

When Allyson's firm, Rad Campaign, developed a year-long, hard-hitting online ad campaign targeting members of Congress to support the labor movement's Employee Free Choice Act, the firm launched a series of successful geo-targeted mobile ads (delivering ads based on location) aimed at House Democrats while they were at a retreat in Williamsburg, Virginia. The firm chose this approach because they knew members of Congress never went anywhere without their smartphones. Even though the banner ads were small in physical size to fit the size of a smartphone screen, they were designed with a strong message to members of Congress: "stop squeezing the middle class," a tagline from the labor campaign that was being reinforced in print materials, petitions, and other online and print ads targeting Congress.

The mobile banner ads significantly beat the industry average click through rate because they were very targeted and had a clear message about an important legislative bill members were in the middle of reviewing.

Mobile Applications

It's easy to get excited about mobile applications. But your app will rarely get downloaded and used if it does not provide incredible value to your constituents. Lauren DeLisa Coleman of Mobile Marketer says too often brands and organizations fall into an app trap when they put out an app for the sake of doing something cool but in reality it's actually boring content or games that even the organization's employees themselves would not engage in if they were not paid to do so.[27] Don't get dazzled by shiny objects and fall into the trap of creating an app for your staff or board members just for the sake of making one. Why? Because 80% of apps fail. Take a popular app you have probably heard about—Angry Birds. It failed to catch on 52 times before the creators, Riovio, got it right.[28] If you don't have the stomach or the money to iterate on your app, don't bother creating one. It's like flushing twenty thousand or more $1 bills down the toilet.

However, some nonprofits, such as the Monterey Bay Sea Aquarium, have gotten it right by focusing their app, which we highlight in Figure 3.6 on providing value and fulfilling a need for their community. For example, the Seafood Watch mobile application helps people make sustainable seafood choices. This app has been downloaded more than 500,000 times because it provides great

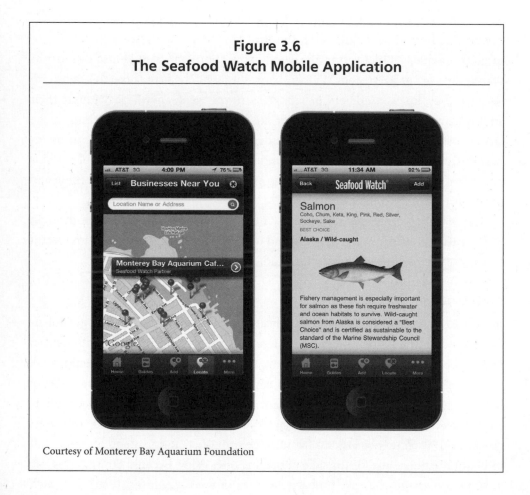

Figure 3.6
The Seafood Watch Mobile Application

Courtesy of Monterey Bay Aquarium Foundation

value, is easy to use, and is focused on an easy solution for individuals that want to make a difference to endangered fish species through their eating habits.

The app informs people about overfishing and health issues by:

- Using a phone's GPS to load the corresponding regional seafood watch guide based on the user's location

- Enabling people to search for seafood by common market name

- Allowing people to sort seafood rankings by "Best Choice," "Good Alternative," or "Avoid"

- Providing a Sushi guide list

- Providing alternatives to seafood on the "Avoid" list

- Letting people contribute to a new "FishMap" feature by adding the names of restaurants and stores where they found ocean-friendly seafood and by locating businesses where others have found sustainable seafood

Sunlight Labs, a part of the Sunlight Foundation, is a prominent open source community of thousands of people dedicated to using technology to transform government. It has several apps, including Real Time Congress, which is aimed at busy grassroots organizations, government affairs, and lobbyists. The app provides House and Senate Committee schedules and key policy documents as soon as Congress and the White House release them. Although the mobile app serves a smaller and more niche audience than the Seafood Watch app, members of the intended target audience want this information at their fingertips, and the app delivers it to them no matter where they are, any time of day.

Blogs

There are over 156 million public blogs. That's a lot of people using this medium to distribute information, express opinions, and foster lively discussions. Niche blogs can be helpful to reach your target audience anytime and everywhere, as many people now get their news online rather than via traditional print media, according to the State of News Media 2011 report by Pew Research Center's Project for Excellence in Journalism.[29]

BLOGGING TIPS

Here are a few ways to write more engaging and informative blog posts. In fact, these tips may be useful when crafting most any public-facing communications:

- Use the inverted pyramid style, which outlines the critical news first, followed by important details and then additional background information. This style focuses on how users prefer to see the key information you want them to know up front. Again this is especially important because many of your constituents are accessing online content from multiple devices, ranging from laptops to the iPad.

- Quickly get to the point. Blog posts should be framed around a central theme.

- Give people an opportunity to take action when appropriate.

- Use short and catchy headlines that summarize the post's content. Blog headlines also impact social sharing. If people share your blog posts on social media channels, you want your headline to stand out and grab people's attention so that they click on it, read it, and reshare it.

- Provide fresh and relevant content. Use your blog posts to provide commentary on the latest news, resources, reports, policies, summits, or events you attended or held, and how they impact people's lives.

Dealing with Trolls

A word of caution: blogs can attract trolls (people who post inflammatory comments or harasses others online), particularly around advocacy issues. And while it may be tempting to respond to the trolls, we usually don't recommend it because they will continue to attack you online. If you build a strong community, the community will help keep the trolls in check and often drown them out. You can also consider closing comments after the post has been live for a certain length of time (two to four weeks, for example).

Video

Video can be an incredibly powerful way to tell your story. Since YouTube is one of the most trafficked sites on the web, it's an important channel that nonprofits should use. When producing videos about your issues, it's especially important to communicate authentically, and think about how you can empower your

- Use an active voice.

- Consider the target audiences. Who are the target audiences of your blog post? Activists? Policymakers?

- Have a conversational tone. It's a blog, not a press release.

- Make it compelling. Remember, no one likes to read boring content. Blog posts are a great way to use a few of your organization's key data points or share a couple of pertinent statistics from your work. However, don't overload people with too much data in a single post.

- Be easily scannable. People like to skim blogs for key points. Utilize bullets, lists, short paragraphs, and bolded headlines to make the blog posts easy to scan. This is also good for search engine optimization (SEO).

- Pose questions to audiences and give them the opportunity to share their own opinions on the blog.

- Integrate social share buttons or widgets so people can easily share your posts on Twitter, Facebook, Pinterest, Google+, and LinkedIn.

- Incorporate captivating photos, videos, audio, infographics, and even presentations that you can embed through SlideShare (an online community for sharing presentations and documents).

- Link to other blog posts and organizations doing good work in the space.

target audiences to express themselves, too. Sometimes the passion your supporters share vocally for your cause is the most powerful expression of why your work is important. While high-end polished videos can be helpful in telling your story, nonprofits working on a budget shouldn't despair.

If you have a good story to tell and access to decent video and editing equipment, do-it-yourself videos are an efficient and effective option. Video equipment has become a lot more affordable, and there are inexpensive editing programs such as iMovie that you can use. If you have additional funds, make audio equipment your first higher-end equipment purchase. Your community can bear with your more impromptu video quality, but people will tune out quickly if they can't hear what's going on.

The "It Gets Better" campaign, started by syndicated columnist Dan Savage, leveraged user-generated video submissions to give hope to Lesbian, Gay, Bisexual, and Transgender (LGBT) youth facing harassment and abuse. The site's visibility gained momentum steadily across platforms quickly: over 200 videos were uploaded in the first week, and the project's YouTube channel reached the 650 video limit in the next week. The project now exists as its own website, the It Gets Better Project, and at the time of this writing it comprises more than 30,000 video entries, with more than 40 million views. The campaign is also active on Facebook and has over 250 thousand people "liking" their page, spurring conversations about the videos, and offering words of encouragement.

SEIU USES VIDEO TO COMMUNICATE AND RECRUIT MILLENNIALS

Over the years Labor Unions have experienced a significant decline in their membership. The Service Employees International Union (SEIU) recognized this problem and the need to focus their efforts on recruiting and connecting with a new and younger, progressive audience. They used video to tell the story of why public employees are valuable and showed how losing certain public services would have huge consequences to the issues that this target audience cared most about. "We started from a research point, asking ourselves: where is this target audience currently consuming content and who are they listening to on this issue… if anyone? Eventually we developed a target list of influencers, editorial sites, and video sharing channels where our audience would be receptive to content on this issue," said Amy York Rubin, founder of Strategic Productions.

Through partnerships with stakeholders in these spaces, such as the comedian Sarah Haskins (popular at the time for her CurrentTV series *Target Women*) and the top YouTube channel Barely Political (which has average monthly video views of 46 million), SEIU were able to tap into a new, targeted audience in the context of the channels they already consume and through the stakeholders and influencers they trust. The result was a video with over 325,000 views in less than a week, and coverage on culture blogs such as Boing Boing. Rubin said that the grassroots momentum not only spurred the homemade creation of campaign-related swag and unsolicited user-generated content but also created enough momentum to pass legislation in California to save public libraries, one of the first public services under attack.

Social Networks

Sometimes organizations forget that social media is about being social and having conversations. "Social media is like a cocktail party," says Colin Delany, editor of Epolitics.com and director of Outreach and Online Communications for the National Women's Law Center. And if you're hosting the cocktail party, a central part of your job is responding to your guests' needs. Apply the same etiquette to your social media program. These back and forth conversations can be instrumental in your advocacy and outreach. If you foster community and attend to your supporters' needs on these channels, social networks can amplify the breadth of the movement and show the community's passion.

By 2012, Greenpeace Brazil had created one of the largest online communities in the global conservation community. How? In large part, this growth came through relentless interaction. Greenpeace Brazil attempts to respond to every inquiry and question on Twitter and Facebook. It takes work but the effort has helped build the community and is a key element in moving from a list of fans to a mobilized community.

While there are many social networks that your organization can have a presence on, you may not have the luxury to spend a lot of time and resources on all of them. Pick two or three networks that you know your target audiences are on. And if you're just starting out and aren't quite sure where your target audiences are hanging out, it's worth noting that Facebook, Twitter, and YouTube are three networks that rank in the top five most trafficked sites on the web, so that would be a good place to start. LinkedIn groups can also be beneficial to reach and share information with niche communities and stakeholders who are interested in specific issues you are working on.

HOW JDRF USED SOCIAL MEDIA FOR A PETITION DRIVE

"Easily our biggest and most successful social media effort to date was a petition drive [targeting the FDA] in support of [running outpatient trials for an artificial pancreas, the next significant advance in diabetes treatment technology] in the winter of 2011," said Mike Kondratick. JDRF embedded a Convio petition on their website that they drove traffic to via email, Facebook, Twitter (with a program-specific hashtag), and mobile text messages.

JDRF's goal was to get to 40,000 signatures in a month. They generated 106,000 signatures in 30 days. About 60% of these signatures were generated directly through Facebook. "I was truly astounded. We wound-up with more 'likes' on our petition page than we have on our existing Facebook Page," said Kondratick.

What made this campaign so successful? They did a good job of building community daily, as well as raising awareness around the campaign by utilizing multiple online channels and mobile in the months leading up to the petition drive. "We were careful to make sure that our messages were tied to a specific person rather than just our organization, which I think helps tremendously. So, we could make our mobilization appeals directly from those people. Once we gained some momentum, the regular Facebook posts, tweets, and mobile messages pretty much did the rest," said Kondratick.

This was also a watershed moment for JDRF. They had the opportunity to set aggressive interim signature goals, which they ended up exceeding. JDRF finally had the evidence they could use to prove that what they do everyday via social media and online channels matters tremendously and that, if they want to be successful in advocacy or fundraising, they have to use these social media channels to manage conversations and relationships.

Design for Distribution

You may approach your advocacy campaign from an organic perspective. The places where the content or calls to action get shared are the places that the community and the network take it, not necessarily where you've already posted it or asked for your community to engage. Maybe you have a good sense of the tools and messages that your community will respond to, or maybe you don't have the lead-time to recruit supporters to get involved on your behalf across the web. Compared to the previous approach, with this strategy, what you lack in a networked approach you can make up for with tools and technology to help spread your advocacy campaigns.

Whether you hope you reach citizens in the next town or on the other side of the world, you can support sharing and distribution of your content and calls to action by embedding sharing tools at the start of your campaign. Widgets provided by platforms themselves (the "like" button, tweet button, Google's +1 button, and others), which we also discussed in the blogging section earlier, can easily be added to your website with a small bit of code. You can also use widgets like the "ShareThis" plug-in,[30] which allows visitors to select the channel they wish to use from one button to share your campaign or content.

Just adding share buttons isn't enough though. Test different buttons, locations of the buttons, and sharing messages. Pay close attention to which buttons get used. There is a science to sharing, and making sharing easy for users can make a big difference. Recently, Upworthy (a progressive social venture started in 2012 by former leaders of MoveOn, Facebook, and the Onion) shared data on its social sharing tests. The results showed that catchy headlines and the inclusion of buttons and photos make a big impact on how sharable the content is.[31]

Since some of the most popular content to be shared across social networks are photos and videos, make sure that compelling photos or videos that support your campaign are front and center on your website and ready to share via email and social media. Make sure you're set up on any social platforms you plan to use, too. If you have a key video you plan to use, for example, make sure your YouTube account is active and working, and post the video there in addition to your site. You can also model the content sharing process with other social accounts you have and content you produce—include the same hashtags or key words, using the same (succinct!) call to action, and providing a link to the campaign or organizational website.

A great example of this method for multichannel advocacy is the Occupy movement. Very quickly after the first occupy camp started in New York City, people posted information about issues and actions on Twitter and Tumblr, live-streamed video on Vimeo, and shared pictures on their mobile phones. This allowed people to join the movement from wherever they were—they could share and repost updates on social networks, tell personal stories on Tumblr, and "occupy" anywhere. People all over the world used Meetup.com's Meetup Everywhere feature to register a solidarity event in over a thousand cities.[32] The online visibility of the hashtag and stories, combined with the map of Meetup Everywhere events, helped the movement build rapidly even without a central organization supporting and creating the messages and calls to action. Four months after the launch of #OccupyWallStreet, there were over 2,800[33] "Occupy Together" events on the Meetup Everywhere Map.[33]

Deliver Your Messages to Advocacy Targets Across Multiple Channels

There are a variety of ways to deliver your messages to your advocacy targets. Before deciding on a delivery method, think about what you want the message to achieve. Is it to put pressure on members of Congress about a legislative bill? Is it to publicly hold a corporation accountable for bad actions? Or perhaps it's to generate publicity, like when MoveOn.org sent John Hlinko, one of its members, to hand-deliver 30,000 printed messages from constituents to Senator McConnell's office wearing cling-on socks, boxer shorts, and other evidence of static, after McConnell publicly stated that Americans care as much about campaign finance reform as they do about static cling. Here are some delivery methods and factors to consider:

- *Snail mail is the old-fashioned way of delivering messages to advocacy targets, but it can still be used effectively in campaigns*. For example, if your goal is to have constituents' personal letters read by members of Congress, Congressional staff members still read handwritten notes and often respond.

- *Email delivery of petitions or letters is the fastest and most cost-effective way to deliver messages*. It's worth noting that when you target members of Congress, "most government systems either hide the email address or simply reject bulk actions to it," says Dave Leichtman, vice president of services and support at Salsa Labs. Leichtman suggests organizations look for Constituent Relationship Management (CRM) providers that submit emails through members of Congress's webforms, which also verify constituents' zip codes. "That tends to be even better for guaranteed delivery than either email or fax," said Leichtman. Several CRM providers that specialize in advocacy do this, such as Blackbaud (including tools gained in their 2011 acquisition of Convio), ActionKit, Engaging Networks, and Salsa Labs. Many corporate targets operate similarly.

- *There is an ongoing debate in the nonprofit community about how much weight blast-email petitions carry with members of Congress compared to handwritten notes and personal calls*. According to the Congressional Management Foundation Study "Communicating with Congress: Perception of Citizen Advocacy on Capitol Hill,"[34] which surveyed 260 congressional staff, email and postal mail are considered with the same weight, but what matters most is the content, not the channel. However, 53% of Congressional staffers still believe that advocacy campaigns of identical form messages are sent without constituents' knowledge or approval, showing that there is still a great deal of misperception among Congressional staff. This doesn't mean that petitions are unimportant. Petitions are just one tactic, and it is important that you are able to demonstrate power in multiple channels.

- *Social media can be a great way to publically put an advocacy target in the hot seat or even thank a target for doing something positive for your cause*. For example,

"Tweet bombs" where people tweet the advocacy targets with a central message in a specific time period. You can use a similar tactic on the wall of a target's Facebook Page.

- *Act.ly is a free Twitter petition tool where organizations and individuals can petition advocacy targets such as corporations, government agencies, members of Congress, etc.* The app tracks and publically displays people on Twitter who have signed the petition and if the target responds to the petition. While social media as a listening and communications tool is gaining momentum among Congressional staffers, comments from social media applications have little influence on undecided members, because members cannot tell whether comments are made by their constituents, according to the Congressional Management Foundation Study.

- *Faxing is another viable delivery method.* And while it can be more expensive (some vendors can charge up to 10 cents per fax delivery) and slower than email, thousands of legitimate faxes being sent to a target's office can certainly get your target to pay attention. Of course, some offices have been annoyed by the fax jams these types of campaigns can cause and have turned off the fax machine for a day.

POPVOX PLATFORM

POPVOX is another platform to consider for delivering your advocacy messages to members of Congress around specific legislative bills. People take action on POPVOX by selecting from bills pending in Congress, choosing to support or oppose, and writing a message to Congress. Comments are then forwarded to members of Congress with a constituent's real name, address, and phone number, which is information they need to verify that the messages are legitimate.

METRICS: MEASURE IMPACT ACROSS MULTIPLE CHANNELS

No multichannel advocacy plan focused on creating social change anytime, everywhere would be complete without establishing realistic metrics that measure how well you are achieving your short-term and long-term goals. While there are several metrics that you may consider for your advocacy campaign (which we will highlight below), the most important metric to measure is your overall impact. Did you meet the goals you set out to achieve? Did it make a real impact on policy, lives, and the planet? The best tool you have at your disposal to measure results is yourself. No tool can ever replace a human being's capacity to assess real impact on the ground. Young at charity: water says, "the most powerful analytics tool is the human brain."

A good place to start your measurement plan is to identify Key Performance Indicators (KPIs) that are unique for your advocacy campaign. KPIs will help you determine whether you are succeeding or failing so that you can quickly tweak your advocacy campaign or change course if something isn't working.

A few KPIs that we have found useful for multichannel advocacy campaigns include the following:

Conversion Rates

Are your people taking action on your campaigns? For example, are they signing your petitions online, responding to your text messages, calling their members of Congress after you send them an urgent email, signing up to volunteer, texting to donate, downloading your apps or toolkits, meeting with their member of Congress as part of your big lobby day, or whatever else may be the focus of the call to action?

Website Visitor Loyalty

Many nonprofits set up campaign landing pages and even microsites as an entry and focal point for advocacy campaigns. One of the signs of an active online advocacy campaign is a high number of repeat visitors to your website, especially on the campaign landing pages that you promoted. Repeat visitors can be indicative that people are coming back to your site even after they have taken an action.

Share of Search Across the Web

When you are promoting multichannel advocacy campaigns to reach your target audiences, it's important to assess your organization's share of search (proportion of search clicks for a keyword or issue) across the web and compare it to your "competition." In addition, share of search is now influenced by your success on social networks, especially Google+. Google's "Search Plus Your World" now integrates Google+ profiles, pages, and updates into search results by using social signals to determine relevancy. This means that you can earn a greater share of search by engaging your audience and sharing valuable content on social networks.

Your share of search is usually keywords associated with your campaign, such as the name of your organization, campaign name, and issue area. There are many types of vendors you can use to assess share of search. For example, Compete.com, which has both a paid and free version, can show you unique monthly website visitors and web traffic patterns for a website over the course of a year and compare them against your competitors.

Google Insights is a free tool that can show you search results for keywords about campaign issues. For example, when we searched for the term "climate change," Google Insights showed that the top search term is "global climate change," followed by "global warming," "what is climate," and "climate change effects." It also shows regional interest of the search term. Furthermore, it highlights a detailed graph on how the search term has generated interest over the years relative to the total number of searches done on Google. So in this example, an environmental nonprofit working on climate change could use the Google Insights information to bid on Google Adwords and to target people in geographic regions where climate change is generating interest.

Radian6 is a paid tool that helps you measure important keywords related to your advocacy campaign on social media sites, blogs (including the comments), forums, and online news outlets, as well as sentiment and other comparative metrics against competitors. Small Act's Thrive and SpotRight, a social CRM aimed at the nonprofit community, also helps nonprofits measure keywords across social networks and identifies the influencers talking about your issues so that you can reach out and connect with them during your advocacy campaign.

Impact on the Ground

Ultimately, KPIs must measure impact on the most important metric of all: the social change you seek to create on the ground. For example, if you were an animal rescue organization, this KPI could be how many rescued dogs were adopted. If you were a policy organization focused on climate change, this KPI could be how many related climate change bills with no loopholes passed to reduce carbon emissions.

More Metrics to Consider

- Open rates, click through rates, and conversion rates on email alerts.
- Completion rates on your advocacy action landing pages.
- Social media sharing statistics on your advocacy campaign landing pages.

- Click through rates on short URLs (created via bit.ly, goo.gl, etc.) that you use in social media. If you use a third-party app such as HootSuite to manage your Twitter accounts, consider upgrading to its pro account to access your analytics. These are especially useful if you send people to special landing pages associated with these URLs so you can track action and conversion rates.

- Top web traffic sources: referring sites, search engines, direct traffic. What percentage of visitors come from social networks, and which networks send the most traffic?

- Average time on site.

- Mobile application downloads. Positive reviews in the app store to track how many people found the app valuable.

- Active user rate on mobile apps.

Once you begin to find measurable successes across multiple channels, rinse and repeat. But don't be afraid to experiment even after you've tasted success. Think about testing new strategies, measure them, and rinse and repeat again.

Nonprofit Industry Standard Metrics

Many KPIs are typically judged by industry standard benchmarks. A couple of great benchmark studies to consider as you go through the process of developing realistic goals for your own advocacy campaign are the eNonprofit Benchmark Study,[35] which analyzed 44 nonprofits online and mobile data, and the Social Network Benchmark Report, which surveyed 3,500 nonprofit practitioners.[36] Consider using them as a guide and see how your own organization measures up.

Online Advocacy and Email

According to the 2012 eNonprofit Benchmark Study, advocacy emails have the highest open, click through, and response rates of any type of email, as well as the lowest unsubscribe rate. These statistics are not surprising and show that many people on your list are willing to take some sort of action on behalf of your organization, but they require a deeper level of nurturing and engagement to turn them into donors.

The advocacy response rate was 3.8% in 2011. It's worth noting that from 2010 to 2011, advocacy response rates increased by 28% for the first time in several years. The study says the response rates increased significantly in 2011 because more organizations are adopting best practices online to optimize their email campaigns for better open rates and response rates.

The average study participant sends about 4.7 total emails per subscriber per month. Advocacy actions and items of personal interest tend to result in higher click through rates from newsletters. Advocacy open rates were 14%, while the click through rates were 4.2%, and the unsubscribe rate was 0.16%. Accordingly, it was the environmental organization category that had the highest click through rates in the study.

Why Churn Rates Are Important

Churn refers to the rate at which people unsubscribe, opt-out, or otherwise leave your lists, and it is an important metric to pay attention to.

According to the annual eNonprofit Benchmarks Report and the Facebook Extra report from NTEN and M+R Strategic Services, the average churn rate for

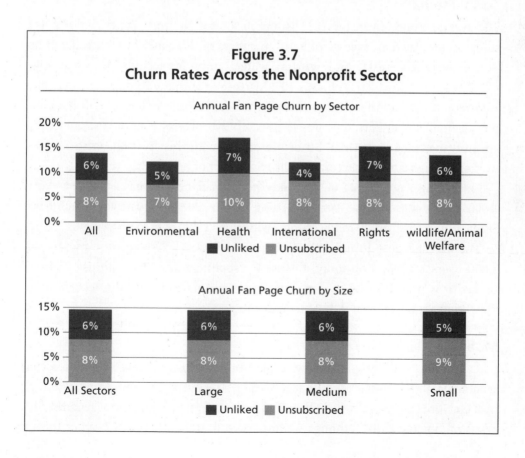

Figure 3.7
Churn Rates Across the Nonprofit Sector

email lists is 19% generally in the nonprofit sector. You can see the comparison data in Figure 3.7.

Research has shown that unsubscribes can be a sign of a healthy list, but it is natural to wonder how to maintain a good list and a strong community. The metrics you track should include both unsubscribes and opt-outs, as well as the shares, "forward to a friend" uses, and other direct response and engagement. Without the full picture of how your constituents are interacting with you on email, as well as across different channels, looking at the churn rate doesn't make sense. For example, it may be that you had someone connect on your Facebook Page who then realized that you focus broadly on all of the aspects of your organization's work in your Facebook Page engagement. If that person's interest is limited to a single program area, they may disconnect from your presence on Facebook but sign up through your email channel to receive specific action alerts related to the program they care about.

Social Media

The average nonprofit in the 2012 Nonprofit Social Network Benchmark Report study accumulated an average of 8,317 members on Facebook, which is about an 81% increase from 2011. And over on Twitter, nonprofits accumulated an average of 3,290 followers, which is about a 30% increase in community size. However, the study could not indicate whether these Twitter followers overlapped with the nonprofit's email subscribers. One way to research that overlap is to do a social media append (matching your email list of subscribers with their profiles on social networks) through a reputable company like Small Act or SpotRight.

On average, nonprofits in the study had 103 Facebook page fans for every 1,000 email subscribers. And according to the 2012 eNonprofit Benchmark Study, nonprofits had 29 followers on Twitter per 1,000 email subscribers.

The average post to a Facebook page received 2.5 likes or comments per 1,000 users, and 98% of nonprofits use Facebook versus 72% who use Twitter. LinkedIn is used by 44% of nonprofits participating in the study, according to the Nonprofit Social Network Benchmark Report.

Mobile

Since mobile is still relatively new to the nonprofit space, there are not a lot of reliable data and studies on mobile advocacy. The average nonprofit represented in the eNonprofit Benchmark Study had a total of 19,665 text message subscribers as of January 1, 2012, though it's important to note that only 12 out of the 44 nonprofits in the study provided mobile data. Nonetheless, those numbers are continuing to see healthy year-over-year growth. Between 2010 and 2011, text messaging lists grew an average of 46%. The median percentage of a nonprofit's mobile list is 1.2%. And the median annual churn rate is about 12%.

METRICS FOR YOUR MOBILE ADVOCACY CAMPAIGN

The open rate for text messaging is about 95%. This is because of the strict laws around people having to opt-in to receive text messages from your organization. The top three actions people respond to via texting, according to Angela McIntosh, director of business development of MobileCause, are:

1. A poll (replying to a question)

2. Replying to donate money

3. Clicking a link to watch a video

SPECIAL FOCUS: ADVOCACY REACH GLOBALLY

We have heard organizations say they want their video, hashtag, or even entire campaign to "go viral" more times than we can count. While "going viral" isn't something you can simply decide to do, reaching a global audience is—especially when using the multichannel strategies and tools we have just outlined. Social networks, mobile applications, and even websites are adopted at different levels by various segments of the population, depending on where you are in the world. As such, you can't assume that your campaign site or your photo will be picked up and shared without cross-pollinating and supporting that redistribution.

There are two approaches to using multichannel strategies in a global-reaching advocacy campaign. The first is proactive, relying on a core group of volunteers or community members. The second focuses on resources to support anyone participating in the advocacy campaign.

Seed the Channels

When you know you want to incorporate not just a multichannel approach but also a global reach to your advocacy campaign, you may choose to proactively seed various channels for engagement. Depending on the channels, tools, and platforms you plan to use, this initial groundwork will vary on specifics but will include a few crucial steps.

First, you will need to work with your volunteers, key community members, or active contributors. Unless you have a very large staff, it just isn't possible that you will have the capacity internally to create and maintain content on every single channel that we have discussed in this chapter. A strategy that many organizations have found to be successful is to recruit volunteers and supporters specifically to create and distribute content for the campaign; this way there is no confusion about what someone is signing up to do and the collaboration is deliberate.

Working closely with a subset of your community in this way is also important if you want to consider translating messages into different languages before you launch the campaign. Even if you do have the capacity as an organization to operate in multiple languages, translating crucial information about your campaign ahead of time can help support the sharing and distribution of content across languages by those who may or may not already be connected with you.

Most important, make sure your messaging is consistent. The more examples and templates for content that you can provide to your community (both for posting and translating), the more you ensure that you are creating a uniform call to action and message, regardless of the channel or distribution mechanism. If you don't, then it is like starting a global game of telephone in which the action and information can very quickly go awry.

350.org's Global Advocacy Reach

350.org is a terrific example of an organization that cultivates a core group of advocacy supporters, provides consistent and translated content before and during campaigns, and successfully mobilizes people in record numbers around the world.[37] When they are preparing for a day of action or a major campaign, people can sign up on the organization's primary website to join in, and they are given options to volunteer to do more—lead an event, organize locally, and so on. In this way, they are creating various groups of volunteers who have opted in at different levels of involvement, instead of having one big list that receives messages and calls to get involved that they don't want and that may burn them out before the campaign even begins.

Once people sign up for their preferred participation level, they are then provided with the resources and templates, as well as basic bulleted instructions, on what they should do next. If someone signed up just to stay informed, they may get prompted to share the campaign on their preferred social network. If they signed up to organize an offline event in their city, they may receive instructions on how to post the event details publicly on the site and messages to use to invite people to join them. The people who volunteered to organize events or post about the campaign help carry the message and catalyze action, especially for a campaign that focuses on one day of simultaneous action. Others who sign up to stay informed can receive messages preparing them for the day and reminding them to participate when the campaign or day of action launches.

Because 350.org's campaigns focus on a global issue and urge communities small and large around the world to get involved, it is not reasonable to think that information would be available on the website in hundreds of languages. This is the beauty in the core message of 350.org's campaigns: "350." The global Days of Action that 350.org has organized focuses people all over the world on calling for one thing: climate legislation and action that brings CO_2 in the atmosphere from its current level of 392 parts per million (ppm) to below 350 ppm, the number climate scientists note as the highest safe level. The campaigns urge people to take action locally however they want—some organize bike rides and others march on the streets, some plant gardens or create parks and some organize rallies—and share their action with a photo and a 350 sign.

These images are aggregated on the website, shared on Flickr and Facebook, tweeted and posted, and even emailed. Some are taken on a smartphone, others on simple cameras, some even on professional equipment. However people take action, in whatever language or culture, they can capture it and share it in real time to be part of the campaign and part of the movement.

Measurement Challenges for Global Advocacy

With a global reach, messages in various languages, and actions both online and offline, there are a few major challenges to advocacy campaigns of this size. For many organizations, translation of campaign materials into multiple languages is beyond feasible capacity. There may be volunteers who step up to provide translation, but it can't necessarily be checked for accuracy or cultural context. When this is the case, rely on the universal language of images. Like 350.org, consider focusing participation or the call to action around an image that can be shared, personalized, and remixed. Or consider making a video about your campaign that relies on graphics to explain your message instead of a talking head. Whatever universal types of images you end up using, make sure it is positioned centrally in your campaign messages and website so that your message is understood immediately.

Another sticky issue for organizations running campaigns beyond their on-the-ground presence is the reporting of participation and impact. For example, with the Occupy movement, just because someone puts a city on the Meetup map doesn't mean an event is taking place there. But if those activists take photos or video and share them with the rest of the network, it is easier to count not just cities participating but also the numbers of individuals around the world taking part. Even though it is not a guarantee for accuracy, incorporating easy ways for participants to self-report can help you have a more accurate projection of your impact than simply counting tweets or email responses.

Photos and video, especially user-generated content, help document growing campaigns and movements. As Shadia Fayne Wood, founder of Project Survival Media, put it when talking about the role of photos and video in the early days of the Occupy movement, "Seeing the photos has been really, really powerful.... How one visualizes and feels a part of a movement is by being able to see what you're a part of and how it's growing. It is absolutely critical in terms of people feeling urgency and understanding why people are going to get arrested, why people are putting their bodies on the line, and why they should be there to join them."[38]

PUTTING IT ALL TOGETHER: YOUR COMPLETE MULTICHANNEL ADVOCACY CAMPAIGN

Remember our core principles for any multichannel campaign:

- Use multiple channels to engage people.
- Use stories that move people to action.
- Always measure, learn, and iterate.

As you develop your advocacy campaign, you will be identifying where your supporters are, the channels they use, and the stories that inspire them to become involved. With so many channels at your disposal (email, mobile, blogs, video, social networks, and more) the options can overwhelm campaigners. That is why it is critical to build in time to test, evaluate results, and tweak your plan. Always be learning and you will better understand the channels, your supporters, and what messages work.

Now that you have a guide to creating and implementing an advocacy plan across different channels, and understand how to measure performance and assess results against nonprofit benchmarks, you are almost ready to start crafting your own plan. But before you dive in it's important to know how to plan for fundraising anytime, everywhere—the topic of the next chapter. This will help ensure that your advocacy and fundraising work together, rather than as competing priorities.

DISCUSSION QUESTIONS

Spark a conversation with your team or organization about these core advocacy principles with the following questions:

1. What are the short-term goals that your supporters can have a direct impact on?

2. What are the powerful stories from your community or work that you can use to highlight a short-term advocacy goal that you can promote across multiple channels?

3. What are the core actions and the ladder of engagement you will use to engage current and new supporters for your next campaign?

4. Which groups or super supporters will you tap to help you seed content or engagement when you launch your next call to action?

5. What are three metrics you want to watch in your next call to action to measure impact or increase actions rates?

chapter FOUR

Fundraising Anytime Everywhere

Creating social change is no easy task. It takes people, planning, resources, and money. This chapter is about the money. Truth is, today's organizations and campaigns rely on fundraising to build community, communicate with supporters, tell their story to the world, and provide direct services. Done well, fundraising not only provides resources, but also gives people an opportunity to invest in the process of change. This rewards donors, organizations, and communities.

Today, we look around and see unstable local, state, and national economies. We see governments slashing support for cultural programs, education, and social services. Nonprofits and their donors are needed more than ever. In 2011, $298.4 billion were raised for charity across multiple channels, about 2% of the GDP according to *Giving USA 2011, the Annual Report on Philanthropy.* The majority of money raised from the private sector came from individuals. As we have seen, online channels and mobile have created more ways than ever for people to access and interact with organizations.

Your organization needs to master multichannel communications to identify supporters, engage them in the cause, and give them ways to invest time and money.

FUNDRAISING IS LIKE BAKING BREAD

Think of fundraising as baking bread. You can't mix only one or two ingredients like flour and water together, toss it in the oven, and expect a warm, crusty bread to come out. Baking bread requires time and several key ingredients that make up the perfect chemistry to get the right consistency, make the dough rise, and ultimately end up with the best loaf of bread. Similarly, in fundraising, there are several strategies (or ingredients) for raising money. The best fundraisers we know focus on building a steady stream of donors by nurturing relationships with their constituents and moving them up the engagement ladder.

Equally important, they understand what motivates people to donate, and they craft strategies and tactics with that information in mind. For example, storytelling is a psychological marketing tactic that's used to emotionally connect us to one individual's (or animal's) plight, and tends to increase donations. In contrast, data driven messages cause people to use the analytical parts of their brain and can suppress giving. In addition, organizations need to show donors how their donations are making an impact on the ground, as we discussed in Chapter Three. Organizational fundraising communications (such as emails, donation pages, social media, and mobile) also need to be navigable, readable, and understandable. To sum it up, fundraising is part community and relationship building, part psychology, and part marketing and usability.

In this chapter, we first examine what drives people to donate money to charity. Next we discuss the different giving channels that supporters use today. Then we drill down into a variety of strategies, tactics, and examples to show you how they work in action. We don't expect that you will integrate all of these strategies and tactics, but it's good to understand all of the options so that you can determine which ones are realistic for your organization's budget, resources, and staff.

PSYCHOLOGY OF GIVING: WHAT MOTIVATES PEOPLE TO DONATE?

We believe that if we are truly going to change the world, we need to be realistic about the power and influence of money and how it impacts real social change. In this section we invite you to expand your understanding of why people typically donate to causes and take a look at data that we think is worth testing in your upcoming fundraising campaigns.

If you're an organizer, social media campaigner, or even a web manager reading this book, you may feel that people give money to charities because either they want to help people or communities in need or because they want to be a part of a movement and feel connected to something bigger than themselves.

While these reasons are certainly logical and factor into why people donate their money to charity, several studies have been done around the psychology of giving that tell a partially different story—the findings may surprise you.

People Want to Save One Person

You might be thinking: How could donors prefer to save one person instead of hundreds or millions? Peter Singer, a professor of bioethics at Princeton University and author of the book *The Life You Can Save: Acting Now to End World Poverty*, says people are motivated to give when you show them a single person in need that they can personally and emotionally identify with. For example, in one test that involved a children's advocacy organization, one group of participants were given the opportunity to donate money after they viewed messaging and data such as, "Food shortages in Malawi are affecting more than three million children." A second group with another set of participants viewed a photo of Rokia, a little girl from Malawi, who was very poor and struggling to get by. The photo was reinforced with messaging that indicated a gift to support Malawi would change her life. Guess which group gave significantly more money? The second group, which saw the photo of Rokia and were told how they could make a difference in her life. Typically, people emotionally connect with individuals rather than large groups of people.

People Are Ruled by Their Emotions

In the book *Science of Giving: Experimental Approaches to the Study of Giving*, edited by Daniel M. Oppenheimer and Christopher Y. Olivola, various authors and researchers outline several studies by psychologists and economists who researched donors' giving patterns and the psychology behind their decision to donate money, which we shall highlight.

Allyson, in her graduate school days, was focusing a lot of her art and web interactive projects on social justice issues, especially domestic violence, homelessness, and animal welfare. Some of her go-to resources for research were organizational websites and email updates, which were filled with staggering statistics but not real stories. One day after completing an exhaustive amount of research on the web, she went home feeling overwhelmed and powerless. There was so little emotion being conveyed for such emotional issues, she remembers. She took a paintbrush and painted on a canvas, "Don't Make Me Think." What does this flashback have to do with fundraising? Everything. When we rely on people thinking rather than feeling, we lose a chance to connect with donors emotionally—and a donation opportunity.

Researchers Stephan Dickert, Namika Sagara, and Paul Slovic say their studies show donors are driven by emotions and empathy toward others when they donate to charity and choose how much money they will actually give. For example, one study they conducted, "Affective Motivations to Help Others: A Two-Stage

Model of Donation Decisions," asked participants how they felt about children who were sick and suffering. Participants were also asked to think about the value of those sick children's lives. Researchers found that when participants saw a painful situation such as the sick children, they wanted to turn those sad, guilty, or negative feelings into something that made them feel good, like donating money to help the sick children. Michal Ann Strahilevitz, one of the other researchers in the book, confirmed a similar theory and said part of a fundraiser's job is to sell happiness to donors. Donating money makes people feel happier. The happier they feel, the more they will donate. Oppenheimer says that we're not just raising money, we are helping donors feel good about themselves.

The participants' empathy for the children also had a direct impact on how much they donated. The more participants were approached with empathy messaging, the more money they donated. But when participants were asked to think about the value of a sick child's life and thus tap into the analytical side of their brain, they gave less. The desire to donate is emotional and empathetic, not analytical and rational. Data and statistics may support a policy argument but they don't motivate people to give. Emotion and drama in your messaging and storytelling inspire people to act and give money.

Donors Are Influenced by Their Peers

Researchers found that exerting "peer pressure" influences people to donate more money. For example, volunteers who were managing the phone lines during a public radio station fundraising drive raised 29% more money by telling callers who were phoning in a pledge gift that a previous caller had just donated more money than the caller on the line was intending to give. And even more interesting were the results when a volunteer said that the previous caller was of the same gender. Gift size then increased by 34%. A similar impact was also seen in direct mail. These types of studies show that people are not just "caving to peer pressure" but want a sense of belonging. Our peers provide validation that a cause is important or that our beliefs are shared by others like us.

While this particular study was not tested in online channels, spurring competition (which is a form of social peer pressure) through online peer-to-peer fundraising campaigns has been very successful throughout the nonprofit community. For example, walkathons and runs such as the AIDS Walk or Susan G. Komen Race for the Cure that gained popularity in the 1980s and 1990s utilize online peer-to-peer fundraising platforms like Team Raiser.[39] They rely on an organization's ability to mobilize their constituents to compete with each other to raise money by collecting pledges from their friends, family, colleagues, and even followers on social media.

SPRING2ACTION SPURS FRIENDLY COMPETITION

It's not just walkathons that use social peer pressure to raise money. It is also a tactic seen in social fundraising campaigns. ACT for Alexandria, an organization dedicated to fostering social action and philanthropy in Alexandria, Virginia, launched a social fundraiser in 2011 called Spring2Action that helped its local organizational partners raise over $104,156 in 2011, and over $300,000 in 2012.[40] Using the Razoo online fundraising platform, 47 nonprofits set up donation pages and rallied their supporters together to donate $10 or more. Nonprofits weren't just competing locally for donor dollars, but were also competing for numerous prizes ranging from $30,000 in additional cash prizes to a barbecue party for ten, donated by a local business. Organizations and constituents collaborated to generate donations. Participating nonprofits were raising money for various programs, including an afterschool program, scholarships for a summer camp, and a new arts facility. In 24 hours nonprofits and supporters crowdsourced a huge sum of money by sending out personal emails to their networks, encouraging people on Twitter and Facebook, and making phone calls to personal contacts. Campaigns like Spring2Action demonstrate how you can utilize friendly competition to raise money and remain tactful in the process.

The More You Ask People to Suffer, the More Money You Will Raise

You may think asking people to suffer to raise money sounds crazy, but it works. This is one reason an extreme athletic event like the Boston Marathon is so popular and raises over $10 million a year for charities in Boston.[41] For example, Olivola's studies found that people feel okay with suffering physical discomfort for the privilege of then giving money. "When people anticipate that they're going to have to suffer to raise money for a charity, then their willingness to contribute to that cause actually goes up."[42]

Essentially, when "pain" or "suffering" is endured it can be motivating in part due to social pressure. People tend to feel that if all these other people running the marathon can do it and put up with it, they can too! We do things in groups that we could never motivate ourselves to do alone.

This connection between raising money and people feeling the need to suffer also speaks to other types of peer-to-peer fundraising that involve discomfort or humiliating situations. For example, when blogger and author Geoff Livingston was raising money for the nonprofit Invisible People, which documents and shares stories of people experiencing homelessness across the United States, he organized a personal fundraiser called the "Punish Geoff Fundraiser," hosted on the online fundraising platform Razoo.[43,44] Livingston said he would let someone throw a pie in his face, film it, and post it to YouTube if 56 people donated $18 as seen in Figure 4.1. Livingston pitched to all of his friends, colleagues, family, and followers throughout his personal fundraising campaign via email, social media, and his own blog. While having a pie thrown in one's face may not be painful physically, it's humiliating for many people.

People Want to See Their Impact

Donors may be driven by emotion and peer pressure and willing to endure physical exertion but they are also perceptive. They know that their $10 or $100 gift alone is not going to change the plight of Rokia, the little girl from Malawi. But they know that, collectively, their gifts will help her have a better life for now, and they expect your organization to show them the tangible impact. In fact, demonstrating impact increases donations. This is an easy win for nonprofits. You already have access to this information; now share it with your community.

Paull Young of charity: water says one of the organization's secrets to fundraising success is to show donors exactly where their money is going through documentary photos, videos, and GPS coordinates. This helps donors see exactly which village and water project they helped support.

People Want to Be Appreciated

There's an old Stone Roses song called "I Wanna Be Adored" in which lead singer, Ian Brown, sings his heart out about how all he wants in life is to be adored. Like Ian and every other human being on this planet, donors want to feel adored and appreciated.

When Craig Newmark, founder of craigslist and craigconnects, donated money to the New Organizing Institute (NOI) to support a mobile app that helps U.S. voters register to vote, NOI didn't just send Newmark a typical thank-you note. They took the time to be creative to show how appreciative they were of his support and designed a craigslist-like ad with the same look and feel of craiglist.org, which you can see in Figure 4.2.

NOI posted it on a webpage and sent Newmark an email with the link. Newmark said his immediate reaction after seeing it was, "It's definitely novel and it made me feel appreciated as a supporter."

Of course nonprofits don't have the resources to thank every single donor in a similarly unique way. But that doesn't mean you shouldn't always be thanking your donors, even for the little things. Treat them like VIPs, whether they donate $10 or $1,000 dollars. Greenpeace International is a great example of an organization that has set up processes to ensure that both low-dollar and high-dollar donors are thanked often and personally:

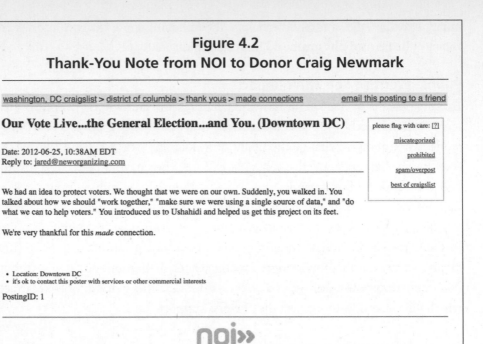

Figure 4.2
Thank-You Note from NOI to Donor Craig Newmark

washington, DC craigslist > district of columbia > thank yous > made connections   email this posting to a friend

Our Vote Live...the General Election...and You. (Downtown DC)

please flag with care: [?]

miscategorized

prohibited

spam/overpost

best of craigslist

Date: 2012-06-25, 10:38AM EDT
Reply to: jared@neworganizing.com

We had an idea to protect voters. We thought that we were on our own. Suddenly, you walked in. You talked about how we should "work together," "make sure we were using a single source of data," and "do what we can to help voters." You introduced us to Ushahidi and helped us get this project on its feet.

We're very thankful for this *made* connection.

- Location: Downtown DC
- it's ok to contact this poster with services or other commercial interests

PostingID: 1

noi>>
EDUCATION FUND

Copyright © 2012 new organizing institute   terms of use   privacy policy   feedback forum

"Our victories are due to our supporters' work and donations. We are constantly thanking them," said Dionna Humphrey, senior email campaigner for Greenpeace International. "We have a supporter care team that serves as our frontline to answer questions, and who also call donors to thank them for their donations whether it was $5 or $499. This is so important in making them feel validated."

To ensure your donors always feel appreciated be careful not to treat them like ATM machines that dispense $20 bills whenever you ask. charity: water does a fantastic job of showing their donors how much they appreciate them. Each donor that they have a phone number for is called and wished a happy birthday by a staff member no matter how much they donated to the organization. And they are not asked for a donation on this call, ensuring that the outreach is focused on building the relationship and thanking them for all that they have done.

Seasoned fundraising strategist Nick Allen says, "On the one hand, you won't raise much money online if you don't ask your supporters often. On the other hand, they did not sign up for your list, take your advocacy action, or donate because they wanted to get more fundraising appeals in their in-boxes. They engaged with you because they cared about your organization, or mission, or effort—so you need to continue engaging them and take them along an engagement path, not just ask, ask, ask."

FUNDRAISING CHANNELS

Now that we've covered some of the complex emotional factors that go into your donors' decision making, we'll drill down into the different channels supporters are using to make donations and how much these channels raise.

Offline and Direct Mail

In the past 10 to 15 years the Internet, social media, and mobile devices have truly transformed the way we communicate and do business, yet 79% of donations are still made by personal check, according to the Association of Fundraising Professionals (AFP).[45] And veteran fundraising consultant Mal Warwick confirms that the majority of new donations, which account for a large proportion of all philanthropic gifts, come through direct mail.[46]

While the majority of donations are coming from offline, the average multichannel donor (someone who donates both online and offline) contributes $197, compared to an offline-only donor who contributes $63, according to 2011 donorCentrics Internet and Multichannel Giving Benchmarking Report.[47] These statistics demonstrate why we need to focus on creating multichannel fundraising campaigns, and implement and adapt messaging for each channel to reach donors wherever they are at anytime.

Online

About 6.3% of donations come in through online channels such as an organization's main website, online fundraising appeals directing people to specialized campaign donation pages, and social fundraising platforms ranging from Causes to Razoo, according to the 2011 Online Giving Report.[48] And up to 40% of all online donations come in during December.

Although 6.3% may seem low in comparison to offline fundraising, online fundraising is one of the fastest growing channels. In fact, most sectors in the report saw double-digit growth since 2009, as highlighted in Figure 4.3.

According to Network for Good, 65% of the people surveyed said that they planned to donate money online in 2011 versus only 4% who donated online in 2001.[49] This is significant because it shows how comfortable and willing people are to give online today. Furthermore, online donors are typically younger, earn

Figure 4.3
Online Giving Growth Since 2009[50]

Sector	% Change
Arts, Culture, Humanities	21.8
Education	40.0
Environment, Animals	38.4
Health Care	13.0
Human Services	41.8
International Affairs	75.3
Public/Society Benefit	21.0

higher incomes, and give bigger donations than offline donors, according to the 2011 donorCentrics Internet and Multichannel Giving Benchmarking Report. The average online donation is $145 per online gift, according to the report.

"Digital is a key channel for us, with more than 70% of new supporters joining us online last year," said Tobin Aldrich, who works with the World Wildlife Fund (WWF) in the United Kingdom.[51] Organizations like charity: water say that in the past two years 75% of their revenue has come in through digital channels.

In 2010, $22 billion dollars were raised online in the United States, a 34% increase from 2009, according to Steve MacLaughlin of Blackbaud.[52] The massive response and donation level was largely a result of online donations, but the numbers are slightly skewed due to the unusually large scale of the Haiti disaster we discussed in the preface.

In 2011, online revenue for nonprofits increased by 15.8%, down from 20% in 2010 but above the increase of 14% in 2009, according to the Online Marketing Nonprofit Benchmark Index Study that examined data from over 700 nonprofits.[53] But again, it's important to remember that the numbers were a bit skewed in 2010 due to the significant fundraising around disaster and international relief.

Similar to the findings of the donorCentrics Internet and Multichannel Giving Benchmarking Report, a Visa study that examined cardholder's data found that when people donate online they tend to give more money.[54] The Visa study also found that those donors who contribute $500 or more use online bankcards more than personal checks. Online donations also have a positive impact on recurring donation programs. Visa reports that 90% of people live up to their commitment of making recurring donations versus 79% who set it up through personal checks.

Another important reason that online fundraising is important for an organization's overall fundraising, as studies such as the donorCentrics report show, is that online fundraising has a positive impact on direct mail programs. Every year, about 32% of donors acquired online switch from online giving to offline giving via direct mail. "They then continue to give offline in similar proportions in subsequent years. Eventually, just under half of all online-acquired donors convert entirely to offline, primarily direct mail giving," said the report. "Over time, the high giving amounts of online donors coupled with the high donor retention rates provided by direct mail make for a powerful combination."

Social Media

Of the 6.3% of online donations, how much is being raised through social media and texting? Not too much yet. A look at the data in Figure 4.4 from the 2011 Nonprofits Social Network Report shows that only 0.7% of nonprofits have raised more than $100,000 using social media platforms Facebook, Twitter, YouTube, and LinkedIn.[55]

This is not really a surprise given the evolving relationship between donors and nonprofits via social media. And while we believe that it will gain more momentum as more organizations look to social media as part of their engagement and outreach (which will have a long-term impact on organizations' fundraising strategy), it's important to remember that social media is about being

Figure 4.4
Fundraising Across Social Media Channels

	Not Fundraising	$0 – $1K	$2K – $9K	$10K – $100K	More Than $100K
Facebook	52%	35%	11%	2%	0.4%
Twitter	80%	17%	2%	1%	0.1%
YouTube	91%	8%	1%	0.4%	0.1%
LinkedIn	94%	5%	1%	0.1%	0.1%
Flickr	98%	2%	0.2%	0.1%	0%

social. The channel is best used to foster relationships with prospective and current donors rather than as a channel to raise money.

"Making a value judgment on [social networks like] Facebook based only on donations received completely overlooks the inherent value that [social networks like] Facebook offers," says communications consultant and author of *Facebook Marketing for Dummies* John Haydon.[56] He's right. Social media should be used to get people so excited about your organization that they want to join your movement and share it with their friends, family, and colleagues. If you build a strong relationship with prospects on social media (or any channel) and move them up the engagement ladder, you can convert a percentage of them to donors during the course of your relationship with them.

Social media can also help you build a more personal and social relationship with your current base of donors and activists. Social media's strength is in the reach that's created as users talk about your campaign, said Haydon. "Your fundraising strategy should include ways to get people to converse about the cause. The more they talk about it, the more their friends become aware of your fundraising campaign."

Mobile

Up until 2008, mobile fundraising wasn't utilized in the United States very much because, historically, the carrier fees were too expensive and charged up to 50% in donation fees. However, in 2008, the Mobile Giving Foundation made it possible for nonprofits in the United States to use text-to-give donations at a much more affordable rate, only taking about 10% in donation fees (excluding mobile vendor setup fees) at the time of this writing.

This news attracted the attention of organizations such as UNICEF, the Salvation Army, and the American Society for the Prevention of Cruelty to Animals, who began testing the integration of mobile fundraising in their campaigns, said Katrin Verclas in an article on the MobileActive.org site, a nonprofit she founded.[57]

Organizations raised about $500,000 via mobile in 2008, which is about $300,000 more than online fundraising brought in its first year in 1997, according to James Eberhard of Mobile Accord in an article on the MobileActive.org blog.

Then, in 2010, mobile fundraising made history after the world witnessed the photos, video footage, and stories of the tragic earthquake in Haiti that killed and injured hundreds of thousands of people, displaced over one million, and devastated the country's infrastructure. Organizations such as CARE, Catholic Relief Services, and the International Rescue Committee rallied the public to come together and donate money to the relief efforts. As we discussed in the preface, this was the first time the United States witnessed the power of multichannel campaigning that included text-to-give programs to immediately allow people to donate money. It was also a critical turning point for mobile fundraising; the public finally recognized mobile as a safe and secure channel for making donations.

It was during this time that the American Red Cross raised a record-setting $32 million in two weeks through their text-to-give campaign to support Haiti relief efforts, according to Josh Kittner, senior marketing consultant of Digital Engagement at the American Red Cross. The text-to-give campaign was promoted via

- Email campaigns
- Peer-to-peer online fundraising drives through social fundraising platforms such as Causes, CauseVox, Crowdrise, JustGive, and Razoo
- Online marketing and advertising
- Public Service Announcements, including ones that featured President Obama

However, it's worth noting that a study by Pew Internet Project, in partnership with the Berkman Center for Internet and Society at Harvard University and the mGive Foundation, found that the donations raised through the Haiti texting campaign were motivated by "impulse giving" in response to the tragic events people were witnessing.[58] The study also found that mobile giving is a social networking activity, but more through word of mouth than through online channels. Approximately 43% of the Haiti text donors encouraged their friends or family members to text to donate and 75% pitched to them in person, while 21% encouraged them by posting to social network channels.

As of this writing, 64% of U.S. adults use text messaging and 9% have texted to donate from their mobile phone, according to the same Pew Internet study.

Text-to-give programs also encourage multichannel giving. Another study by mGive concluded that 79% who donate money via texting have also donated to other channels such as email, website, or direct mail.[59] In addition, the study said that 86% of people who texted to donate considered donating higher amounts of money via other channels. While mobile fundraising certainly has grown as a fundraising channel in the United States over the past few years, it still has not been widely adopted. We think it will continue to mature though, and is definitely worth testing if you have a sizable list and the right opportunities to fundraise around.

PLAN A MULTICHANNEL FUNDRAISING CAMPAIGN

Now that you understand people's motivations behind giving and the channels they use, how do you go about planning a multichannel fundraising campaign?

Establish Fundraising Goals

Set your total fundraising goals up front. When determining the "magic number," it's important that you set realistic expectations. For example, if you are experimenting with social media fundraising for the first time, it's important to remember that only 0.7% of organizations raise more than $100,000 through that channel. Be very conservative in your goals, and consider the staff time and vendor fees you'll need to support your campaign.

Develop Campaign Goals and Messaging

Sometimes it helps to crystallize your campaign goals by doing a simple exercise. Answer the question, "What three or four main goals will we achieve by raising X dollars for Y campaign?"

For example, here are some campaign goals that we answered internally for a neighborhood soup kitchen whose mission is to provide warm meals and job training to people who are experiencing homelessness.

"What goals will we achieve by raising $50,000 for the neighborhood soup kitchen?"

Goal One: Illustrate that homelessness has risen 25% in our city over the last year, resulting in a rising demand for our free meals and job training services. We want donors to understand that every night there are lines of hungry people outside our door waiting for a hot meal.

Goal Two: For every $50 donated, 25 homeless people will get a nutritious dinner for one week at our soup kitchen, beginning next week.

Goal Three: For every $25 donated, our soup kitchen will provide computer-training classes to 10 homeless people we are serving for one month.

Goal Four: Tell the personal story of a soup kitchen volunteer who has benefitted from eating regularly at our soup kitchen and participating in our job-training program.

Again, be realistic when setting campaign goals. Think about smaller, achievable goals like we discussed in Chapter Three. Also remember these goals are for

When you're creating a fundraising campaign calendar, think about your "asks" in terms of moving people up the ladder of engagement, where every step doesn't necessarily involve money. Start with easy ones like signing a pledge, and as they take more actions, move up to the harder, more committed ones that involve some financial commitments. This is particularly important when you are trying to move your advocates into becoming financial supporters too.

internal purposes. When your organization designs and rolls out its campaign publicly, you can still convey the fact that there are lines of hungry people waiting for food by telling an *individual's* story.

Define the Messaging Hook

When developing your campaign and messaging, you will need to share the compelling story behind the issue you are fundraising for and discuss the immediate need, as we outlined in the soup kitchen example. Tell donors how their donation will benefit the organization, program, and those served. Remember, people want to see a tangible impact. You will raise more money if this is clearly highlighted in your fundraising messaging. Fundraising appeals that have urgent deadlines and matching gifts have higher open rates and average gift amounts.

Identify Your Target Donors and Their Channels

Who will you be targeting with your fundraising campaign? Existing donors who have donated to a similar campaign appeal before? Primarily new donors with whom you have built a relationship through Facebook around a certain campaign?

Since often each online channel has different demographics, it's also important to understand prospective and current donors' preferred channels for donating and communicating. Do they prefer to donate via online fundraising appeals that are signed by your organization's executive director? Direct mail? By phone? Through peer-to-peer online fundraising campaigns?

Set up a Fundraising Calendar

A fundraising campaign calendar is one of the most important parts of multichannel fundraising plans. It maps out the timelines for the entire campaign, helps you plan an engagement ladder with your constituents, and outlines staffing and resources. A good calendar outlines a schedule for drafting, editing, and implementing the campaign and considers the goals, audiences, and channels for each component, including

- Email appeals and graphics
- Welcome series for new donors
- Website donation landing pages, graphical callout boxes, and homepage hijacks
- Direct mail
- Telemarketing
- Social media strategies and messaging
- Text-to-give messaging if appropriate
- Online or print advertising to promote the campaign, if appropriate
- Fun interactives that don't ask donors for money
- A/B testing, which analyzes two versions of a webpage, appeal, or message to see which is more effective
- Segmenting
- Thank-you messages and fundraising campaign updates

Farra Trompeter, vice president at Big Duck, a branding and communications firm, also notes how essential it is to consider other communications going to your community during a fundraising campaign because you don't want to message your supporters too much. "Be sure your story is strong, and that each element or message makes sense on its own, as well as builds on the other channels. [And remember] while your campaign is certainly significant, it is not the only thing your donors, advocates, and other supporters will see. Consider the other communications going out from your organization (newsletters, reports, event invitations), as well as other campaigns from similar causes, holidays, and general news happenings."

Figure 4.5 is a great example of a campaign calendar for the Baldacious campaign by the Leukemia and Lymphoma Society that Trompeter helped create.

Staffing and Resources   As part of this fundraising calendar process, it's also important to establish staffing resources and identify how this fits into the overall timeline.

Figure 4.5

Campaign Calendar for the Baldacious Campaign by the Leukemia and Lymphoma Society

Target Date	Goals				Project	Audience	Theme/Creative Concept
	Names	$$$	Action	Good will			
February							
2/8/10					Totallybaldacious.org		Site launch
2/8/10		X		X	Campaign email #1	eNewsletter subscriber campaign; Alumni campaign	Encourage people to go Totally Baldacious and set up fundraising pages; note: Local Chapter template available for current participant promotion
2/8/10					LLS.org website	Site visitors	Post homepage feature barker; post press release; post Top Story blog post
2/8/10					Facebook, Twitter, YouTube, and Flickr	Fans, followers, and subscribers	Conduct social networking sweep with campaign announcement; active ad for TB Fan Page; cross-promote TB Twitter account
2/8/10			X		LLS.org website—Community	Site visitors, blog readers	LLS to post special announcement and write about campaign on @LLS blog all month long
2/8/10	X		X		Facebook, Google	External audiences	LLS ads launched for Totally Baldacious
2/8/10			X		LLS.org website—Community	Site visitors, blog readers	LLS to post special announcement and write about campaign on @LLS blog all month long
TBD			X	X	Shavertown	Media, local politicians, community	Invite press and others to event in town
2/14/10			X	X	Campaign email #2	eNewsletter subcribers; TNT Alumni	Be Baldacious for Valentines Day; Donate, Feature on Your Profile, Share
2/14/10					Campaign email #3	Participants	Fundraising Competition, Share Your Story
2/14/10			X	X	YouTube, Facebook, and Flickr	Viewers and fans	Donate, Feature on Your Profile, Share-Promote Twitter rally at 2:14PM on V-day
TBD			X	X	Terri Cousin	Media, local politicians, community	Press conference and kick-off of Totally Baldacious weekend
2/14/10	X	X	X	X	Valentine's Day		Post messages on Facebook and Twitter to get people to Donate and Bald Yourself; host

"A tight team that's worked together, knows their stuff, and understands what everyone else is doing probably doesn't need to muddy a calendar with project management details, dependencies, and broken down tasks. But the typical nonprofit fundraising team is working with outside developers, designers, and writers, plus staff, spread across the country, some of whom just started in the past year because of typical nonprofit turnover," said online strategy consultant Ted Fickes. "And the weekly team meeting and countless emails to everyone, just doesn't get you organized enough. So, a calendar should to the extent possible specify the relationships between people and tasks."

ROLL OUT YOUR MULTICHANNEL FUNDRAISING CAMPAIGN

After you have gone through the steps of creating a plan for your fundraising campaign, the fun part begins: doing it.

Write a Series of Fundraising Appeals

Fundraising campaigns are often done as a series of cohesive online and offline fundraising appeals because they generate higher response rates and more money than stand-alone appeals. The most common fundraising series is done via direct mail, telemarketing, and email but can certainly incorporate mobile texting and even social media.

While there should be an overall campaign theme to your series, each individual fundraising appeal should be crafted differently to show the breadth of your campaign work, the critical need, and your impact.

A fundraising series often comprises three appeals, though it can certainly be more, particularly for year-end fundraising campaigns. The first appeal tells the story of the overall campaign, laying out the campaign goals and the impact donors can expect to see from their donation. The story should be woven into all of the fundraising appeals in the series.

The second appeal updates people on the campaign's progress. It also reminds people of the story you shared in the previous appeal. This message tells them that you still need their help to make an impact and meet the campaign goals.

The final message is another update and one last ask for help to truly make that tangible impact and meet your goals.

Once a donor has given money to your fundraising campaign, do not ask them for more money as part of this fundraising series. Donors will get frustrated and feel like you are taking advantage of them. Twenty-year veteran fundraiser Tony Poderis said it best: "Prospects and donors are not cash crops waiting to be harvested; treat them as you would customers in a business." "No successful businessperson deals with customers as if they had a responsibility to buy. Prospects and donors have to be courted as you would court a customer. They must be told how important they are, treated with courtesy, and respect."[60]

Your fundraising series should also include thank-you messages that are sent to the donors who contribute, as we discussed earlier in this chapter. Personalized thank-you emails or letters should be sent within 24 hours after your organization receives the donation.

Remember to consider other online audiences and content channels such as social media, blogs, and mobile. These channels need different text formats and styles, unique donation pages, and other special considerations to maximize conversions.

Segment Your Donors and Prospects

Identify your donors and prospects by segmenting them to personalize your campaign and make your ask more appropriate to their interests and level of engagement. For example, you want to avoid sending the same appeal to members of your list who have never donated to your organization and those who have donated $250 three times in the past twelve months. These two segments are connected to your nonprofit very differently. Therefore they should receive different appeals that match their level of engagement.

Cultivate and segment your activists in your fundraising. Frank Barry, who does Internet marketing and strategy at Blackbaud, says, "Key industry benchmarks and trends show that engagement online through advocacy is an effective springboard for raising money because advocates are seven times more likely to give compared to non-advocates."[61]

Conduct A/B Testing

Many organizations run their fundraising program in a vacuum. They don't do enough testing with their fundraising to find out what strategies, variables, and

SEGMENTING YOUR COMMUNITY

There are myriad ways you can segment donors and prospects by slicing and dicing data through your CRM. Here are a few suggestions of data you might want to segment by

- Past donation amounts. For example, does this group donate at the $25 level, $50 level, $100 level, or $500-plus level?

- Location. Is your campaign local or nationally focused? Could there be different asks based on different donor locations?

- Specific areas of interest. By running a query in your CRM, you can identify what issues donors and prospects have taken action on, and possibly answers to survey questions that may provide insight into their interest areas.

- Gender.

- Lapsed donors or recent donors.

- Prospects who came in through social media channels: Facebook, Twitter, YouTube, and so forth.

- Prospects and donors who you have mobile numbers for and who gave you permission to communicate with them through texting.

- Donors who came in through a text-to-donate campaign versus a social network like Twitter or Facebook.

tactics in their fundraising appeals, messaging across multiple channels, and landing pages increase donations. Don't assume because a campaign tactic was successful for another organization's fundraising campaign that it will be equally successful for your own. That is not necessarily true, and this is why A/B testing is so critical to your fundraising campaigns.

All organizations, regardless of size, should do some A/B testing with their email fundraising appeals. If you have a mobile texting program or a very active and large social media following, A/B testing can be valuable too. It's worth noting, however, that for A/B testing to be statistically significant you will need to test your campaigns with thousands of people, not just a few hundred.

HOW DOES A/B TESTING WORK?

An A/B test should always have a call to action, a control, and one or more variations of the control. For the most credible results, it is recommended that you test fewer variations. The most basic process is to test a couple of factors—the success rate of the control and the success rate of the variation(s)—and then, finally, complete a comparison between them to determine which is most effective, recommends Jono Smith, VP of marketing and sales at the event fundraising consulting firm Event 360.[62]

There are a variety of tools that you can use to track the results of A/B testing, including your CRM and Content Experiments, a newer test tool, which integrates with Google Analytics.[63]

A/B TESTING IN ACTION

The Clinton Bush Haiti Fund, which formed to provide aid to Haiti after the earthquake, had a 10.2% increase in donation amounts overall (about $1.02 million) after testing two different versions of their website donation landing page, which we highlight in Figure 4.6.

Version A featured

- A two-column layout with a prominent photo showing people in Haiti receiving help from humanitarian workers on the ground with text above the photo that read "Support Haiti Relief and Recovery Efforts."
- Below the photo were six short sentences of explanatory text.
- Two fewer form fields than Version B.
- Button copy that read "Support Haiti."

Version B featured

- A single-column layout.
- No images, just explanatory text and the donation form fields.
- Button copy that read "Submit."

Version A outperformed version B significantly. Check out some of the specific donation increases the Clinton Bush Haiti Fund experienced by changing just a few variables to their fundraising appeal and donation form.[64]

- By changing the button from "Submit" to "Support Haiti" in the form field, they experienced a 15% increase in dollars raised per page view to about $59.38.
- By making the donation form a single column and adding an image, donations increased by 8% per page view.
- When the organization did not show a "Verified" icon on the site, donations decreased by 5% per page view.

Keep in mind that an A/B test may not give you the data quickly enough to make changes to a current campaign (though it could). An organization that tests consistently, however, will always be learning and have information that can help improve future campaigns.

Figure 4.6
Version A: Clinton Bush Haiti Fund Website Donation Form

Suggested Elements for A/B Testing

The following is a list of common elements that have been tested in online fundraising campaigns that will provide your organization with the necessary data to tweak and optimize your fundraising appeals and donation landing pages:

- Subject lines and whom the message was from
- Layout, graphics, font sizes
- Donation page landing flows
- Number of donation form fields
- Fundraising copy in the main message, headlines, and form fields, including the submit button
- Donation amounts
- Placement of donation asks in the fundraising appeal
- Deadlines
- Matching gifts
- Appeals from celebrities
- The text that makes up tweets, Facebook updates, and text messages with calls to donate
- Length and phrasing of Tweets, Facebook updates, and text messages with calls to donate
- Time of day and days of the week that donation appeals are sent to donors and prospects

STRATEGIES TO RAISE MORE MONEY ACROSS CHANNELS

So you've got a multichannel fundraising plan and a rollout strategy but you're not sure how to best promote campaigns across all the different channels and synchronize them. Here are some strategies we've seen that work well.

Direct Mail Channel

While direct mail is getting more and more expensive to produce, print, and mail, it's still the number one channel for bringing in donations, so don't abandon it altogether in favor of online fundraising or social media. In fact, you can use direct mail to enhance online fundraising.

Use Direct Mail to Enhance Online and Offline Giving   Nonprofits that integrate direct mail and email fundraising typically raise more money than stand-alone appeals. The next time you send out a direct mail piece, kick off the campaign series with an email appeal 24 hours before the direct mail piece is set to arrive in your donors' mailboxes. The ACLU tested a fundraising series that leveraged direct mail and email, and the average gift was $64, compared to $48. Direct mail, email, and telemarketing raised the most money, with an average gift of $80.[65]

Capture Donor Email Addresses Through Direct Mail   Over the past few years, direct mail response rates have declined, which has raised concerns for many nonprofits that rely on it as a major funding source. As nonprofits continue to communicate more with donors and prospects online, it's important that you capture direct mail donors' online contact information too. When you send out a direct mail piece, give donors the option to make their donation online, including setting up recurring donations. You can also offer premiums (tied to your mission) to encourage them to make the donation online or simply to provide their email address with a tear-off card that they can mail back to you.

While it's good to focus on getting offline donors' email addresses, don't ask for additional information, such as their mobile numbers or Twitter handles. Adding too many requests can depress response rates in direct mail.

"As in all direct response channels, we have to carefully test additional asks (like requesting more contact info) on fundraising reply slips. We must make sure that the additional asks don't distract and then depress fundraising response," said Mwosi Swenson, vice president of the online fundraising firm Donor Digital.

Swenson says that nonprofits are finding it increasingly difficult to collect more data from direct mail. "Everyone is increasingly sensitive about giving out their telephone/mobile numbers; there's no way to get around that. And for mobile numbers or social media account information, we must offer a great reason *why* a donor would give up that additional contact information—what useful, interesting, pertinent information is the organization going to provide in return," said Swenson.

Promote Your Website and Social Media Channels in Direct Mail   Just because you need to be careful about not asking your direct mail donors for too much information doesn't mean you can't promote information about where your direct mail donors can connect with you online—share information about your website and social networks.

Email Channel

As we discussed earlier, research shows that organizations that have their donors' email addresses raise more money. Nonprofits such as the ACLU say that donors on their email list give about 25% to 35% more money than other channels.[66]

In today's battle of the in-boxes, Tweets, Facebook updates, text messages, and banner ads flying across the screen, organizations can't afford to ignore the basics of crafting a good email appeal that motivates and inspires supporters to donate money.

TIPS FOR RAISING MORE MONEY WITH EMAIL APPEALS

1. Use Short, Catchy Subject Lines.

Hook your supporters right off the bat with a short and catchy subject line.

Example of Bad Subject Line:

"Renew Your Commitment to End Dog Homelessness"

Aside from this subject line being *boring*, you are also intimidating your members to shoulder a very big issue—that they alone are responsible for saving all dogs. Bad idea!

Example of Good Subject Line:

"Help Keep a Puppy Safe in DC's Blizzard!"

This is a good subject line because it's focused, local so the organization can segment the appeal to their DC supporters, timely because there is a blizzard coming, and a bit emotional. Who doesn't want to keep a puppy safe from a terrible blizzard in their hometown?

2. Focus on One Issue in the Email Appeal, Not Multiple Issues.

Focus people's attention on the single and most important issue of your fundraising campaign. Don't dilute it with several issues or different asks—don't have a call to donate money on one line and a call to volunteer two sentences later. It adds a layer of complexity and decreases response rates.

3. Keep Your Email Appeal Short and Sweet.

So you hooked your members with a short and catchy subject line, now continue to engage them in the body of the text with a brief (three to five

(continued)

paragraphs), straightforward appeal that tells one story and appeals to their emotions. Since your goal is capture your donors' attention in just a few short paragraphs, it's important that you not muddle the story with every little detail. You will have the opportunity to spread your story out over a series of fundraising appeals

Tell your members how their $50 donation is going to make a specific impact. For example: "Your $50 donation will help feed puppies like Lita, one of the sweet black labs we rescued yesterday, for an entire month."

4. Ask for the Donation Upfront.

People typically skim appeals; so provide an opportunity for people to donate (with a link) within the first paragraph of the appeal. You want to make sure you frame the story first, before you ask for money. Then repeat the call to donate at least two to three more times.

5. Make It Timely and Deadline Driven.

The most successful organizations raise a lot of money around timely issues. Any opportunity that your nonprofit can connect fundraising campaigns to current news, seize it! Adding deadlines also gives a sense of urgency.

Figure 4.7
Picture of Lita, One of the Rescued Black Labs That
Allyson and Her Husband Adopted

6. **Add a PS at the Bottom of Emails.**

Adding a "PS" at the end of emails is sometimes one of the most read content in an email appeal. Boil the campaign down into one key message and test this as a PS in your next fundraising campaign.

7. **Follow Up and Thank Your Donors.**

Don't forget to close the loop. We can't stress how important this basic cultivation strategy is to engaging and sustaining donors. All too often nonprofits forget to thank their donors (or don't thank them soon enough) and close the loop in online fundraising campaigns. Donors want to know if you met your goals, or if you didn't meet them. So take the time to build better relationships with them and schedule follow up emails. Also make sure you include any stories, successes, and photos or videos so that donors can see how their donation made a difference. This relationship-building strategy is important to your overall fundraising strategy. Donors are more loyal to organizations that show their appreciation, follow up, and share results.[67]

WEBSITE CHANNEL

Your organization's website serves as the most important funnel for connecting with donors and generating online donations. But if your website isn't optimized for fundraising, with prominent calls to donate that lead donors to easily navigable donation landing pages, your organization won't raise much money through its website.

Here are some key fundraising strategies to implement on your website to bring in the money.

Utilize Homepage Hijacks and Donate Callout Boxes

When you have a very important fundraising campaign, it's critical that you promote it across your website. There are two simple strategies you can implement to encourage your web visitors to increase donations.

Homepage hijacks, as you can see in Figure 4.8, are a graphically designed fundraising pitch that sits on top of the homepage. When users click to make a donation, they go to a unique fundraising campaign landing page that tracks

Figure 4.8
Homepage Hijack Example by Humane Society of the United States

donation response rates. You tend to see a lot of homepage hijacks around year-end fundraising, but they can be leveraged for any big or urgent fundraising campaign any time of year. It's important to be strategic about homepage hijacks. They should be used for the biggest fundraising campaigns of the year only or else you may annoy web visitors who are coming to your site for information and content. And if you use one, consider adding a web browser cookie to it so that web visitors who come back to your website often don't see it multiple times in a short period. Alia Mckee of Sea Change Strategies recommends that organizations use a cookie so that repeat web visitors only see the homepage hijack about once a week.[68] You should also always give visitors the option to close the hijack window through an "X" button so that they can access your main website immediately.

Display Callout Boxes on Your Homepage

When your organization is in major fundraising mode, consider placing call-out graphic boxes around key areas of your site such as the homepage, your blog, and campaign landing pages (especially when it relates to the issue you are fundraising for) that ask people to donate to the campaign. The graphic callout box can fit into the size of an ad space or whatever dimensions work best for your site.

Optimize Your Website Donation Landing Pages

What's the secret to creating a successful donation-landing page? Make it short and user-friendly, with the most important form fields as far above the fold as possible. Follow these simple tips from the *Procrastinator's Guide for Year-End Fundraising* (which we refer to as *The Guide* from here forward) by Sea Change Strategies and Care2, and you will see more donations come through your website all year long.[69] Important: You will also want to test and make sure that your donation page is mobile-friendly and works properly on smartphones such as the iPhone, Android, and BlackBerry.

Collect Only the Information You Need

It's easy to get caught up in collecting a lot of information about your donors. But don't fall into that trap because for each extra form field you add, you will suppress donations. Focus on collecting the most important information you need to seal the deal, such as first name, last name, email address, mailing address, and credit card information. As you build a relationship with your donor, you can continue to collect more information over time.

Focus Your Website Donor on the Task at Hand

If you asked a supporter to donate money to a specific campaign, that is what your donation landing page should focus on. Don't muddle the page with a lot of other options like "join our email list," "become a monthly donor," or "renew your membership." One exception might be testing the inclusion of a link to a "why give" page on your website, according to *The Guide*. Suppressing your global navigation on the donation page focuses your donor even more and can lead to more donations. If you suppress the global navigation, remember to provide a navigation link back to the home page.

Use Consistent "Donate" Language on Your Website

If you want people to donate money to your organization, don't mince words, particularly in your buttons and links, which are key cues for people to click on to donate. The best words for your donate buttons and links are "Donate," "Give," or "Contribute." And be sure to track each of these donate button terms to see which one performs the best with your community.

Look Legitimate

The nonprofit world is no stranger to fraud. Make sure that you provide your organization's contact information, privacy policy, Verisign seals or similar verification seal, and any ratings from the nonprofit evaluation providers, such as Charity Navigator, Guide Star, and Great Nonprofits. Milo Sybrant, managing director of engagement media at Amnesty International USA, said the organization experienced a 5.11% increase in their fundraising after adding the Better Business Bureau seal above the donation form.[70] This is an easy tactic to raise more money.

Don't Make Donors Jump Through Hoops to Make a Donation

Donors get infuriated when donation pages don't work properly or they have to click three times to access the proper donation form. Poor online donation experiences can ruin a donor relationship forever. With that in mind, test your donation page, and try to break it. Look out for broken links. What happens if you don't fill out the required information; do you receive an error? From *The Guide:* "If at all possible, make sure donors thrown into error hell don't have to re-enter all their personal information."

Display a Thank-You Page After the Donation Has Been Processed

Thank your donors immediately by directing them to a thank-you page upon completion of the donation form. Be sure to include Tell-A-Friend forms to encourage your donors to share the campaign with their friends through email and social networks.

Within 24 to 48 hours, send a personalized thank-you email to your donors. These are easy to set up in most all CRM systems.

Social Sharing

You can also test integration of social sharing on the thank-you pages, where people can edit and post updates to social media such as Twitter ("Join me in donating

$25 to @humanesociety to provide blankets to homeless puppies like Lita in DC shelters—sourced link").

"People that just gave are your most passionate supporters. Give them the opportunity to share the good word while they're most excited," said online strategy consultant Ted Fickes.

Show Fundraising Results in Real Time

If you want to raise money on any channel you need to share your fundraising goals and demonstrate impact in real time, says Blackbaud's Barry.[71] One of the most effective ways to do this online is to integrate a thermometer or graphic on a donation page that displays the fundraising goal and updates as people donate. The graphic also quickly tells people what percentage of the fundraising goal has been met.

"Seeing the goals and the impact does two things. First, it helps website visitors further understand what the project is all about by seeing real data. Second, it allows visitors to connect with the fundraising efforts on a deeper level. By seeing the impact people start thinking, 'Wow, that's amazing . . . I think I can help here!'" said Barry.

MOBILE CHANNEL

With the rapid adoption of mobile technologies, nonprofits should evaluate different options to integrate mobile into their fundraising plans when it's a good fit and a good investment. Between text-to-donate campaigns, using QR codes in print ads or posters, and optimizing email fundraising appeals for mobile devices, there are plenty of avenues to explore and test to start raising more money with mobile if you have enough staffing and resources to support a mobile program.

Text-to-Donate

One of the biggest areas nonprofits are eyeing these days in the mobile channel is text-to-give programs. There are two basic routes nonprofit staff can explore to setup a text-to-donate campaign in the United States—both require shortcodes, five- or six-digit special telephone numbers used to route text messages from mobile phones to mobile messaging applications.

Proprietary Shortcode

Acquiring a unique shortcode can take time to secure and is more expensive than sharing one. The advantage is that you get the opportunity to brand yourself around your unique shortcode code and to launch different types of fundraising appeals and action alerts.

Shared Shortcode

A cheaper route is to use a shortcode that is shared with other groups but the key word is unique. This route can be problematic—if donors mistype the keyword, the donation will not go through—but some vendors such as Mobile Commons have tried to address these issues by designing their app to pick up common misspellings. They also do not allow similar keywords for other campaigns. As of this writing, people can't donate more than $10 at a time.

Many organizations (outside of the American Red Cross during natural disasters such as the earthquake in Haiti or Japan) that have experimented with text-to-donate campaigns have not raised a significant amount of money. However, if your organization is seeing traction with mobile fundraising and you want to take it to the next level, consider hiring staff or consultants who are trained to engage with people via mobile to build deeper relationships with those constituents.

Raise More Money by Leveraging Mobile and Email

As we highlighted earlier, if you have a large enough list of supporters' mobile numbers, texting can be a great strategy to boost your overall fundraising response rates. In an A/B split test, the Humane Society of the United States experienced an increased response rate of 77% during one of their year-end fundraising drives by texting an appeal to their donors with mobile numbers 24 hours before an appeal hit their email boxes. Of course the organization has a very large and active email list, so it's not surprising to see how well this A/B test performed.

Using QR Codes at Offline Fundraising Events

Oxfam International used QR codes in one of their London retail stores as part of a fundraising campaign that involved celebrities donating sentimental items and clothes. When potential buyers scanned a QR code on a sales tag with their smartphone, videos of celebrities popped up with a personal story behind that item for sale. For example, when someone scanned the QR code on a dress that songwriter and activist Annie Lennox donated to the auction, it showed a video of her telling a story of how she wore it to Nelson Mandela's 90th birthday party in London.

The Juvenile Diabetes Research Foundation uses QR codes in their brochures at their offline fundraising events. "The QR code links to our lead advocacy volunteer, telling her story and briefly describing the benefits of joining our advocacy team," said Mike Kondratick at JDRF.[72]

One of the metrics they track for measuring the effectiveness of QR codes is their walk-related sign-ups. "Our mobile sign-ups were up noticeably in 2011 walks, about 8% or so. This growth via mobile accounted for the vast majority of our walk day growth overall," said Mike.

SOCIAL NETWORKS CHANNEL

While most nonprofits have a presence on social networks, the majority of them are only raising enough money to fill a small piggy bank. However, a few organizations, such as Humane Society of the United States (HSUS), are starting to raise hundreds of thousands of dollars a year. "HSUS is the third most successful nonprofit on Facebook Causes (the largest social fundraising app on Facebook) in terms of fundraising," said Carie Lewis, director of emerging media at the Humane Society of the United States.

At the end of 2011, HSUS reached their goal of raising $500,000 on Facebook. HSUS deployed a number of strategies and tactics to raise money on Facebook. The simplest strategy they used was to repurpose all their email fundraising asks on Facebook. "People on Facebook want to stay on Facebook. We notice considerably higher conversion rates when we bring 'the ask' inside of Facebook. We also provide other ways to donate, either by a sourced link to our website or via Blackbaud/Convio's donation API on a custom Facebook tab. Some people just don't trust donating on Facebook yet, much like they didn't trust the donate button on our website in the beginning. But it's important that we position ourselves for growth in this area, too, as the trust forms and the tools mature," said Lewis. "But the real key is engagement. By providing our fans what they want like fun contests, polls asking for their opinion, listening to their feedback on posts, thanking them, answering every question, and other engagement opportunities, we believe that our fans will feel enough of a connection with the brand to do what we ask—such as making a donation."

Lewis also says that every one of the organization's emails, thank-you pages, and auto responders are shareable on social networks. "Within only months of us making our emails shareable, Facebook became the number one referring site to our website, surpassing Google. The number and amount of donations made on our website sourced originally from Facebook also continues to increase over time."

When Frank Barry at Blackbaud analyzed how the 0.7% of nonprofits were raising more than $100,000 on social media (what he calls Master Fundraisers), he attributed the following patterns to their successful fundraising.[73] (Note, this is not an overnight process and it will take a big staff investment.)

Nonprofits Who Invest in Social Media Staff Raise More Money on Social Media

Organizations such as the Make-a-Wish Foundation, Best Friends Animal Society, Chris and Dana Reeve Foundation, American Red Cross, National Wildlife Federation, and HSUS have at least one staffer "that owns their social media program. Some even have full-blown teams," said Barry.

It's not just large organizations that are raising over $100,000 on social media. According to the Nonprofit Social Network Benchmark Report, 30% were considered small organizations.

The study also found that 30% of successful social media fundraisers dedicate at least two staff members to managing their social media presence—compared to 2% for the rest of the nonprofit industry.

Other factors contributing to social media success are shared staff knowledge and how social media roles are distributed across staff teams. We dive deeper into these issues in Chapter Seven: Equipping Your Organization for Anytime, Everywhere.

Allocate a Social Media Budget

Organizations that raise money on social media spend money on Facebook ads, Facebook apps, promoted tweets, blogs, content creation, campaign integration, etc. "It doesn't have to be an enormous amount of money, but if you want to raise significant dollars, you'll have to invest," said Barry.

Add Social Media to Fundraising Appeals

Barry recommends experimenting with Facebook to generate two-way engagement. For example, ask people to share why they financially support your organization. Post a video to YouTube with a personalized thank-you video for all those who donate as part of your fundraising campaign.

If you happen to know some of your donors' Twitter handles, thank them personally on Twitter and tell them how their donation will be supporting your organization. This will also let your other Twitter followers and your donors' followers see your tweet about the campaign.

Tailor Fundraising Pitches to Multiple Channels

When drafting fundraising pitches, you will need to tailor messages to each channel, since each one has a different tone, length consideration, and nomenclature, as we discussed in Chapter Three. "Donors are looking to hear about you in many places—some may just want to communicate in one channel; others will [want to] connect with you in several. The messaging and visual story of all these channels should reflect one another, while also taking into account the unique aspects of that channel and how people use it," says Trompeter.[74]

Evaluate Your Fundraising Campaign

Evaluating your fundraising campaign as you roll out your various fundraising appeals is critical to your organization's success raising money anytime, everywhere. Measuring results during the live campaign will help you tweak your fundraising plan along the way or even change course if a strategy is clearly not working. This will help you maximize engagement and donations.

Email Fundraising Appeals

There are some terrific nonprofit fundraising industry benchmarks that have been developed over the years, which we shall highlight. As you review them, note that results will be different for each nonprofit organization. While understanding these data is important, you should identify metrics that are realistic for your organization.

According to Convio's Online Marketing Benchmark Study:[75]

- Median open rates for online fundraising appeals are 18.4%.
- Median click through rates are 1.7%.
- Median donation rates are 0.16%.
- The average online gift via email appeals is $93.67.

- The median amount of funds raised from first time online donations was $136,625.

- Average sustainer gifts were $25,474. This is a 38.7% increase from 2010.

Fundraising Metrics on Social Media

If you are doing any fundraising on social media, it's important to establish your own metrics, since many organizations still aren't raising much money through this channel and there is little data available. And the organizations that are raising some money are seeing vastly different results, so the data are a bit skewed and inconsistent. Here are four metrics you should review as part of your social fundraising campaigns at least once a month:

1. Analyze your follower growth by reviewing your Facebook members, followers on Twitter, Google+, and other social networks.

2. Analyze your engagement with people on social networks. As we discussed earlier in this chapter, fundraising is about building a community and relationships with people. It's not always about the money. Add up the Facebook likes, comments, Twitter shares, @mentions, retweets, +1s on Google+, and metrics on other social networks. Did you see more or less engagement during your fundraising campaign compared to other times? Were the comments positive, negative, neutral? Don't rely heavily on paid and free tools that analyze sentiment, as they are not 100% reliable. If possible, try to analyze sentiment manually. While these specific metrics won't paint the entire picture in terms of how your organization is engaging constituents, they are valuable to review in conjunction with other data.

3. Create unique source URLs for your fundraising pitches for each social media channel. This will help you determine donation rates for each social network and associated fundraising pitches. Divide the number of donors by the donation page visitors based on the unique URLs.

4. Determine the average donation size by dividing the total amount of donations by the number of donors.

Mobile Fundraising

Similar to social media, mobile fundraising is still in its infancy stage. As of February 2012, there are many gaps in the data and statistics that mobile vendors and nonprofits are collecting and sharing. Despite the gaps, there are a few metrics that are worth considering if you plan to test mobile fundraising.

On average, the size of an organization's text messaging list is 1.2% of its email list, as we mentioned in Chapter Three. This number is expected to grow considerably over the next few years and is something you will want to track at your own organization.

Both opt-in and opt-out rates to receive texts from organizations are low, according to Angela McIntosh, director of business development at MobileCause. Opt-ins range from 1% to 7%. Opt-outs hover around 1%. "Carriers have greatly restricted the amount of communication that can occur after a text-to-give donation. Most of our clients choose to use a mobile pledging service rather than text-to-give so that they can more easily communicate with their donors and cultivate longer-term relationships," said McIntosh. An estimated 75% of text-to-give donations are completed by the donor, meaning individuals replied with the word "yes" to confirm their gift, according to McIntosh; 25% of text-to-give donations are not completed by the donor.

Currently, for most organizations, mobile fundraising is not a cost-effective fundraising source. Most donors prefer to give money to nonprofits through other channels. Unless you have a large email list and you are ready to invest in staff, consultants, and vendor fees to support a mobile fundraising program, we recommend holding off until mobile fundraising matures.

Be Realistic

As you know, there are never any guarantees with fundraising; so while we encourage you to test a few of these fundraising strategies and tactics, raising money anytime, everywhere is no easy task. Be prepared to

- Set realistic goals and benchmarks
- Tell stories that appeal to people's empathy
- Show donors their impact
- Cultivate your community across multiple channels

Now that we've looked at advocacy and fundraising, in Chapter Five we discuss building community. We show you how other organizations are using a variety of channels to share their message, tell their story, and build strong, engaged communities, as well as point to how you can start building community anytime, everywhere today.

DISCUSSION QUESTIONS

Spark a conversation with your team or organization about these core fundraising principles with the following questions:

1. What are the top three goals for your next fundraising campaign?

2. What stories do you have of individuals impacted, served, or otherwise representative of your work that you can highlight in a fundraising series or appeal?

3. What data can you share with donors to show the impact of their financial support?

4. How can you personalize thank-you messages or other follow-up communications with donors to show that you appreciate and recognize them as part of your community?

5. Which channels do you want to utilize in your next fundraising appeal to remind supporters of a donation opportunity within 24 hours?

6. How can you streamline your current donation landing page to make it as easy as possible for a donor to complete the donation process? Which form fields can be eliminated, knowing that you can continue to learn more about your donors as you build a relationship with them over time?

chapter FIVE

Community Building
Anytime Everywhere

We all know that our supporters, volunteers, donors, and advocates are integral to our success. They take action, give money and time, and help us move our mission forward on and offline. After so many examples of using multiple channels for advocacy and fundraising, it's important to remember that you can't build real community around your work and move the needle on your cause if you invest in doing so only during campaigns or fundraising drives. Community building has to be an anytime, everywhere goal too.

How do those supporters find us, how do donors hear about our work, and how do interested citizens become our advocates? How do you use multichannel approaches to build a community around your mission? When you continually post updates and valuable content, listen and learn, and create opportunities for engagement that are meaningful and important all year long, you develop a community that is primed for taking action when you have a larger goal to reach or a call to action to share.

There are four essential elements of a multichannel strategy for building community. The first is to build trust between your organization and your community—both old and new supporters. Second, you need to use the same language, in the same places that your community does; you can't connect with supporters if you use language that they don't understand or relate to and post to platforms they don't access. Third, plan to connect the community through conversations across channels. And finally, it's critical as you build community around your mission to recognize that practice is critical, and that takes planning and organizational support.

TRUST IS REQUIRED

Building a community that supports and promotes your work isn't something that happens in a single day. It requires trust, and a lot of it. For your organization to succeed in advocacy and fundraising, or to build a strong community, you need to focus on building trust in a multichannel way, too. A fitting technique to use for trust-building across channels is to engage with your community in ways that show you are listening, sharing your data, and modeling your behavior to serve the community.

Listen for Action

We all know listening is important—we are told as much in school, in relationships, and in our work. We've heard all about listening. But what's missing from what we do (that we may think is listening) that would help us make our messages, our events, and our conversations more effective in changing and shaping the world? Listening for action, or listening with the intention of engaging with the community.[76]

Most organizations are listening in the most basic ways: examining news alerts, social media tracking, blog searches, and even market research to learn about what the community and the public at large are saying about them, their programs, and their cause. Organizations track mentions, identify the most vocal contributors, and try to analyze trends and hot topics. This is listening to learn. It's incredibly important but it is just one part of the equation. It fills you with information and data, ideas and understanding . . . and a lot more questions.

The next step organizations take is to listen enough that they can start conversations—this is a good thing. How many times have you heard someone say, "Join the conversation that's already happening online"? We know our work, our issues, our services, and our ideas are being talked about, and we want to be part of the group that's doing the talking. So we start commenting on blogs and posting announcements and updates to social media about our work to let people know all about the impact we've made, the campaigns we've created, and the ideas we like. This level of participation is still incredibly important, but it is just one part of the equation, like listening to learn. We are pulling everything in and then pushing everything out. But there is more to social media and mobile channels than that—they provide a way to listen to your community in a deeper way.

Listening for action is the trigger for collaboration, building a movement, and making change. This means listening to learn where the opportunities are for collaboration, then sharing the needs you have and inviting the community to shape the vision for the world you want to create. Listening to act is like thinking aloud, in public, with a community of people listening and suggesting opportunities to act together. But how do you do it?

Organizations that want to engage in community building using online and mobile tools have a great opportunity here to go beyond monitoring Twitter or tracking who the influential bloggers are that discuss your programs or issues. For example, you can ask direct questions on your Facebook Page, then stick around to respond, "like," or otherwise participate in the conversation that follows. It could also mean that you build clear ways for people to give you feedback either as quick evaluation questions via email after transactions or participation, or social feedback mechanisms such as ratings, or a "thumbs up" and "thumbs down" indicator on your blog.

HOW NTEN LISTENS FOR ACTION

Listening for action can sound like a pretty theoretical topic. Here's a quick overview of how NTEN listens to online conversation to pick up on themes, issues, and opportunities to take action.

- Identify popular topics: Use website analytics to see what posts are popular, and look for high numbers of retweets on Twitter or shares on Facebook.

- Create surveys: Include short online surveys in email communications with event participants, and gather feedback and ideas from donors and campaign participants.

- Make staff accessible: List email and social media links for each staff member so supporters can connect directly to give feedback, ask questions, and start conversations.

- Share what we see: Post to the blog and social channels with updates and data from events, organizational experiments, and the lessons learned using various tools and applying different strategies.

No matter how you listen and gather feedback, share ideas, and make proposals, if the organization doesn't plan to act on what the community says, there's little purpose in listening or trying to build community in the first place. The community will see that you aren't making changes, aren't communicating, or aren't collaborating and will disengage at best, turn against you at worst.

The co-creation cycle highlighted in Chapter Two as part of the principle to build a movement is especially important with community building. Even though you may not think your organization is co-creating a product or program, a piece of content, or even a campaign, you are creating something important: an engaged community! Doing so means you do need to listen for the hot topics, areas where needs aren't being met, or opportunities to get people involved. Listening to take action means that you take what you hear to the next level and start engaging: share back what you're hearing and learning to see what resonates and where you can start creating something together.

Share Data

One way to begin building trust with both current and prospective supporters is to share your data. Sites such as Charity Navigator,[77] GuideStar,[78] and GreatNonprofits[79] make it easy for people who are interested in learning about your organization's data and history to find it. Do not assume that if a potential donor or volunteer wants to learn about your work, impact, or financial history they will download a massive annual report to read in their free time. Make your information—both qualitative and quantitative—easy to find and understand directly on your website.

Share stories of your impact, but make the numbers just as accessible, too. For example, CARE: Cooperative for Assistance and Relief Everywhere, Inc., provides information about its expenditures and program area financial distribution directly on their donation form pages.[80] Similarly, the American Jewish World Service (AJWS) provides a basic financial expenditure chart in the footer of its website so it is accessible from every page, as well as links to download financial statements and 990 reports.[81] Figure 5.1 is a screen shot of the AJWS website.

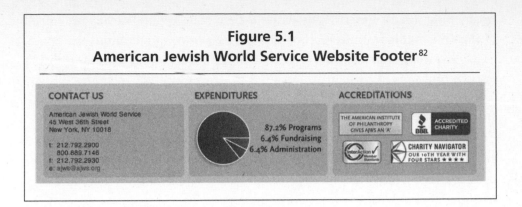

Figure 5.1
American Jewish World Service Website Footer[82]

Include Signposts to Your Website

While you're being transparent on your own site, be sure to connect your various online profiles back to your main website. It doesn't take many clicks for someone to get lost on the web—we've all experienced that! So, make it easy for people to find out more about you wherever they come across your presence online. Ensure that your Facebook, Twitter, YouTube, Google+, LinkedIn, Pinterest, and any other online profiles include a link back to your official website. This signposting helps people quickly and easily navigate to your official homepage on the web, and also helps signify that your various profiles are real accounts from the organization and not those set up by others.

Even better, link your individual profiles to a welcome page (a simplified landing page) designed for people who find you elsewhere on the web, and may not know about your work. Often, an organization's homepage provides only a generic introduction, or tries to cover everything the organization does, making it overwhelming. A welcome page gives you a chance to greet visitors who found out about you on social media with a more direct message. This can build trust, but can also increase engagement by providing relevant calls to action on the very first click.

Similarly, you can provide a welcome message on your online profiles for new visitors, encouraging them to get involved with any actions you are currently promoting or evergreen opportunities (that is, opportunities that are always available or are not going to change or fade in value or relevance). For example, the California State Parks Foundation uses a custom tab on their Facebook Page to provide supporters with direct links in case they want to follow the organization on Twitter, or even access their mobile application. Even though, at the time of this writing, Facebook no longer allows organizations the option to automatically redirect visitors to a custom tab, the option to use these tabs for custom content is still valuable.

Build Trust into the Community

There are many different ways to build trust, some of them more active than others. The approaches we have just discussed serve as a solid foundation for more dynamic communications or engagement. Next we examine options to marry trust building with active community building.

Every organization we have worked with, no matter how small or how new, has some fans and favorites (even if they are also your friends or family) that rise above the rest in their dedication or support. Invite those super fans to form a community advisory team that provides feedback, ideas, direction, and even leadership or organizing support. This doesn't have to be something that creates more work for your staff. Do you already have a group of people outside the organization who are regularly providing feedback? Or supporters that you or your staff check in with or send updates to? Simply formalize that role and connect those supporters with each other. Try inviting them all into the office once per quarter for a lunch to discuss new ideas or hold a conference call or webinar so they can respond to possible new initiatives. You could connect them together in a Facebook Group to brainstorm about your current or potential programs. Create an email list for them and your staff or leadership team so that connecting and discussing new ideas can be done easily and quickly.

Are you releasing your annual report? Did you recently secure some new funding? Are you launching a new program or campaign? Announce it to the community with an invitation to join an open conference call or webinar where you will provide more information, allow people to ask questions, and give an overview of the next steps. Even if there isn't a huge turnout on the call or webinar, record it and provide the video or audio file on your website for others to listen to in the future. Showing that you are available and transparent about your operations will build trust in real time on the call and going forward, and provide an opportunity for the community to have a direct line of communication with you about your work.

As much as it helps build trust by making your organization's leadership accessible, it's even more important that the program staff—those driving and building the day-to-day impact of your programs and services—are connected directly with the community. This connection can take many shapes: monthly community calls, an ongoing series of posts or stories on social media platforms, staff interviews and blog posts (be sure you allow for comments!), or regular program updates via email.

USING A BLOG SERIES TO BUILD TRUST

Meyer Memorial Trust (MMT), a private foundation serving Oregon and Southwest Washington, has an ongoing blog series called "Two Way Street Tour." Program officers from the foundation travel to different parts of the state to meet with the nonprofit community (both grantees and others), share Meyer's work and vision, and (the two-way street part) learn all they can about what groups are doing locally. The program officers enjoy the opportunities to meet with people throughout the service area in person and connect with them directly.

By sharing recaps and highlights from the visits on the trust's blog, program officers help change one visit and a dozen conversations at a time into a larger conversation with the whole community. MMT also builds trust with the community by sharing their notes and observations in a place where those involved can weigh in to agree or disagree, and everyone can track where program officers spend time (demystifying the idea that energy is concentrated in Portland, the city where the trust is based).

This is a great example of using content already available to start conversations and connect your community!

Beyond accessibility, you build tremendous trust with your community when you are accountable to them. In the summer of 2012, while record-breaking heat waves were sweeping across the United States, 350.org president and cofounder Bill McKibbon announced a new action and a call for donations to fund it:

putting large pieces of ice that spelled out "hoax?" in front of the White House. It was intended to make the statement that these heat waves were just another sign of global climate change's impacts and that the idea of climate change was not a hoax. The community responded, saying that this wasn't the kind of action they wanted to support and that they wanted to donate funds to help communities hardest hit by the heat and storms. McKibbon sent out a message the following day apologizing, and explaining that through the community's feedback the 350. org team was able to understand their perspective and would cancel the action, sending all funds to relief efforts.

Whatever you do to build trust, be sure that you operate transparently, and operate in an authentic way with your community, knowing that you will continue to find opportunities to do even more. Social and mobile technologies are changing and evolving every day, which means you will discover new ways of sharing, new ways of collaborating, and new ways of understanding your work. Often, our communities start using new tools before we figure out how to adopt them as organizations. This gives you great potential to build deeper connections with your community when you, too, begin using these new tools, knowing your community is already there when you join them.

Focus on the Needs of the Community

In Chapter Two, we outlined the guiding principles of operating in an anytime, everywhere world. Understanding your community—especially recognizing who is in it, what those people are like, and what kinds of content and actions resonate with them—is critical if you want to be able to interact and engage with your advocates and supporters. When it comes to building community using multichannel strategies with an anytime, everywhere goal for engagement, knowing your community's preferences—and acting on them—can help catalyze passive followers into active supporters.

SPEAK THEIR LANGUAGE

Imagine you're at home, it's early evening, and like many Americans, you're multitasking: the television is on, you are checking email and Facebook on your mobile phone, and sending texts to a friend or two. Then you receive a text message from an advocacy organization urging you to share an update with your friends and family about a national issue that could impact you. One more thing:

the message is not in your first language. Do you share the message or just go back to your other conversations? Or perhaps the message that you received from the organization is in your preferred language, but it came as a Facebook message instead of a text or an email. If you rarely check or respond to Facebook messages, what are the chances that the important information really reached you?

Those are the kinds of questions many organizations ask themselves when evaluating tools and applications, designing their communications plans and campaigns, and even when setting up their subscription forms and communication opt-ins. Building community through anytime, everywhere communication (especially two-way communication) is achievable first and foremost by knowing your community members' preferences for where, when, and how you communicate, which we also discussed in Chapter Three.

Some organizations create separate online or communications spaces based on language, location, or content type, allowing individuals to opt in to the one that matches their preference. For example, if you have diabetes and want to connect with others to share your experience, there's a social network for you; actually, there are two: one for English speakers (tudiabetes.org), and one for Spanish speakers (estudiabetes.org), both created by the Diabetes Hands Foundation.[83] Alternatively, some organizations choose to maintain just one channel and use a growing set of options and functionality that platform providers are creating, like Facebook's ability to filter posts and updates by language or location.

Recognizing the language preference of individuals in your database or community is the first step. What comes next is ensuring that you have the capacity to communicate appropriately in that language. Simply translating word for word can get you into trouble, sometimes in a big way. Here's an example from Immigration Reform for America (IR4A):[84]

IR4A offered text message alerts in both English and Spanish to connect mobile phone numbers to other user data in the database. They regularly tracked message response metrics such as opens, replies, and so on. Just as with email, organizations are legally required to offer opt-out or unsubscribe information to recipients as we discussed in Chapter Three. Though, when you have such a small space in a text message to begin with, it can be tricky to figure out.

Jed Alpert, the CEO of Mobile Commons, shared that one of IR4A's text messages read:

> *Immigration Alert: BIG White House meeting w/pro-immigrant advocates tomorrow. Text 2246 your question now. Top Qs will be asked! Txt STOP to unsub Please Forward*

The message received the highest number of opt-outs of any message in the campaign (about five times more). As they analyzed the data, IR4A realized that the vast majority of those unsubscribing were from the Spanish-speaking list. They revisited the Spanish version of the message and noticed that the word "ALTO" was used in place of "STOP" in English. In their community, especially during this campaign, that word had been used as a rallying cry against certain immigration legislation, and its use in the text message was mistaken by the recipients. Many thought they were sharing support for a stop to a certain political action, not to stop receiving the text message updates.

IR4A issued a clarifying message to the Spanish list to allow those who did want to opt out to do so. Since the opt-out language was clear in English, IR4A has since continued to include the same unsubscribe language in messages to the English-speaking list, while separating unsubscribe notifications from other communications to the Spanish-speaking list to ensure the message is clear.

Let the Individual Pick the Platform

Whether you're using text messages where space is limited, or have unlimited options on your own website, blog, or even email, providing language options is a great start to building community. Just like any content in any language, though, the message needs to be clear, relevant, and appropriate. When new supporters sign up to hear from you, just like language options, you can provide them with options for the platform of their choice. Some of that comes with the territory: if they connect with you on Facebook, they are saying that's where they want to engage, or if they sign up via text message to keep receiving messages that way, you know that's the platform they prefer; but you can also provide a sign-up link from your Facebook profile or embed a sign-up form directly on a custom Facebook tab so those that find you there but don't prefer to get your messages on Facebook can opt in to your emails, blog, or other types of message alerts.

Preferences for various technology or communication channels are not established solely by you sending messages out, but also by supporters sending messages and updates back to you! For example, the Alliance for Climate Education (ACE) educates high school students on the science behind climate change through school assemblies and classroom presentations and inspires them to take action to curb global warming. At the end of assemblies, often with hundreds of young people all in one place (and equipped with mobile phones), ACE teachers ask participating students to share a "DOT" or a way that they will "Do One Thing" to help the environment.

Many students share their DOT via a text message short code, while others do so on the web.[85] As students text to share their pledge, they also sign up to the ACE list, where the organization can send them reminders and helpful information for successfully completing their action. ACE aggregates and shares the pledges on the web so students new to the network can see what their peers are doing and get inspired to take action, too.

The students pick the channel they prefer not by signing up just to get messages from ACE, but by sending the organization their pledges, plans, and results. The channel they choose, whether text messages, email, or the web, then becomes the method ACE uses to support them, provide them with more opportunities to take action, and to move them up an engagement ladder to develop leadership and make more local impact. The results? At the start of 2012, ACE reports over 173,000 DOTs pledged from students across America.

What is crucial about ACE's approach is that it starts with the students; they are the ones that take the first action by texting in their DOT or signing up on the web to be a leader in their school. Instead of the organization prescribing what actions to suggest to students and how to communicate with them, ACE puts the community in the driver's seat to pick a communication channel and tell the organization just what they want to do.

You may not have the chance to be in person with your community the way that ACE has. And you may not have such a hot topic as immigration in the news like IR4A. Regardless, start asking your community how they want to communicate with you and build those options into your registration and sign-up processes. It can make a huge impact on your success if you communicate with your supporters the way they want to hear from you.

ENGAGE SUPPORTERS IMMEDIATELY VIA TEXT

When ACE educators invite hundreds of students in school assemblies to pledge to make a change to help the environment, they know many of them will pull out their phones and send a text message right then and there. That's only the first step, though. Just like with email confirmation messages that you set up to send automatically to your donors and supporters who take action on your website, these mobile subscribers need to be engaged with immediately to help establish the connection and start building a deeper relationship. Here are some examples of messages that ACE uses to engage students right away, and to follow up with them later to get them back in action:

Immediate conversation when a student texts DOT to 30644:

1. Not done yet! Txt back 1 thing you'll do (turn off lights, unplug gadgets) 2 help stop climate change! Msg&DataRatesMayApply TxtSTOP2quit HELP4info.

2. Awesome—great idea! With everybody doing 1 thing 2 stop climate change, we can make a big difference. 2 complete your DOT, pls text back ur email & zip code.

3. Thanks for joining ACE! More at acespace.org/dot. Tell friends 2 text DOT to 30644 or forward this message to double your impact!

ACE also sends reengagement messages after 3, 8, and 15 days to pull supporters back into more actions. "We use the "ACE" opt-in to help segment our users based on their level of interest and engagement. This not only helps us customize our content, but also tailor the frequency with which we communicate based on their preference," explained Kara Muraki, Marketing Manager at ACE.

1. ACE here-thx again 4 sharing ur DOT. Did u know u can do more than 1 thing? Life Academy has already collected 1,137 DOTs! Can u beat that? Txt bck ACE 4 more.

2. What projects are you most interested in? a. ACE's Biggest Loser Energy contest b. Solarizing your school c. Recycling Rply STOP2quit HELP4info Msg&DataRates.

3. ACE here. Ready 2 up ur game & take on fun climate projects like solarizing ur school? Last chance 2 txt bck "ACE" to get project ideas & exclusive opps via txt.

Keep Shared Goals Prominent in Communications

One of the principles discussed in Chapter Two was the need to stay focused on real impact and goals, despite the shiny-new-thing attraction with many social and mobile tools. Ultimately, the action we want our community to take is not to "like" something or "download" something but to learn, share, and change. When it comes to using these tools to build community, this is especially important to remember. You will not be able to bring people together and keep them connected to your mission if they do not see value in the work you do and the way they contribute to your impact.

The Alliance for Climate Education (ACE) aggregates the DOT ideas students submit via the web or mobile phone to inspire other students to take action. They also count them up. The DOT ticker is a prominent part of the action center on ACE's website, making it easy for any visitor to see how important the number of actions is to the organization and community.

ACE's approach has two catalyzing moments for the students to truly become community members. The first is at the initial assembly or presentation when they are invited to text a DOT and take action. Many organizations use the same approach when they have a fundraiser, a live event, a rally, or even a local government meeting where they can invite potential supporters to join them. The second opportunity is when the students see their DOT or the pledges from other students and are inspired to do more. This second opportunity is critical because this is where community members can see ACE's focus on the impact they can make together.

CONNECT THE COMMUNITY ACROSS PLATFORMS

When you create opportunities for your community members to connect with you in the languages and channels they prefer, you present your staff with a challenge. In an anytime, everywhere world, where supporters are communicating

SHOW THEM THE NUMBERS

Many organizations are familiar with the idea of a thermometer or other visual gauge on a fundraising campaign page. Just as the Alliance for Climate Education does with the Do One Thing pledge counter, there are many ways you can aggregate or display data to continue to inspire your community and reinforce that every action they take does matter. Here are some ways you can show the community all that they're doing:

1. Total community members or subscribers, etc.

2. Number of signatures on a petition, or responses to a call to action

3. Number of people served that day, month, or year

4. Number of hours of volunteer time

5. Mission-specific data like the number of books purchased through a campaign for a school

6. Fun facts that show your impact like the number of miles all of the donated pencils would stretch when put end to end

7. A map with the locations of participants or contributors

8. The minutes it takes to complete various actions to make a difference

with you using various technologies, you can't just write one message and push send. Instead, you need to work across platforms, crafting relevant messages, listening to the various subgroups of your community that congregate in each area, and responding accordingly.

Make It Easy to Find All Your Channels and Chapters

It may be that your organization has chapters across the state or country, maybe you have volunteer groups working at a local level, or even state affiliates. A common question we get from organizations or groups that have partners and affiliates serving other areas is how to direct people to the right place for local content.

One great example of a multichapter organization that is doing this well is AARP. There are benefits to connecting everyone in the United States, for example, with the national AARP presence online. Often, individuals can benefit more from a direct connection to the local chapter versus the national organization. AARP recognizes this value and includes a custom tab on its Facebook Page so that visitors, even without "liking" the AARP Page, can quickly find the appropriate link to the Facebook profile for their local AARP organization.

By creating an easy path for visitors to find the organization or chapter profile that they are most interested in, the AARP hands over the control to the visitors to decide what kind of relationship and content they find most valuable. It also creates an opportunity for community members to opt in to the community group they want to be part of, whether it's national or local. As such, staff managing the profiles for their chapter can speak more directly to the community members there, knowing they are interested in the AARP work and news related to that level of the organization.

Another example is the American Museum of Natural History (AMNH), based in New York City, which epitomizes the idea that various channels present entirely new relationships with the organization. The AMNH gets around four million visitors each year[86] entering the physical museum across from Central Park. The Museum describes itself and its mission this way:

> The American Museum of Natural History (AMNH) is one of the world's preeminent scientific and cultural institutions. Since its founding in 1869, the Museum has advanced its global mission to discover, interpret and disseminate information about human cultures, the natural world and the universe through a wide-ranging program of scientific research, education and exhibition
>
> The Museum is renowned for its exhibitions and scientific collections, which serve as a field guide to the entire planet and present a panorama of the world's cultures.

It would be easy to assume that an institution like the AMNH, where the focus is on its physical space, including 46 permanent exhibition halls and over 32 million specimens, would have only one offline channel for connecting with the community and serving its mission. However, thanks to social media and mobile technology, the AMNH has a way to let people that are standing in front of a dinosaur fossil in the New York museum, as well as those who have never been to the United States, explore exhibits and learn about our world anytime from their Apple iPhone or iPad.

The AMNH has four applications for the iPhone and one specifically for the iPad.[87] With over one million downloads so far, these applications are helping the museum reach its mission to provide information about the wonders of the world to people everywhere. The applications cover topics including the physical planet, dinosaurs, outer space, and even the inside of the Museum itself through a guided tour. The museum's community can now be defined not just by those four million people physically walking through the exhibits, but also by all those downloading the mobile applications and exploring the AMNH's exhibits and collections from anywhere—geography no longer impacts a visit to the Museum.

SUPPORTING SUBGROUPS IN YOUR COMMUNITY

There are many ways to empower your community to connect and collaborate with each other through your work, even when you aren't creating the content or the events. Here are some ways you can keep groups connected within the full community:

- Create an online group for volunteers to share their knowledge, experiences, and encouragement with each other on Facebook, LinkedIn, or even an application like Ning, a white-label application (meaning it is customizable and private) allowing you to brand and maintain a private social network.

- Host or participate in regular Twitter chats focused on a specific aspect of your cause or programming and bring in contributors or supporters as the guests and moderators.

- Create a group blog on your website where content comes from a specific group or is focused on a specific program area—host the blog or display the posts on that group or program's area of the website in addition to the general blog.

- Use subgroup features on LinkedIn, Meetup, or even your own website to set up location-specific groups for community members to find each other locally.

- Set up a shared Pinterest board for supporters to share photos and blog posts from an event, or to collect examples of your mission in action.

Support Smaller Groups Taking Action

For many organizations, building community across platforms means creating relationships with supporters, and helping community members create groups and connections between themselves. For the organization Do Something,[88] young people can find or create actions they want to take locally that don't require a car, an adult, or money. The DoSomething.org website houses thousands of actions created by the organization and community members, as well as nearly 50 national campaigns each year.

Do Something encourages members to grab their friends and take action together, even if those friends haven't signed up yet. Participants act locally, donating used jeans, starting petitions, or even educating others about an issue they find important. While they are out in their local communities, they can use their mobile phones to take pictures and videos, and are encouraged to share their experience back on the DoSomething.org website. By 2010, Do Something had engaged over 1.2 million young people in campaigns, and in 2012 it set a goal of hitting 5 million participants by 2015.[89]

The only way to reach that number was to expand beyond their website, and that is just what Do Something has done. Community members share the responsibility of building community and maintaining connections across platforms with the organization by using the website, text messages, and offline action interchangeably. Maybe you sign up for an action one day and complete it; six months later you receive a text message about a similar action and recruit your best friends to show up with you. Three more months go by, and you send a text to the organization telling them that you want to do something at your school and they send you materials that you and your friends can use to start up a canned food donation drive. And so the chain of actions and engagement continues.

For many organizations, Do Something included, the community is actually made up of smaller groups. We don't want to focus on only connecting with the community as a whole, but need to also create ways to nurture the smaller subcommunities separately, and help them connect with each other. Do Something shares the accountability with community members for connecting supporters and making impact across platforms. By encouraging participants to create their own group and lead their friends in an action, Do Something supports forming subgroups and gives over responsibility for making an impact to group leaders.

Ultimately, we are building community around our work to increase our potential for impact. Building community is the first step to building a movement.

Connect Impact Across Channels

We need to connect our community across platforms and campaigns. We also need to connect the community by our impact, reflecting the total influence of the community's efforts; after all, it isn't the work of just your Facebook followers or only your newsletter subscribers when you have success. It's the combined influence of all your subcommunities. Some people often mistake the total size of a community for the ultimate impact it can generate. Creating the most impact in the real world, versus signing up the most people, should fuel the growth of the community. Using multichannel communication and collaboration technologies, you can support your community in catalyzing change within their networks, sometimes without even bringing those new constituents into your community.

Survivors Connect is a nonprofit organization that empowers survivors and grassroots activists working against slavery, trafficking, and violence by leveraging the power of innovative information and communication technologies. Survivors Connect uses an online social network to bring activists and supporters together from around the world.[90] They describe this online group, Freedom Connect, as "a web-based public meeting place that provides survivors and activists with a shared calendar, discussion forums, member profiles, photo gallery, resource library, subgroups, and more." They use a white-label social networking tool called Groupsite. Instead of creating a group within a commercial social network like Facebook, the Freedom Connect social network is its own social space, and Survivors Connect can set the permissions for the entire network and designate certain site functionality and shared resources as private or public as necessary for the group's goals.

By creating a space where all of the members of the community can see and connect with each other, the organization is able to step out of the way as a gatekeeper or roadblock. Don't make collaboration between members of your community difficult or time consuming by trying to facilitate every interaction. In this case, Freedom Connect allows activists to share their experiences and knowledge with each other directly, which in turn strengthens the entire community and increases the effectiveness of activists' work locally.

Similarly, Do Something supports their community's impact by encouraging young people that sign up for an action to grab their friends and do it together. Knowing you have a friend to participate with increases the potential for community members to complete the actions. After these small groups make change together, those that were not already signed up on the DoSomething.org website may register to show that they participated. At that point, they are encouraged to complete the cycle again, with more friends—those that are and are not already connected to Do Something.

The way you connect with and create connections within your community is less important than the fact that you do it. There are organizations using combinations of public pages and private groups on Facebook, others using white label vendors to build custom online networking spaces, and still others that have built-in functionality on their own website. If you know your community and the subgroups well enough from the very beginning so that you can set up various tools at the same time, great. But most organizations will need to focus on creating the overall community connections and then work with their supporters to find the additional groups and tools necessary to keep everyone engaged.

EXERCISE YOUR VALUE IN THE COMMUNITY

We've all seen the infomercials where a couple of people have sculpted their bodies into ripples of muscle and it seems all they've done to achieve such impressive results is use a Shake Weight. If it seems too good to be true, it probably is. The point is, you can't compare your organization and your community to the ideal; create opportunities to practice and improve using benchmarks from your own community and the goals you've set as an organization.

From time to time, you may run a campaign focused solely on building your list, getting more people signed up for your content or alerts, and registering potential supporters and donors. These kinds of community member drives are valuable as opportunities to grow your list and exercise in engaging your community, and can also add more data to your benchmarks and give you a good check-in point for goals on larger campaigns. Efforts to find and connect with new potential members should also be part of the way you operate year-round. Community building with multichannel tools should be something that you build into your practice anytime, everywhere, too!

Staffing to Support the Community

There is no way that you will be able to recruit and engage your community, or manage content across platforms (especially considering that you need to tailor messaging for each) unless you have the organizational support for that work. Social media has spurred a fast increase of community manager and social media staff roles and jobs, specifically focused on managing and engaging (and promoting the organization or brand) on social media channels. Increasingly, these roles are truly focused on multichannel engagement by supporting content and interaction across the web and offline, as well as by identifying more engaged members that may want to take on more formal volunteer roles with the organization.

If your organization does not have a formal community manager role of some type, other departments or staff need to have the capacity to take on those duties. When we say "capacity" for those duties we really do mean full capacity. Monitoring, managing, and operating strategically with multichannel community building is not something that you can add to someone's plate unless you're taking some other duties away. The duties should be included in their job description and evaluation. Working with your community takes time. Beyond staff time and salary, it can also require a budget, especially if you are using or building your own tools.

Not everyone in your organization may be directly connected to or working with the community. Regardless of the number of staff you have, there are bound to be different perceptions of who the community is, and how the community should be engaged, from staffer to staffer. As such, there should be staff with community engagement in their work plan and job description, and there should be opportunities for all staff to come together to discuss the community's role in the organization's work to ensure that all staff can provide input and insight from the segments of the community they know and connect with most. We will cover more details about staffing in Chapter Seven.

The Need for Flexibility

Creating ways for your existing community members to stay engaged and to recruit new community members outside of a specific campaign or action requires flexibility. We can apply some of the same thinking we use with specific actions for more open-ended engagement opportunities. For example, if we have an action campaign running, we should know just which action we want people to take, and what we will ask them to do once they take that action. Maybe we want them to sign an online petition, and then we follow up via email with a prompt to share their story in video, photo, or text. After that, we encourage

WHAT'S THE MAGIC NUMBER?

Community managers, nonprofit directors, and even consultants have asked us what the "right" number of tweets or Facebook posts is per day to keep the community engaged but not annoyed. Here's the catch: there is no magic number!

The frequency of your posts, whichever channel you're looking at, should not be based on a special calculation but instead on the type of community, the frequency of the community's posts, and the kind of response or engagement you receive when you do post. Here are some general guidelines to help you find a balanced frequency for your posts:

1. Limit posts broadcasting information and links, unless it is live reporting, emergency communications, or something else requiring a stream of broadcast-type messages.

2. When thanking people for responses, retweets, or other general engagement, consider including multiple people in one tweet to decrease the number of very similar messages.

3. When answering questions from supporters, be sure the reply (@username) is first in the response if it is a user-specific question (Did I renew my membership? Am I signed up to your email newsletter?), or, for questions that many users may be asking (How do I join? Where do I sign up for your newsletter?), include some text before the @username so you don't overwhelm followers with messages that don't relate to them.

4. When providing resources from another organization, mention them in your post so they can further support follow-up questions or comments.

5. Track your posts and the responses to inform your goals and set limits for the number of posts each day or week. For any social platform you are using, whether Facebook or Twitter or something else, your tracking document should include either the total number of or the percentage of:

   • Your organization's outbound posts with a link and the number without a link.

   • Replies and retweets to your posts with a link and those without.

   • Inquiries from the community and number of general messages (on Twitter, for example, @yourorg great campaign! or @yourorg we love that photo!).

them to post their story and the action to their network via social media channels.

Like focused campaigns, year-round engagement should align with your mission and goals; the difference being you can continually maintain relevance and promote mission-appropriate action without a break because the campaign is over. Say you are an organization working on providing more affordable and safe alternative transportation options in your city. This might involve creating an online space for members to report unsafe intersections or transportation issues. In this way, you can keep your community engaged, tap them to stay on top of any newsworthy issues, and have an opportunity to leverage user-generated content across your online channels.

People may come across your organization on social media and want to learn more about your work elsewhere. Links that connect your various social media profiles and your website, as well as links from your email messages to those same channels, can help funnel people toward the kind of engagement they want to have with you, without your having to know (or, more likely, having to guess) from the beginning. In a multichannel approach, you can also start identifying the subgroups within the community and crafting the kinds of year-round engagement options on each channel to the group or groups in that space.

The Role of Customer Service

The role of customer service in community building is one that many organizations overlook, thinking "customer service" is only for companies selling products or utilities and trying to please its customers. As Paull Young at charity: water has said, "Giving your constituents the best customer support is undervalued by nonprofits." It is actually a core component of building community, especially in day-to-day communications outside of campaigns. Customer service for many nonprofits means answering questions and providing support on various channels, from navigating the website to using the blog, finding resources or identifying other organizations, and even responding to questions that aren't about its work with information that is relevant (even if it isn't pointing people to the nonprofit's website).

Providing quality customer service is a terrific way to build trust. It also creates a positive cycle where you are actively connecting with and helping your community, which keeps them busy connecting with you as a reliable resource.

Craig Newmark, founder of craigslist and craigconnects, has spent over 20 years in customer service. He puts it this way:

> Customer service is about the people who provide a service or product fulfilling their commitment to the community of their customers. It means treating their customers like they want to be treated. Personally, I regard it as a kind of public service, since when you provide reasonable customer service that raises the bar for everyone.

Providing great support and customer service to your community, in a public way on social platforms and on your website, sets the tone for the community. By engaging with people, sharing resources (whether they are developed by your organization or not), and generally helping them succeed in using a tool, learning about issues, or taking an action, you lead by example, and indicate that the community can and should do the same.

Plan for Churn

As we discussed in Chapter Four, churn (the number of subscribers and supporters who leave your database or other list) impacts email, direct mail, social media, and anywhere else people may be directly connected to your database or communications. Despite our best efforts to create flexible and valuable engagement opportunities for our community, and no matter how great our customer service and interaction is, churn is inevitable. Even though it is unavoidable, it is something that good community managers should plan for, pay attention to, and try to decrease.

Consider the Legal Concerns of Building Community

Just as with advocacy and fundraising, using technology for community building comes with risks, liabilities, and legal parameters. You may have donors or supporters that are more informed (and more vocal) about issues that relate to the way they donate, their personal or payment information in your records, or the way you track the actions they take to support your organization. Even if your community is not versed in the issues enough to ask about them, you need to consider potential risks associated with building community in the ways we've described here to ensure all that work you did to build trust wasn't for nothing.

Buy Contact Lists

One of the biggest potential risk areas for organizations using social and mobile technology for community building is around selling and buying lists. Churn is a real issue, as we discussed above, so organizations sometimes consider buying a list of potential supporters from a likeminded organization. Some organizations share (sometimes this means buying or selling) lists with similar or partner organizations, especially during a shared campaign. These lists usually contain information about people's email, phone, or mailing address.

These practices are not illegal, so long as organizations inform individuals upfront. We recommend providing an option for people to elect (opt in) to have their information shared with similar organizations, instead of doing so by default. We also think that a double opt-in process is best, especially if you hope to convert these new names into real donors or community participants. A double opt-in process means that although these individuals checked a box with the first organization, authorizing them to share contact details with similar organizations, once you receive the list you should message them with an opportunity to sign up with you.

Create Clear Ways to Unsubscribe

That kind of opt-in process brings up another sticky area for organizations using these tools to connect with the community: opt-out. Especially when we are working to build community, it's hard to imagine anyone would want to unsubscribe. According to NTEN and M+R's research,[91] unsubscribe rates can actually be an indication of an active community—the community had to pay attention to the fact that you were sending messages, recognize the ones they wanted and didn't want, and then change their subscription settings. There are legal parameters to providing opt-out information in your messages and it is important to understand the options before deciding on the messages themselves.

During the IR4A campaign, the unsubscribe information was confusing when put together with a call to action in one message. But in the effort to provide that opportunity to subscribers, IR4A sends opt-out messages independently of other actions. Many email marketing tools, databases, and even third-party applications provide you with the functionality to manage lists related to message types. Using these options you can encourage subscribers to sign up for the types of messages that they would like to receive from you and, consequently, encourage them to unsubscribe from the messages that they aren't interested in.

Receiving too many messages from you or a similar organization is a small complaint for many nonprofits compared to the issues around privacy. No matter how big or small your community, it is important that your supporters know what kind of information they've provided you and what information is stored in your database. Many organizations provide community members with the option to create a profile on the organization's website or microsite for a campaign. It is important in these cases to provide information and guidelines about the public or private levels of profile information, who has access to the network, and even how people can protect themselves from spam (even if it isn't associated with your organization).

As we said at the beginning of the chapter, trust is crucial. Being transparent and proactive when it comes to helping members of your community protect themselves and control their information means you will build more trust with them. And as our tools continue to evolve, the legal risks and potential pitfalls do too.

So far, we've showcased advocacy, fundraising, and community building separately. Not only do multichannel strategies include the integration of various platforms and messages, they also connect the kinds of engagement—from a fundraising ask that leverages an action alert, to advocacy appeals tied to hot topics in the news asking people to join the organization in building up the community. In Chapter Six, we dive into two real case studies for an in-depth look at how multichannel strategies come together.

DISCUSSION QUESTIONS

Spark a conversation with your team or organization about these core principles with the following questions:

1. What data, whether hard numbers or qualitative information, do you already have on hand that you could share on your website or as features on your blog and social channels?

2. What are the language, platform, or other preference options you would like to explore providing for your community?

3. What are the subgroups in your community and how could you support them being closer to your work and more connected with each other?

4. What upcoming campaigns do you have planned that can include a community-building component as one of the individual appeals?

5. How does your staff share in the process of engaging with the community now? How could others across the organization benefit from learning about the content, messages, responses, and goals of this work?

chapter SIX

Multichannel Strategies in Action

Now that we've covered the "why" behind using multichannel strategies for advocacy, fundraising, and community engagement, let's dive into some of the ins and outs of real campaigns. This chapter is designed to give you the behind-the-scenes tour of real campaigns from a few organizations to show what multichannel strategies look like in action. These three case studies, from National Wildlife Federation, Surfrider Foundation, and Iraq and Afghanistan Veterans of America, show how organizations bring everything together to incorporate advocacy, fundraising, and community building across channels.

OIL SPILL CRISIS: NATIONAL WILDLIFE FOUNDATION'S MULTICHANNEL CAMPAIGN RESPONSE

When an explosion on the Deepwater Horizon oil drilling rig ignited a fire that could not be extinguished on April 20, 2010, resulting in the oil rig sinking two days later, the oil well continued gushing at the seabed.[92] The spill was the largest offshore oil spill in U.S. history, and the National Wildlife Federation (NWF) jumped to action with a multichannel disaster response campaign.

Goals

NWF's campaign had two overarching campaign goals:

1. To quickly organize a multichannel advocacy and fundraising campaign to protect the wildlife covered in oil and impacted by the spill spewing into the gulf and heading into Louisiana's fragile coast.

2. To channel the communities' concern for the oiled animals toward NWF's campaign actions so that supporters could make a real impact on the wildlife in the Gulf.

Within those two areas of focus for the campaign, NWF identified a number of short-term goals that would influence messaging, provide context for calls to action, and ultimately give structure to their strategy.

Get Information About the Spill to as Many People as Possible   With NWF staff and volunteers near the oil spill area, NWF was one of the primary resources for distributing information to the public about the spill and its impact on wildlife. "People wanted to know what was happening and how many wildlife were being hurt," said Kristin Johnson, senior manager for online integration at NWF. Within the first 24 hours of the spill, NWF created a microsite to aggregate the news, blogs, and other information about where the organization needed people's help.[93] They also created a Flickr group featuring oil spill photos and invited a number of people taking photos of the oil slick to join and share their images. This was an important tactic, especially with BP shutting the public out of most coastal areas due to safety reasons. Since local NWF staff immediately started seeing inconsistencies in the numbers BP reported, it was crucial to have an easy and fast way to spread on-the-ground information to the public. This was especially important in order to hold BP accountable for the full extent of the disaster.

Get Resources to Where They Are Needed   NWF's work focused on determining what was needed on the ground to help wildlife and connecting those needs with resources. They recruited volunteers to help monitor wildlife rescue efforts. They asked for gloves and other supplies for volunteers who were working in the Gulf area. They urged people to attend important events and to send messages to their members of Congress when relevant legislation needed to be passed.

Fix the Damage   In the first few months of the oil disaster, most of NWF's focus was on the direct response needed to help wildlife. For example, when hundreds of sea turtle nests needed to be moved to a safer beach, NWF helped fund the effort and recruited volunteers. When the hotline for reporting injured wildlife wasn't working, they enlisted their supporters to let BP know about the problems and got it fixed by BP in a timely manner.

Help People Cope   In times of tragedy social media channels can be used as an emotional support system for people who are looking for comfort. NWF saw many people in their community who were feeling helpless and sad about the tragedy. "We provided comfort where appropriate, or just allowed people a place to just express how bad they were feeling," said Johnson.

Long-Term Goal

NWF realized that in the long term, the oil spill was going to be impacting the Gulf for decades to come. Over time, they would need to transition their volunteer efforts from surveillance to restoration, and continue to fight for legislative funding to ensure that the Gulf received the financial help it needed. Two years later, NWF's legislative priority was for Congress to pass the RESTORE Act. This is legislation that ensures that at least 80% of the billions of dollars in potential fines that BP pays goes to fixing the damage they caused. Without the RESTORE Act, the fines would go into a general fund and be used for other projects. In June of 2012, Congress passed the bill.

Channels

The oil spill was a huge story in the media, and people were seeing very disturbing photos of oil-covered pelicans, dolphins, and other wildlife. So many people wanted to channel their grief by doing something to help, but it wasn't obvious how. "We immediately found it useful to not only be sharing information about the impact the spill had on wildlife, but also to share ways people could help, even if it was as simple as making sure this catastrophe didn't get swept under the rug and forgotten about," said Johnson. NWF even filed a Freedom of Information Act request to make sure the oiled wildlife totals were made public.

Online and Offline   NWF helped to organize volunteers on the ground and on the water to monitor beaches and the Gulf to report wildlife in distress.

Website Among all the people grieving about the oil spill and sharing with NWF online, many were children. To help parents know what to share with their children and how to share it, the editors of NWF's children's magazine, *Ranger Rick*,[94] pulled together child-friendly web content for their website and also helped advise NWF social media staff as to how they should interact with children who were reaching out to them online.

NWF set up campaign action pages on their website where people could contact their members of Congress to advocate for restoration and for holding BP accountable to fix the damage they caused.

Facebook and Twitter To reach their community and new people interested in protecting wildlife, NWF adapted their campaign messaging across several channels. "We actually sketched out an initial plan of attack and sample messages for each channel. And when we rolled it out, we instantly picked up on what was working and how people were responding or not responding," said Johnson.

NWF posted a couple of links each day. "We had to be careful that they weren't all sad and depressing, or we saw people become immobilized in grief and feeling hopeless. We also saw many people posting to our wall about the fundraisers they were holding for NWF, so we maintained a very thankful, humble, grateful tone—which was completely sincere. We were blown away by people every day," said Johnson.

To spread the information as quickly as possible and keep the momentum going, NWF collaborated with their community to reshare important updates, resources, and data. "Whether or not someone could donate or volunteer in person, we made it clear that it was also important for them to donate their time to share links, articles, and information about what was happening," said Johnson.

NWF also viewed their social channels, blog, and website as a vehicle to connect with reporters and help disperse credible information. NWF's social media and communications staff tuned in to the stories of the day, retweeted articles, shared them on Facebook, and tagged reporters/bloggers in the message. "We even saw articles we were sharing on Twitter being reported as news on CNN, attributed to NWF tweets," said Johnson.

Flickr NWF recognized from the start of the campaign how much their outreach was going to be very dependent on images, so they chose Flickr as the primary platform to post photos that documented the oil spill's impact on wildlife. This enabled their staff in Louisiana and along the coast to upload images quickly, as well as to create a Flickr group for other photographers, as we mentioned earlier. NWF searched daily for new images and photographers to recruit to the group, and also asked photographers for the rights to use their images on the NWF website.

Email NWF sent a variety of email and direct mail appeals to their members and activists that updated them about what NWF was doing on the ground and how supporters could help, such as by donating money, volunteering, and contacting their members of Congress to advocate for restoration.

Immediately after the oil spill, NWF started a restricted fund specific to the oil disaster, and cultivated donations online, by mail, by phone, text-to-give, and from multiple social fundraising platforms. Figure 6.1 shows a screen shot of the oil spill donation page.

Causes As we have discussed earlier in the book, when you build a strong community across multiple channels, your community will support you in times of need. In the case of the oil spill, NWF's community immediately started fundraising for NWF without NWF even asking. NWF's biggest social fundraiser was a page they set up on Causes.org. It was featured on the Causes homepage and immediately embraced by the Causes community, where more than a million people joined and donated.

Supporters sold crafts and created their own birthday fundraisers on Causes. Children organized lemonade stands and bake sales, where proceeds were donated to NWF. "While this wasn't necessarily something that we planned into our outreach from the start, we did our best to thank everyone and make sure they had what they needed for their events. We also shared what people were doing and that inspired even more fundraisers," said Johnson.

Text-to-Give Within the first 24 hours, NWF quickly set up their first ever, major text-to-give campaign where people could text "Wildlife" to a shortcode

Figure 6.1
Example of NWF Fundraising Appeal

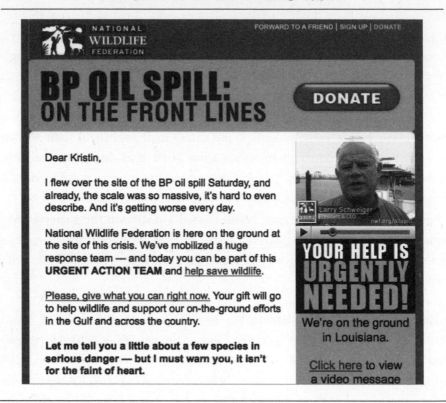

to donate $10. Since NWF was one of the leading experts in wildlife, and were quickly aggregating reports and resources, major news networks and blogs were interviewing and featuring their staff in news stories. This media exposure gave the organization even more leverage to promote the text-to-give campaign to a much wider audience. They also utilized the following channels to promote the text-to-give campaign:

- For the NWF website, they posted banner ads and graphics, which helped get the word out to their website visitors.

- For Twitter, they incorporated the text shortcode in several tweets, which was retweeted by a considerable number of supporters, including by celebrities with very large followings. They also featured and embedded the "Text 'wild-life' to 20222" graphic into their Twitter background.

- For Facebook, they mentioned the text-to-give campaign on their Page and included it in their comments when they were responding to people asking for ways to help. "But our approach with Facebook was to make sure our community always felt like they were getting content that was valuable to them," said Johnson. This aligns with the strategy we discussed in the fund-raising chapter (Chapter Four)—don't always ask your donors for money; give them several ways to engage with your organization.

Ads   NWF was fortunate enough to receive donated ads and travel as one of three charities chosen for the CNN "Disaster in the Gulf Telethon." "Really, we didn't use any paid promotion, and really did our best to make sure the money being donated was going to our work in the Gulf and to on the ground projects that smaller charities needed help with," said Johnson.

Results

Measuring metrics and real-world impact can be challenging when you are in the middle of a rapid response multichannel campaign. Johnson said that while NWF made every effort to set up source codes to track how people were responding to email actions and fundraising appeals, it was difficult to truly track the outpouring of support they saw for the wildlife and communities in the Gulf. NWF said they raised a significant amount of money, including $120,000 from the fundraising effort on Causes. They also had thousands of people sending messages to decision makers, and many people retweeting messages or sharing blogs. However, the numbers that NWF were most concerned with tracking were those indicating the impact they made on the ground to make things better for wildlife, including

- Training and organizing 250 wildlife surveillance volunteers to help monitor more than 2,500 miles of coast in the months following the spill. They even had a scuba group volunteer to take underwater photos off the coast of Florida before the oil got there to capture the current state of the reefs before the oil hit.

- More than 400 volunteers helping with events that included restoring fragile nesting habitats in dunes, building oyster reefs, and replanting marsh grasses.

- Showing reporters from major news outlets the impacts of the spill in remote wetland areas that included key pelican nesting habitats, which generated media coverage for NWF.

- Helping relocate more than 250 sea turtle nests (a nest has about 100 eggs) to safer beaches in an effort with the Sea Turtle Conservancy to give the endangered and threatened turtles a chance to survive.

- Directly impacting the passage of the RESTORE Act in Congress and continuing to make sure that BP will not only pay their fines, but also ensure that those fines go to restoring the damaged habitat.

Lessons

"We had no instruction manual on the shelf called 'What to do when an oil rig explodes in the Gulf.' It was written page by page, on the fly in the weeks and months after," said Johnson. NWF learned that by identifying point people from all departments who would meet daily, they were able to get the information they needed from the field and review and vet reports that NWF staff were seeing on social media channels and blogs. This helped NWF staff be on same page and help each other out, since reports were coming from a variety of sources. Johnson also said that the organization had to organize their internal communications to make sure that any staff that were talking to the media or on social media were properly equipped to talk about the facts around the oil spill and its impact on wildlife.

NWF said that the oil spill was also a lesson in streamlining their website processes and using their website to post the latest news and actions people could take. "We stressed that up front. Wherever you are, whatever you're putting out, redirect people to the oil spill website for the latest information," said Johnson.

Johnson said that had they not streamlined their internal web processes and used their website as the main source of updated information on the oil spill and wildlife, the campaign would not have run smoothly. "We would have had different, possibly inaccurate information coming out on our online channels [social media, email, blog, etc.]. We would have also posted a lot more duplicative or conflicting web content as our media team, magazine team, and online team were trying to get information online as fast as possible," said Johnson.

BAN THE BAG: SURFRIDER FOUNDATION'S MULTICHANNEL ADVOCACY CAMPAIGN

The Surfrider Foundation is a grassroots organization that works to protect the world's oceans and beaches through local organizing. Volunteers often lead Surfrider Foundation chapters at the local level. When the Portland, Oregon chapter was looking to reduce plastic pollution in the ocean, they launched the Ban the Bag campaign.

Goals

The immediate goal for the Ban the Bag campaign in Portland was to get local residents to write Portland City Council members and urge them to support legislation that banned single-use plastic bags in the city.

Channels

After finalizing their goals, they identified their target audience—local Portlanders who cared about the ocean, sustainability, and plastic pollution. Then they used multiple channels such as email, Facebook, and offline events to reach their target audience. According to Tara Gallagher, the Portland Chapter Outreach Coordinator, almost all of their online outreach and organizing was done through their Facebook Page, where they promoted petitions, events, and news coverage. They also sent out action alerts to their membership and asked people to share it with their friends and colleagues via email and social networks.

Offline organizing and promotion was also integrated into their multichannel campaign. For example, they distributed handbills and flyers to advertise local rallies supporting the Ban the Bag campaign that also linked back to their campaign website. They did presentations to conservation groups and recycling groups. In addition, they gathered petition signatures at a variety of events, including local concerts and festivals. And, most important, they got stakeholder buy-in through meetings with the mayor's office, grocers, and other parties who had a stake in the campaign.

Results

It took the Surfrider Foundation about four years to get plastic bags banned in Portland, but it was well worth it since the campaign actually became much larger and evolved into a statewide ban of plastic bags. During the campaign, Surfrider Foundation operated on a shoe-string budget and generated

- 10,000 petition signatures
- 4,924 Facebook "likes," a number that is still growing
- Hundreds of citizens attending the rallies
- Media coverage in *The Oregonian*, which was then reposted numerous times on Facebook, a cover story on the *Willamette Week*, and many more

"Not bad for an all volunteer group with an operating budget of $5,000 to $10,000! Social media has definitely allowed groups like ours to make an impact on a greater scale," said Gallagher.

Lessons

When campaigns grow beyond the initial geographic goal or even action target, it's important to document what you're doing and learning in ways that can be immediately shared with your partners or affiliates. In the case of the Ban the Bag campaign in Portland, as the effort grew to a statewide reach, sharing the successful strategies and tactics with campaigners outside of Portland was incredibly valuable.

Another aspect of campaigns that grow like Ban the Bag did is the impact on messaging. When the campaign launched, the focus was on a Portland-area change and the estimated timeline was much shorter. If your campaign changes its focus or duration, it's important to rescale the messaging to match. This will ensure that you are being transparent and consistent, as well as let you set the tone for the community as more supporters join.

MEMORIAL DAY: IAVA'S #GOSILENT MULTICHANNEL COMMUNITY CAMPAIGN

In the United States, the last Monday in May each year is Memorial Day, a federal holiday in remembrance of the men and women who died while serving in the United States Armed Forces. Iraq and Afghanistan Veterans of America (IAVA), the first and largest nonprofit, nonpartisan organization for Iraq and Afghanistan vets, with over 200,000 members and supporters nationwide, created a multichannel campaign to build community and call supporters to action for Memorial Day 2012.

Goals

Running a community-focused campaign on Memorial Day was an obvious choice for IAVA given that veterans and their families are the core members of its community. "For the veteran community, Memorial Day involves more collective reflection than nearly any other day of the year," said Megan Hemler, digital engagement director for IAVA. Memorial Day weekends for many are not always focused on veterans, though, which meant this campaign was an opportunity for IAVA to advance its mission and bring focus back to the purpose for the holiday. According to Hemler: "For the general public, it is a holiday associated primarily with BBQs and long weekends. Our "Go Silent" campaign was an attempt to bridge those two worlds, by inviting all Americans to honor the fallen."

IAVA decided on the name #GoSilent for the campaign—asking people to pledge to "go silent" at 12:01 P.M. Eastern time in honor of all those who gave their life in service, to coincide with President Obama's remarks at Arlington National Cemetery. Because the action required nothing more than an individual to take a moment to reflect, people could pledge to participate at any time and actually take a moment of silence at any time, even if it was before or after the ceremony in Arlington. This meant that the campaign messages and calls to action could feel timely and specific but the action was something supporters could complete at any time.

The campaign focused on engaging current IAVA members and supporters, giving them an opportunity to feel united and focused. Because of the national focus of the holiday, a campaign on the same topic meant there was opportunity to attract attention from people in the public eye such as politicians and celebrities who wanted to show their support for the cause. For example, Senator Ron Johnson (on Twitter as @SenRonJohnson) tweeted "I'll be 'going silent' at 11:01 CT today, in remembrance of those who gave their lives for America. iava.org #GoSilent." It was also a great opportunity to grow the community organically as people used the web to learn more about veterans and find IAVA's information.

As Hemler explained, "This one action, carrying one message, was crucial to our success—while complex campaigns with multiple tiers of engagement can be successful, Memorial Day was not complex to us. And we knew it was not complex to the veteran community. Stand with us in our silence, we asked—take a single moment from the BBQ or the beach to honor the men and women who have sacrificed their lives for that liberty."

Channels

IAVA staff would be offline at President Obama's presentation in Arlington at 12:01 for the moment of silence. However, they knew that online channels would be crucial to promote the campaign ahead of time as well as to document the offline ceremony and share it in real-time with supporters all over the country. "When deciding the best channels for this campaign," Hemler said, "we knew that we should expect higher than normal traffic to our primary website, IAVA.org, due to Google searches around the word "veteran" and increased Facebook activity around the topic. We also wanted to use our large social media following (over 370,000 Facebook Fans) to bring people into the campaign organically, by tailoring the content and possible actions to different, yet relevant, platforms."

Website

IAVA staff knew where they were connected to their community (Facebook and other social channels), as well as where they would be able to reach new visitors (primarily their website). They made the channel for those new to the organization streamlined and focused on the campaign. "We reached a final decision of a full-screen splash page on IAVA.org as the homepage for #GoSilent, with a simple form to pledge one minute of silence in solidarity with our community, coinciding with the laying of the wreath at the Tomb of the Unknown." You can see the splash page in Figure 6.2.

As Hemler explained, "[The] petition page was directly connected to our database for easy data collection and analysis—and initiated an automatic thank you email to those who pledged, encouraging them to spread the word and sign up for text reminders shortly before the moment of silence." Figure 6.3 is the petition page Hemler mentions. You can see that only the most critical information was requested keeping the form quick to complete.

Figure 6.2
Screen Shot of the #Go Silent Campaign Microsite

HONOR THE FALLEN

Cpl Donald Marler, USMC - Nicole S.

Go Silent.

Pledge a moment of silence at 12:01pm this Memorial Day to honor the fallen.

6,442 Americans have died in Iraq and Afghanistan since 9/11. This Memorial Day, we stand together to remember and honor their lives, legacies and last full measure of devotion for our country. At 12:01pm, IAVA will lay a wreath before the Tomb of the Unknown Soldier at Arlington National Cemetery. Gather your friends and family across the country and pause with us for a national moment of silence in their memory.

Go Silent this Memorial Day.

PLEDGE NOW

9384 PEOPLE HAVE PLEDGED

Figure 6.4 shows the confirmation page after completing the pledge to "go silent." The social sharing buttons are prominent and the number of people who have pledged increases.

Email   Email was a critical component of the campaign both to promote the campaign to those already on IAVA's list and to immediately engage those who signed the pledge. IAVA sent "a series of three emails to [the] membership base, alerting them about the campaign prior to Memorial Day, then thanking them and giving an on-the-ground update on the day itself," said Hemler.

Figure 6.3
#Go Silent Campaign Sign-up Form

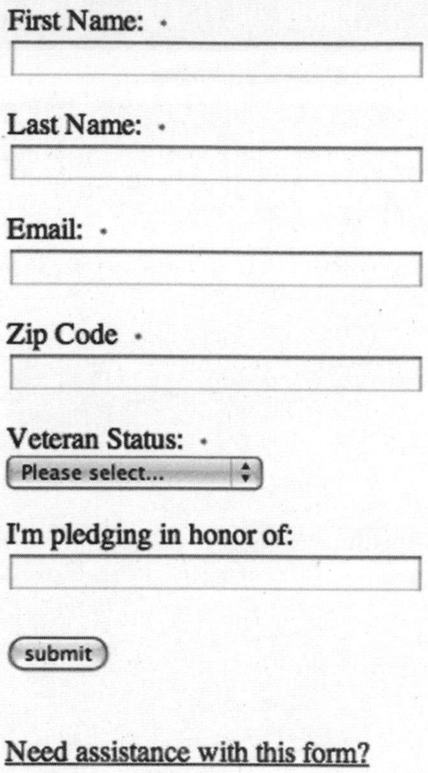

First Name: ·

Last Name: ·

Email: ·

Zip Code ·

Veteran Status: ·

Please select...

I'm pledging in honor of:

(submit)

Need assistance with this form?

Text Messages IAVA used text messages to send reminders to those who signed up to "go silent" and to send live messages on Memorial Day. In Figure 6.5 you can see the email message received after pledging to "go silent"; it encourages recipients to sign up for the mobile reminders, thus ensuring that as many people as possible are in IAVA's database with two kinds of communications options—an email address and a mobile phone number.

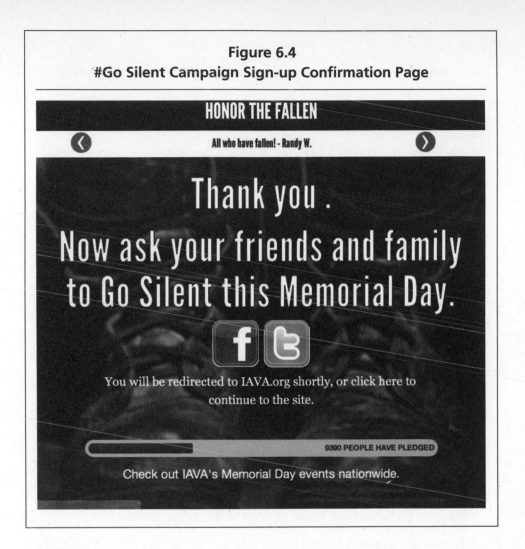

Figure 6.4
#Go Silent Campaign Sign-up Confirmation Page

HONOR THE FALLEN

All who have fallen! - Randy W.

Thank you .
Now ask your friends and family
to Go Silent this Memorial Day.

You will be redirected to IAVA.org shortly, or click here to
continue to the site.

9390 PEOPLE HAVE PLEDGED

Check out IAVA's Memorial Day events nationwide.

Facebook Since IAVA already had such a large community on Facebook, it was important to make sure that the campaign was promoted there ahead of time and supporters had clear ways to get involved on the platform itself. Hemler notes that IAVA used Facebook "to spread the word and encourage Fans to sign the pledge, then share the pledge with their friends." They also updated their profile image and the Timeline cover photo to brand the Facebook Page similarly to the website splash page. You can see what the Facebook Page looked like during the #GoSilent campaign in Figure 6.6.

Figure 6.5
Email Confirmation Message for #Go Silent Supporters

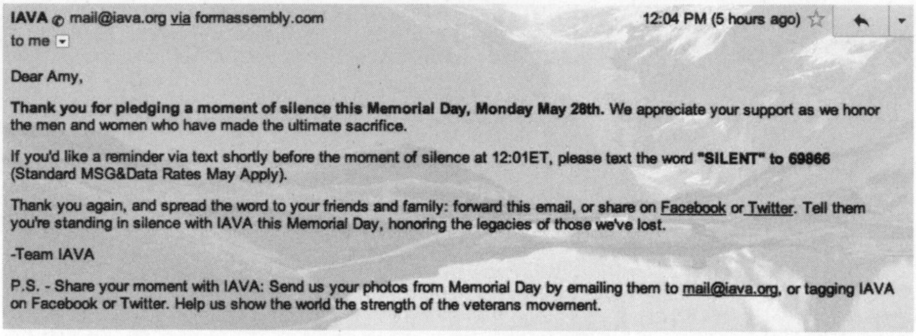

IAVA ⊘ mail@iava.org via formassembly.com   12:04 PM (5 hours ago) ☆ ◄ ▼
to me ▾

Dear Amy,

Thank you for pledging a moment of silence this Memorial Day, Monday May 28th. We appreciate your support as we honor the men and women who have made the ultimate sacrifice.

If you'd like a reminder via text shortly before the moment of silence at 12:01ET, please text the word **"SILENT" to 69866** (Standard MSG&Data Rates May Apply).

Thank you again, and spread the word to your friends and family: forward this email, or share on Facebook or Twitter. Tell them you're standing in silence with IAVA this Memorial Day, honoring the legacies of those we've lost.

-Team IAVA

P.S. - Share your moment with IAVA: Send us your photos from Memorial Day by emailing them to mail@iava.org, or tagging IAVA on Facebook or Twitter. Help us show the world the strength of the veterans movement.

USE CONFIRMATION EMAILS TO MAKE A DEEPER CONNECTION

Many organizations use confirmation emails to let new supporters know that they were successfully signed up for communications or that their donation or transaction went through. Confirmation messages can also be a great way to start building a relationship with a new supporter or donor that keeps them engaged and coming back to do more with you. Consider these tips for your email confirmation messages for campaigns and year-round communications:

- Use plain text to ensure that the first email you send to new supporters does not go to the spam folder (as html-heavy messages often do).

- Encourage recipients to add your email address or domain to their contacts, thus ensuring that future messages make it to their in-box.

- Include suggested next steps based on the kind of action the supporter just did, like sharing their action on social channels or learning more about the campaign.

- Make it personal by introducing yourself as the staff member in charge of that campaign or program.

- Provide a preview of what the supporter can expect to happen next; for instance, mention the kind of email they will receive next or the next planned action for the campaign.

Figure 6.6
IAVA's #GoSilent Branded Facebook Page

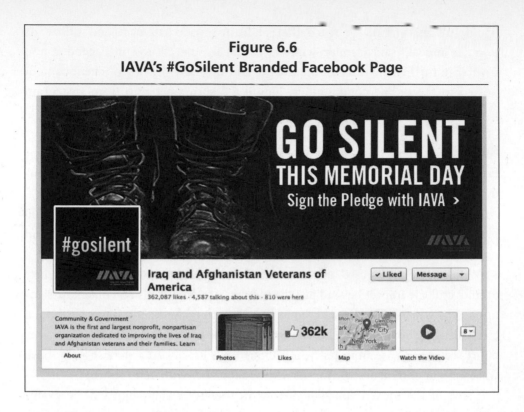

Twitter   IAVA used Twitter to help connect the community across the country, with updates throughout the day, including live-tweeting the wreath laying ceremony in Arlington at the Tomb of the Unknowns. Hemler said, "We shared photos, updates from across the country, and messages of support." IAVA modeled the behavior for the community, using Twitter to share updates, quotes from the president, and pictures of the ceremony. "Thousands of supporters on Twitter added a new level of poignancy to the campaign by tweeting the names of their fallen loved ones and friends. Our team made a conscious decision to retweet their 'In Memoriam' [messages] for thousands more to see and honor," said Hemler.

Instagram   IAVA had well-established communities on Facebook and Twitter before the #GoSilent campaign. It had less of a following on Instagram, an application for iPhone and Android phones for creating and editing photos. Instagram allows for easy sharing of photos from the application to be shared instantly on other platforms, including Facebook or Twitter. This meant IAVA could use Instagram, "to reach that platform's wide fan base and utilize its popular appeal," said Hemler, while also sharing the photos on Facebook and Twitter to further the reach of the images and diversify the day-of-event content posted to the online communities. Figure 6.7 shows a photo from Instagram posted to the IAVA Facebook Page, with nearly 3,000 "likes" in just an hour.

Results

From Hemler's perspective, this was really a campaign focused on building community and "[raising] awareness around the true meaning of Memorial Day." And what were the results? Hemler reported that IAVA "obtained over 5,000 pledges to observe the moment of silence, more than 30,000 page views, and nearly 400,000 people reached on Facebook."

With campaigns focused on community building and awareness, it can be tricky to fully evaluate impact beyond just the number of interactions on content or sign-ups on the website. Hemler said, "to be honest, getting the right analysis has been a bit challenging because we didn't run a similar campaign arc last year. Our donations didn't see an increase from last year, although our email clicks were slightly above what was our current average (opens were about on par with that average)."

Some of the most important metrics in the IAVA campaign will be evaluated over the next few months. "We did see nearly a 10% increase in sign-ups when compared to the same time period last year—and we captured about 20% of those who signed the pledge onto our mobile text list, with nearly 60% of those sign-ups asking for more info from IAVA. All these are positive signs," said Hemler. IAVA can compare this community growth against next year's campaign. Staff can also evaluate messaging responses of these new supporters now that the campaign is wrapped up to identify what topics and actions they are most interested in, and will use those results to inform next year's campaign.

Lessons

Even though IAVA considers the #GoSilent campaign a success, they are already planning how they will do better next year. Hemler explained that they "plan to alter the user experience slightly to make it even easier to sign the pledge, by displaying the pledge form directly on the pledge homepage, and perhaps enabling easier Facebook or Twitter connections."

The 2012 #GoSilent campaign integrated activity across channels for supporters before and during the live event, as well as in real time, by sharing updates

Figure 6.7
IAVA Instagram Photo Posted to Facebook Page

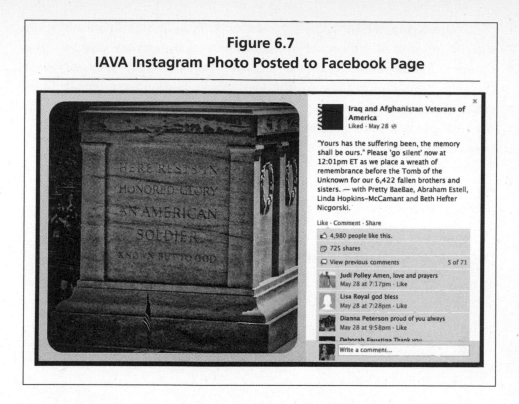

throughout the ceremony and encouraging those around the country to participate. IAVA wants to do even more in 2013, as Hemler reported: "We also hope to bridge the online versus offline experience by working with our program's team to host more ceremonies and events nationwide and encourage civilians to join us on the ground in solidarity."

We think the #GoSilent campaign from IAVA is a terrific example of a multichannel campaign that advances the organization's mission, is based around the channels the community uses and the topics the community cares about, and stays focused on a larger vision that other people and organizations can support. When evaluating a campaign like this, it's important to look at the percentage of people that signed up for more information from your organization, on email and mobile lists, and to track the level of activity from those people after the campaign. Segmenting your list by those that joined during a focused campaign like this can help you orient them to the rest of your work and move them to take other actions—whether advocacy or fundraising related—in the future.

We also recommend that any organization running a campaign like this use analytics tools to identify superfans and influential community members; this can mean looking at the retweets or analytics from URL shorteners on Twitter or the Insights data in Facebook. Identifying those people that were most influential to the community during your campaign now (even if they aren't the "famous" people), will let you reach out to them ahead of the next campaign to prime them for action and provide them with exclusive or early content to share.

Now that you've seen how multichannel campaigns work in action to spark advocacy, raise money, and build community, we'll show you in the next chapter how you can equip your organization for multichannel success.

DISCUSSION QUESTIONS

Spark a conversation with your team or organization about these core principles with the following questions:

1. What struck you about these campaigns? What surprised you?

2. Which platforms have your community members turned to during disasters or major events?

3. Are there platforms you see community members using that you don't yet use as an organization? Are there supporters that would be champions for your content on those platforms?

4. Did anything about the results from these case studies surprise you?

5. Which additional metrics would you have tracked if you were one of these organizations? Which metrics do you want to be sure you track in your next campaign?

chapter SEVEN

Equipping Your Organization for Anytime Everywhere

Operating in an anytime, everywhere world requires more than a suite of profiles on social networks and exciting calls to action. Behind the strategies and tactics is the real backbone of your success: your staff and your leadership. So far we have discussed the guiding principles to create social change anytime, everywhere and how to build community and plan and launch advocacy and fundraising campaigns across multiple channels—and we have provided examples of how other organizations have done it successfully.

In our experience, organizations excel when they invest in multidisciplinary teams with staff that collaboratively manage campaigns, web, email, social, and mobile communications, and strategy. In other words, these organizations (even the small ones) don't put all online communications and campaign responsibilities into one "web" person. That is a recipe for failure because it sentences staff to burnout and leads to turnover. Often a step forward in these organizations results in two steps back when people leave because it forces the organization to reexamine their needs and start over. We have seen nonprofits of all sizes experience this, and it takes a heavy toll on the entire organization and its community engagement.

Preparing your organization to operate in an anytime, everywhere world means recognizing that everyone in the organization ultimately contributes to the success of multichannel strategies. Online campaigns and implementation can no longer be walled off in a separate team on the other side of the office.

Today online channels and social media pervade all positions; staff may be part of a team that is creating content, organizing events, or even planning an appeal, and adapting materials for Facebook or the design of an email alert. This means including staff and teams from all parts of the organization in multichannel thinking and planning. It even means talking to and recruiting your board and funders to join you in these new approaches and models of working. With the principles, strategies, and tactics in place, you need to focus on setting yourself up for success "inside" the office.

In this chapter, we cover the "operating system" of your organization, in a sense. We first guide you through changing your organizational culture to better implement the strategies to create social change anytime, anywhere. Next we discuss staffing models that provide an internal foundation that supports anytime, everywhere action outside of your organization. Lastly, we provide suggestions and examples to help online teams build wide support in the organization for multichannel communications from colleagues, senior staff, board members, and even funders.

TEARING DOWN SILOS: CHANGING INSTITUTIONAL CULTURE

When you think back to the first time you realized that you wanted to do something to change this world, even in some small way, how did it feel? Did you feel inspired and excited to work side-by-side with people who were just as passionate as you to create meaningful social change that truly impacted people's lives? Were you fueled by the possibility of collaborating and brainstorming with colleagues to develop innovative campaigns and programs that connected and motivated everyday people to change the world?

Are you still fueled with that same excitement and hope? If the answer is "no," you are not alone. Too often in our work with hundreds of organizations big and small we encounter staff who spend a lot of their time trying, and failing, to change organizations that are sputtering in an online, multichannel world. Every minute spent working on internal issues is time not inspiring and empowering citizens. Organizational cultures that stifle staff creativity and ideas are often to blame.

Whether you have been working at a nonprofit for a year or over 10 years, you have probably been a victim of rigid, top-down management structures and teams that squash innovation and collaboration along the way. If nonprofits want to meet their missions more quickly and attract the most talented staff, they must change the way they do business inside the office and get rid of silos.

Does Your Nonprofit Have Silos?

Take a look around the office. Does your organizational culture allow staff to take advantage of the multichannel campaigns and strategies with direct input from several departments? Or is staff off in their respective corners of the office planning their own campaigns in isolation? Are colleagues from different departments encouraged to brainstorm ideas to move the needle on your issue? Do these brainstorms come naturally for the organization, or do they feel forced or fake? You can tell this by how comfortable staff are openly sharing new (even crazy or edgy) ideas without fearing that senior management will dismiss their ideas right off the bat. If you answered "yes" to any of these questions, your nonprofit is living with silos (see Figure 7.1).

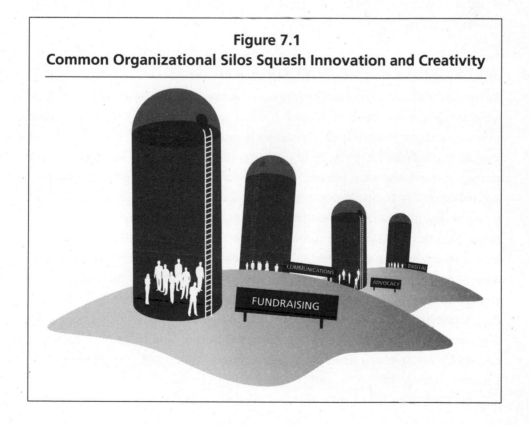

Figure 7.1
Common Organizational Silos Squash Innovation and Creativity

Breaking Silos Leads to Better Organizational Culture

In our experience working with nonprofits over the years, we have found that it's important that nonprofits focus on breaking down departmental silos, encourage more open leadership, and create a transparent environment. This will help create an organizational culture that encourages people to think about new ways of solving problems using the web, social media, and mobile technologies while maintaining the important structure and processes that make organizations run smoothly. And most important, this new organizational culture will help create a safe space that doesn't crush peoples' spirits by punishing them when a strategy or campaign fails or when you think their ideas sound silly.

According to the Nonprofit Digital Team Benchmark Report that surveyed 67 nonprofits, 60% of digital teams are expected to drive new initiatives.[95] And while that is encouraging to hear, staff can't effectively drive new initiatives if their organization doesn't truly embrace a more open and collaborative culture or if the organization does not invest in experienced digital teams with strong leadership skills.

INVEST AND BELIEVE IN YOUR STAFF

As organizations and community leaders continue to tackle some of the world's toughest problems, there is a need to hire, support, and train more people who understand the evolving digital landscape. While online channels, social media, and mobile have made it easier to spread campaign messages, share stories, and connect with people, the channels are also cluttered with competing messages. Activists, donors, reporters, and legislative representatives are being pulled in numerous directions. To create real change on the ground, it's going to take more staff resources and a combination of tried-and-true organizing strategies, creative storytelling, plus developing and testing new strategies to cut through the noise happening online to raise even more awareness about our issues and connect with our community on deeper levels. To achieve this, organizations must also break free from the top-down management style that comes with the traditional organizational culture, and focus on fostering a nurturing, creative, and open work environment where staff can collaborate as a team and innovate.

"All organizations have to contend with gaps between status, power, and expertise. At some point, the best solutions or insights come from those with less power," said Charles Lenchner, cofounder of Organizing 2.0.[96] "Change is too important to be left in the hands of the executive directors, board members, and consultants. Developing a shared language about these matters is key to sharing ownership, all of us together, in the success of our projects and missions. It's about getting the best price in exchange for your 'buy-in.' Now that's change you can believe in," said Lenchner.

Welcome All Ideas with Open Arms

One of the social media strategies we discussed in Chapter Five is to make constituents feel welcome, whether they are engaging with you on Twitter or are part of a Facebook group. The same holds true for your staff. Encourage your staff to brainstorm ideas. Provide the space and time for them to get creative, and we mean supercreative—to the point that they will come up with some whacky or "too edgy" ideas for your organization. Talk through the ideas as a team because it's these types of brainstorms that trigger some terrific campaign ideas in a collaborative environment. And sometimes these brainstorms won't go anywhere, and that's okay, too.

Break Out of Your Comfort Zone

Most nonprofits are averse to taking risks. That's understandable. Nonprofits are dealing with, and accountable to, many different stakeholders, such as major funders and foundations, donors, volunteers, and so on. It can be scary to take risks and put the organization in a vulnerable position, particularly when you are developing campaigns that have a strong social media and mobile component. However, nonprofits can't always play it safe when it comes to getting their issues and campaigns front and center. There is just too much competition in today's "always on" world. As we highlight in Figure 7.2, don't be afraid to take risks and experiment.

John Hlinko, the founder of Left Action and the author of *Share, Retweet, Repeat: Get Your Message Read and Spread,* has this to say:

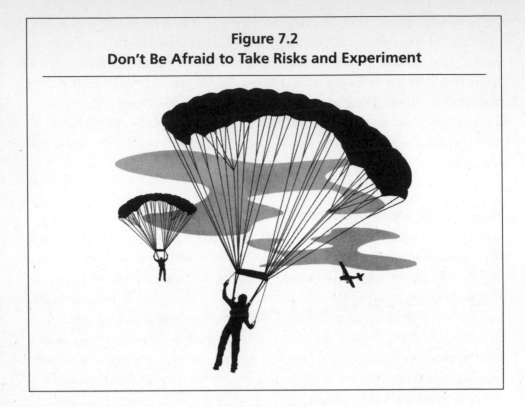

Figure 7.2
Don't Be Afraid to Take Risks and Experiment

The most effective, impactful, spread-worthy messages are invariably the ones that seem at first to be the most discomforting or even downright crazy. But you can't reach and mobilize people unless you get noticed, and in a world of nonstop stimuli you won't get noticed unless you differ from the norm, and cause at least a little bit of a "problem."

Many people play it safe, worrying about offending people, even if just a few. I say, let them be offended. Sure, it's worrisome if a few dozen or even a few hundred people are turned off by something you send them, and unsubscribe from your email list or Facebook page. But if a few thousand new people end up joining because that edgier message was so much more "viral" that's certainly a net gain, right?

Too often, great ideas die in the brainstorm phase because they're a little bit edgy, and no one wants to take a risk. But the proper approach isn't to avoid risk altogether, it's to properly weigh the risks against the potential benefits.

Host Weekly Interdepartmental Meetings

To help break down silos within the organization, host smaller weekly meetings with key people from different departments so that you all know what everyone is working on. These meetings can be extremely helpful for staff to collaborate across multiple channels on upcoming programming priorities and events, legislative bills and advocacy actions, and fundraising so that everything is synchronized. It can also lead to some terrific brainstorming sessions filled with innovative ideas.

Danielle Brigida, manager of social media for the National Wildlife Federation, says, "Our monthly online marketing and communications coordination meeting works to bring people communicating online (through web, news articles, blogs, emails, social media, etc.) together to brainstorm and cross-promote through all the channels. With so many parts of the organization communicating online, we found it important to have these meetings to see where the opportunities overlap."

"We keep a calendar for the group that displays when and what we'll be focusing on depending on the month. It really helps us focus our efforts and it also feeds content for social media," said Brigida.

The National Wildlife Federation has also found that many staff across the organization are communicating online about conservation issues in their free time and most through their personal accounts, which greatly extends the reach of their online communications network.

JustGiving, an online fundraising platform for nonprofits in the United Kingdom, takes it a few steps further. "We focus on creating strong cross-functional teams of experts from different disciplines to deliver products, tools and services—the focus is on ensuring the right people are working together to achieve the optimum output," said Charlie Glynn, head of people.

These teams meet every morning to discuss progress and priorities, and the teams are empowered to make decisions and agree on responsibilities to ensure deadlines are met. It's these teams that make the operational decisions together, not a department director. This also encourages the team to take responsibility and builds a culture of trust. "We have built an expectation around giving each other real-time feedback and holding other team members accountable, so the team feels like they are owners and they are in it together," said Glynn.

Experiment with Tools for Communication and Collaboration Internally

While in person meetings are great ways to share campaign ideas or priorities, using different tools and platforms to collaborate with staff internally anytime and everywhere is essential too. For example:

An operations manual could be implemented as a wiki or Google doc to be edited continually. The Nonprofit Technology Network (NTEN) says that their organization has benefited from creating operations documentation in Google docs. This approach means all their staff have access to documentation—from how to complete various tasks using the database to planning processes for major events—to reference and to update at any time. Periodically, staff and teams also focus on creating or updating certain documentation to ensure that the operations resources available across the organization are up-to-date and could support any staff member jumping into a project or even a new hire accessing knowledge and resources to assist on-boarding. We suggest scheduling quarterly opportunities for teams to work together to review and update documentation to be sure resources are in place and teams are sharing knowledge and best practices with each other in the process.

Yammer, which is similar to Twitter but is aimed at businesses and organizations to discuss internally what they are working on, is great for large staffs or for people who work in different office locations. "Yammer works well in having us all share important content and program initiatives. We use both the monthly meeting and the daily interaction on Yammer to strengthen our efforts and alert one another of our different but equally important priorities," said Brigida.

An online listening dashboard is useful for staff members to get the latest organization information and news, as well as external news. Using an RSS reader like Netvibes (an online dashboard to monitor social media) or iGoogle, you can set up a listening dashboard that pulls in posts from prominent bloggers in your cause area, alerts of staff or program names, commonly used hashtags (a # followed by a word or phrase) or keywords, and even news stories on the issues your services or campaigns tackle. Organizations of all sizes use listening dashboards to help staff manage and identify priorities for responding and engaging online by making it easy to see popular topics, emerging issues, or popular content attractive to the community.

Private Facebook Groups can also be useful as an internal communications tool for staff, particularly at large organizations or when people don't work in a central office. The International Fellowship for Christians and Jews (IFCJ) uses private Facebook Groups for their editorial and new media teams. "This works really well for breaking news types of items. For example, if a breaking news story hits and we see it on our Netvibes or Facebook, we post to the [Facebook] Group and decide if it is going to change our messaging for that week—bump our feature article, change our homepage image, etc.," said Christina Johns, director of new media at IFCJ.

Seize Opportunities

Seize opportunities when they arise, particularly when it comes to leveraging current events that relate to the issues your organization works on. Don't get stuck in rigid processes and long approval chains, as this will derail you from being proactive. Processes are often what prevent organizations moving at the fast speed needed to participate in anytime, everywhere campaigns. Instead, focus on setting up more nimble structures and teams that can efficiently vet information, develop accurate responses, and execute creative and simple campaign ideas. Right now, too many organizations are overly reactive and scramble to respond. By the time they feel that they have all of their ducks in a row, the moment to rally around has long passed.

Commit to Culture Change, Failing Fast, and Mean It!

As we discussed in this chapter, creating a culture of collaboration and innovation within a traditional and rigid organizational structure can be challenging, but it can definitely be achieved. Make no mistake though; it requires a major culture change within the entire organization that must be led from the top. Senior management must focus on breaking down the silos in the organization to have more of an open culture and leadership.

Teams must be integrated, meaning that people in fundraising, advocacy, marketing, PR, programs, and tech should be working together to develop campaigns that are integrated across multiple channels such as email, social media, and mobile. This means putting an end to departments working in isolation and competing for resources and budgets.

And finally you must believe in failing fast or as Paull Young from charity: water likes to say, "do it wrong quickly," and mean it. Don't pretend your organization believes in failing fast and then punish your staff when they do fail. For example, when we met with an organization that swore to us that "failing fast" was part of their organizational culture, when it came down to the campaign plan, it was a completely different story. They looked at us and said, "We can't really fail though." Guess what? No matter how well you plan your campaigns or how creative you get, at some point your organization will fail. And that is okay. Failure is one of the best ways to learn, and it can lead to success the next time around.

Once you are ready to commit to this culture change, you will want to examine staffing at your organization and how to set up collaborative teams that can implement social change anytime, everywhere.

STAFFING

What staffing structures are working today in the nonprofit community that are successful with online multichannel campaigns, fundraising, and outreach? We have found that the most effective way to staff for this is to have a dedicated digital team that is spread across different departments, something that is known as the hybrid model.

The Hybrid Model

The hybrid model is one of the most popular and effective multichannel models for nonprofits in the digital space; though organizations must be silo free for this model to succeed. According to the *Four Models for Managing Digital*,[97] written by Michael Silberman, global director of digital innovation for Greenpeace International and nonprofit strategists Jason Mogus and Christopher Roy, who talked with senior online campaigners from over 60 nonprofits, "the most progressive and the most conducive to producing continuous innovation at the pace of digital change" is the hybrid staffing model. In this model, the digital team is spread across different departments (grassroots, IT, fundraising, communications, marketing, etc.), but all digital staffers are connected to and supported by a central and strong digital experience team that helps direct them toward strategic goals where campaigns are synchronized. "With this model, the culture of the central digital team is practicing . . . open leadership: service oriented, highly collaborative, hyperconnected listeners, who also have the technical and content expertise to be high-value strategists," said Mogus, Silberman, and Roy in the *Four Models for Managing Digital*.

The hybrid model is also a good model for smaller organizations where the staff wear several hats. The bottom line is that we live and work in a multichannel world, and communicating with our people through all these channels should be a part of just about everyone's job within the organization. It should not be siloed off into one part of the organization that works in one corner of the office.

Ideally, your core Internet staff is able to guide and collaborate with a team of campaigners and communicators spread across organizational departments and roles. This could be an official structure, clearly defined in the staffing charts and definitions, or it could be a somewhat unofficial arrangement. The right way to implement a hybrid model depends on the organization but regardless of approach it needs senior leadership support to succeed.

Staffing Your Website and Online Communications

Nearly 40% of nonprofits have one to two digital staff, according to the Nonprofit Digital Teams Benchmark Report.[98] Yet 79% of nonprofits manage more than five online properties (websites, social media channels, mobile apps, etc.). Larger nonprofits manage an average of 24 properties and smaller nonprofits averaged 12. Clearly, nonprofits need to invest in more digital staff if they're going to effectively use multiple channels and platforms to engage with constituents in meaningful ways around their issues and campaigns and create social change.

Here a few options to consider for staffing your organization's online presence:

Internet Director This position leads and directs the technical planning and high-level online campaign strategy for the organization. The Internet director collaborates with all departments in the organization such as advocacy, communications, grassroots, and fundraising to ensure that that all online communications, like email alerts and fundraising appeals, web content, and social media, are synchronized and adapted properly to each channel and timed accordingly. This position also oversees the organization's online marketing and outreach, but does not necessarily implement it.

Web Producer This position manages the day-to-day website and thoroughly understands website best practices, such as search engine optimization, optimizing graphics for the web, and writing for the web. Essentially, the web producer manages website content and ensures that items are posted to the site in a consistent and web-friendly format that is also engaging to your web audiences. The web producer should also have a strong foundation working with the organization's content management system and have a proficient programming background in order to fix day-to-day website issues and bugs. The web producer also works with the Internet director, and with different departments to execute online campaign plans. Finally, the web producer analyzes the organization's website traffic to determine traffic growth, popular content, and website referrals and looks for patterns that show how the organization can better optimize the website for target audiences.

Online Campaigner If your organization works on a lot of online campaigns throughout the year, it's worth investing in an online campaigner position. This position also works across different departments and helps the Internet director coordinate and implement the organization's online campaigns, ranging from writing web copy to action alerts. Online campaigners are also tasked with implementing some of the organization's online marketing and outreach and helping to build deeper relationships with constituents. This includes listening and responding to constituent feedback on different channels and social networks and connecting with like-minded bloggers and influencers to promote campaigns. This position is also responsible for compiling important online campaign metrics, such as response rates on action alerts and fundraising appeals and producing bi-weekly or monthly reports.

Database Manager This position is important for organizations that have several databases running for different aspects of the organization. For example, if you use Raisers Edge for your main donor database, Convio for your constituent relationship management system, and NGP VAN for your voter file management, you are going to need a designated staff person to manage all of the databases and associated data.

Social Media and Mobile Staffing

At this point, you maybe asking yourself, how does social and mobile staffing factor in, given its growing trends?

Social media and mobile can be incredibly time consuming, especially if you are a big nonprofit like the American Red Cross or the Humane Society of the United States. These groups have a lot of people who are constantly interacting with them through social media and mobile. These large organizations can't afford not to have full-time social media and mobile staff serving as "listener in chief," responding to the community, relaying current news, or debunking myths. For example, when the Humane Society of the United States (HSUS) started seeing the mobile trend "come to life," they positioned the organization for the anticipated growth in that area by hiring a full-time mobile communications manager. "We actually repurposed an existing online position so that we could hire the mobile position right away," said Carie Lewis, director of emerging media at HSUS. "In 2012 we will move mobile out from underneath emerging media and treat it as one of our major online communications channels along with social media, website, and email. This will position it for even further growth in the future."

Social Media: A Shared Role   Recalling the hybrid staffing model we discussed earlier, social media can be a shared responsibility within your organization's staffing structure. It does not always have to be done by the "social media person."

Here are some great examples of organizations that have several staff contributing to their social media presence.

NONPROFIT SOCIAL NETWORK BENCHMARK REPORT

Fifty-six percent of nonprofits surveyed allocate a quarter of a full-time employee equivalent, according to the 2012 report. Not good! About 10% surveyed have a three-quarters full-time equivalent staff member. Forty-two percent of nonprofits surveyed said they plan to increase their staffing for commercial social networks, 55% say they will keep staffing the same, and just 3% say that they will reduce staffing.

Forty-six percent of nonprofits have no budgets for social networks.

PETA (People for the Ethical Treatment of Animals) has found success staffing their multichannel campaigns, according to Ashley Palmer, senior marketing coordinator for PETA, by having full-time digital team members spend 50% of their time managing social media. They spend the other 50% of their time creating web features, working on PETA's mobile apps, and coordinating email and action alerts in collaboration with several departments. PETA also has 15 other staff members who promote PETA via their personal social media accounts, as well as help plan out how to utilize PETA's social media accounts when promoting new projects. These 15 staff members spend approximately half an hour on social media strategy or promoting PETA's content each week, with a few participating slightly more at about five hours per week.

While the American Red Cross National headquarters has three full-time social engagement staff, they also have a field network of over 600 chapters and 36 blood regions, and many of them have staff or volunteers devoting a percentage of their time to social engagement. In addition, they have subject

STAFFING ANNUAL CAMPAIGNS AND EVENTS

Not every cause is a full-time operation, and each will need to be staffed differently. For example, Epic Change runs a few different volunteer-led campaigns, like Epic Thanks and To Mama With Love, to raise money to help build classrooms and expand a school in Tanzania, which we discussed in Chapter Three. During these campaigns, Epic Change is very active on social media channels, like Facebook and Twitter, ranging from three to ten hours daily. However, when Epic Change is not in campaign mode, they don't engage on social media networks more than once or twice per week, "and often not about Epic Change, but about our lives as human beings. It's human to connect. It's also human to disconnect. And as long as we're open, our community is very receptive to a drastically and constantly changing level of engagement online. Honestly, I think if we were online 24/7 or every day of the year, our community would burn out—so would we," said cofounder Stacey Monk.

matter experts within their lines of service devoting 30 minutes to 2 hours per day to social engagement in their area of expertise. The American Red Cross is also developing a cadre of digital volunteers to "deploy" during disaster operations, said Wendy Harman, director of social strategy for the American Red Cross.

"Our vision is to make *social* part of the organization's operational DNA, so participating in the social web is a part of many people's existing jobs," said Harman.

Other organizations, such as Conservation International, who have one full-time social media staffer, have also formed a social media content team responsible for submitting content to the organization's social networks. This team consists of three junior staff members, a senior director of online engagement marketing and communications, and a media director. The team meets once a week to brainstorm content, campaigns, plan for upcoming staff absences, and to discuss any issues that arise. In lieu of meetings, questions and concerns are also discussed through the team's email list so that they are in constant communication.

The social media content team has helped break down some of the silos in the organization and has increased their capacity to synchronize communications efforts across traditional communications channels and social media.

Social Media Staff Guide The staff managing and participating in an organization's social media should be the biggest champions of its brand and issue. For some organizations, social media has been integrated into many aspects of an organization, and that is a good thing, but it also presents organizational challenges. Having a social media guide for staff will be very helpful in empowering staff to be even better champions and help senior leadership be more comfortable with transparency around the brand. Here are some ideas for you to think about when drafting your organization's social media hand guide:[99]

- Will you only allow certain members of your staff to post to your social media accounts? Will all staff have access? Personally we prefer for organizations to have more of an inclusive policy that encourages staff from several department to share, which falls into the hybrid staff model we mentioned earlier.

- What are your top five social media goals? Be explicit. Example: "Our goal is to foster discussion around our issues even if people disagree with some of our positions."

- Adopt a "listen, learn, adapt" strategy. "No one can control what is said about your organization. As consumers have a voice and a means to make themselves heard, it is up to you be out there to listen, track, and respond," said Ayelet Baron, director of Cisco Systems, in her presentation *Social Media for Social Good*.[100]

- Are you properly staffed to respond to all questions regardless of how silly or stupid you think they may be?

- Identify what private, illegal, or sensitive information is not permitted to be discussed publicly—including on social networks. For example, it's illegal for 501C3s to endorse or oppose candidates running for office.

- How should staff respond to criticism? Note the answer is not to "ignore it." Arm your staff with suggested tactics and a plan to quickly respond to criticism.

- How should staff respond to personal threats?

- There is no "delete" on the Internet. If your staff accidentally posts something that was not accurate or inappropriate, have them acknowledge it ASAP and post a correction.

- Remind employees that their professional and personal social media activity must be distinct, and they must be aware that even if privacy settings are used, anything posted online has the potential to become public. Suggest that they note that all posts are on their personal accounts, as a social media disclaimer.

Staffing Your Mobile Program   According to Jim Manis, chairman and CEO of the Mobile Giving Foundation, out of 1.5 million nonprofits in the United States[101] there are a little over 1,000 nonprofits and associations using mobile to engage donors.[102] That is less than a 1% adoption rate.

While a much larger percentage of nonprofits in the United States are investing staff in social media, as opposed to mobile, nonprofits should take note that 86% of those who donate money to an organization via text are willing to consider giving larger amounts via other channels, according to the Donor

Survey Report by the mGive Foundation, so this channel should not be ignored.[103]

Admittedly, staffing for mobile can get tricky and expensive. Some larger nonprofits like HSUS have hired one full-time mobile staffer, since they have a significant, growing base of supporters who use mobile to access their sites, respond to appeals, and make donations. Other nonprofits, like the American Red Cross and the Human Rights Campaign, use some of their existing digital staff to integrate mobile into their campaigns. "As priorities shift and mobile activities heighten as they do in disaster scenarios, we typically designate a single individual to be responsible for the mobile channel on a full-time basis, and during non-disaster periods we revert back to shared responsibilities," says Josh Kittner, Senior Marketing Consultant at the American Red Cross.

But some organizations, like Conservation International, that have experimented with mobile texting in the past have not seen a good return on the investment, because their mobile list was not large enough at the time.

Regardless of how you choose to staff your mobile presence, your nonprofit can effectively integrate some mobile tactics and strategies no matter what your budget is. For example, your organization's website, donation forms, and email appeals should be optimized for mobile platforms, like smartphones and tablets. You can also assess whether mobile apps are a good investment for your nonprofit or experiment with QR codes in your marketing and outreach. You can also test text-to-donate campaigns around urgent and timely issues.

ENGAGING LEADERS IN CULTURE CHANGE

You are reading this book because you recognize the importance and potential of multichannel approaches for social impact. But you can't do it all alone no matter how passionate or smart you are. Chances are, you aren't in a leadership position with authority to change job descriptions, redirect resources, and train people to work more collaboratively on digital communications. Or maybe senior staff or a colleague in the next office is pushing back with, "We are doing fine online. Just do your job. Nobody needs more work around here."

Whatever the circumstances, your organization needs multichannel communications to work, and it needs you to help lead it forward. We want to help. From your leadership staff and board to your staff and colleagues and even to your funders, the following examples and suggestions are designed to equip you in rallying both interest and participation for multichannel approaches to meet your mission.

Convincing Your Senior Staff and Board

When it comes to convincing anyone of anything, one of the most successful tactics is to figure out first what is important to him or her and what would influence the decision. When it comes to specific social and mobile tools or multichannel strategies in general, much of the push-back that executive directors and other leadership staff may exhibit in your organization comes from not fully understanding the tools and applications themselves. Strategic direction and relevance to your mission, in addition to the opportunity to engage donors, are some of the most influential topics on their mind. It is your opportunity to share with them not just the ins and outs of a given tool, but also the way these technologies and multichannel strategies will help your organization do more to meet its mission.

First, invite your executive director or a board member to actually sit with you at a computer so that you can really show them what these tools are like and how they are used; and let them hold the mouse! Be prepared for the meeting by pulling up a few tools that you want to show them and log in if necessary to speed up the process for exploring the tools. If you have accounts set up that represent the organization already, be sure to have those open and logged in. If you know that you will be meeting at a specific time, ask the community to say "hello" or send a message at that time or a few minutes sooner. For example, if you know you will be demonstrating Twitter to your board members at noon, post to the account at 11:50 that you are about to show Twitter to the organization's board and would love the community to say hello; when you show them the screen, they will see very recent activity and give you content to demonstrate how to reply and engage.

You know that your organization's leaders are focused on the strategic plan and mission of the organization. Show how the goals and strategies for anytime, everywhere technologies are aligned with the larger goals of the organization and how they can help you achieve your mission. Aligning your goals with the community and the various tools also helps you communicate about why and how you want to use social and mobile tools. This is also an opportunity to frame the conversation around these technologies from the beginning on what is really important: the quality and action versus the sheer number, for example.

One thing you can anticipate your leadership staff or board will ask for is the data. You can share this book with them and show them the infographics from the introduction to help illustrate the general data for anytime, everywhere technology. You can also pull some data together yourself. If you have profiles set up for the organization already, put together a list of the data you have for those platforms. If you don't have profiles for the organization, or haven't actively used them, you can still pull influential data. Use search to pull up example results on topics of interest to your organization or cause. Highlight example messages or interactions that organizations like yours have had online, especially if they highlight missed opportunities for your organization to participate. For example, look for posts on Twitter in which local community members asked for resources or talked about an event they attended where another organization replied with a link to resources or a message of thanks for their participation. That could have been you!

Don't overlook the option of running a test to prove your point. This small test can take place using the channels you have set up for the organization already, or, if you have to, even on a personal or temporary account. For example, open up comments on a blog post or page of your website soliciting feedback or ideas. Then work with coworkers to orchestrate a collaborative multichannel approach to an upcoming message by tying an email message and social media messages together. Circulate a survey via your website and social channels that asks which platforms supporters use and where they want to communicate with you—or even add a field in your sign-up form for a mobile phone number (with a note that it would be used for SMS/text updates, not cold calls).

Be sure to track where you were before the test, what you did and why, and then what happened and what it means. Did you add the mobile phone number field to your sign-up form and see 90% of completed forms include a phone number? Even if you added the field as a test and don't have mobile messaging in place at the organization, that's a great number to show your leadership staff that the community wants to hear from you on their phones!

Convincing Your Staff and Colleagues

For many of the people we've talked to, if convincing their boss isn't the issue, then it's getting their coworkers and colleagues to join them. Just as organizational alignment is key for leaders and board members, for your colleagues the bottom line is the capacity to get it all done. Nonprofit staff are often stretched thin and using new strategies and tools, no matter how shiny and cool or mission-critical, can launch many of your colleagues into the feared realm of "more work." As such, it's important to approach your conversations and invitations to join you in an anytime, everywhere approach from the perspective of helping them meet their goals (maybe even with more participants or in a faster time).

Doing some of the legwork for your team or organization can really help people understand where they fit and how they can contribute without really doing anything new. As Katie Benston recounts from her time as director of annual support for Hospice and Palliative Care Charlotte Region, "I created a calendar for one month and populated it with messages we already had from other communications. This helped me show that creating content wouldn't take much time."

Try creating a shared calendar just for messages and sharing it with others so they can add links and updates they think could be distributed across various channels. You can also jump-start some of the multichannel options available by creating a content map that coordinates types of content and the channels that they align with.[104]

If you aren't in a position to enforce adoption of anytime, everywhere tools and methods, you may want to start your convincing efforts on a strategic colleague. Find a friend outside of your team and get them on board with the value and alignment of these tools. You can then show that it isn't just an opinion you have, or even something just from your team or department. And, even better, have that ally be someone at a management level to support your point that buy-in is already coming from staff with a strategic focus on the organization's mission.

For those readers who are organizational leaders but find staff are the ones pushing back, remember that for this group the bottom line is really getting things checked off the to-do list and completing work as effectively and efficiently as possible. So, these tools and strategies need to be presented as a better way to do our work. There are also a few things you can do to build it into the structure, beyond the staffing models we discussed earlier in the chapter.

Provide incentives for participation. In celebrating making it through a big milestone or a hard day, we can celebrate together and provide team or individual incentives for advancing the organization toward an anytime, everywhere operation. Create goals that can only be achieved by using multichannel approaches and engaging staff across the organization to invite participation from many teams and focus all staff on a shared goal. Whether you meet the goal or not, be sure to celebrate and document what you learn from the whole process.

It's also important that the various contributions each staff person makes toward achieving a successful multichannel approach to all your work be included explicitly in their job descriptions and evaluations. Even if a staff person does not use any of the tools or post content directly on behalf of the organization, that person may be responsible for or help with the content, events, or even internal reporting that ends up shared via email, social media, mobile, or elsewhere. Whatever the role an individual plays, supporting multichannel approaches to the organization's advocacy, fundraising, and community engagement should be seen as part of every staff member's job.

In 2010, Shelley Zuckerman, the executive director of North York Community House (NYCH) in Toronto, Ontario, started wondering if there were channels NYCH could use to better showcase their impact beyond their basic website. She did some research and investigation of her own, looking at how other organizations were using new channels, then brought her idea to her management staff that NYCH dive in to social media. "We all looked at her like scared children," said Rabia Din, NYCH Settlement and Education Partnerships Toronto program manager. "Most of us not even being on Facebook (the simplest of tasks), were all terrified at the idea of Twitter, LinkedIn, and all other social media and networking tools."

Recognizing that not only did the management staff have fears of adopting and managing these new channels, but so did the rest of the organization, Zuckerman prepared an inspirational presentation for the annual all-staff meeting, showcasing how other organizations were successfully engaging and growing their community. As Din explains, "She used real examples of how social media has changed people's lives around the world, as well as the impact that it can have locally. We were all very impressed (and shall I say, even touched) by the presentation and began to see social media in an entirely different way. That night I, who was completely against anything 'social media related,' created my Facebook account—and it kind of sky-rocketed from there."

Zuckerman ensured that the strategic use of these new channels was successful for the organization, not just individual comfort zones and use, by investing in professional development and capacity building. Din recounts, "The management team started to have meetings that were focused on reading and debriefing chapters from 'Social Media for Good' types of books, we were encouraged to attend social media sessions all over the city, we hired a communications administrator that was able to help all the staff get comfortable with different social media channels, created social media policies and procedures, and more."

Zuckerman didn't just train staff on a new communications tool or community building platform. She actually shifted the culture of the organization and expanded their opportunities for meeting their mission. Din confirms, "We are now able to share our wonderful digital stories and videos on YouTube, advertise our programs throughout the city (and world), connect with other people/agencies in our field, and most importantly, tell our story of impact."[105]

Simply because you are the organizational leader, you can't expect everyone to share your enthusiasm for new tools and new channels, especially when staff feel stretched thin. Recognizing where the hesitations or opportunities lay first, and then building the support for your staff from there, just like Zuckerman did, can help you create multichannel champions of all your staff.

Convincing Funders

Nonprofit organizations often feel at the whim and mercy of the philanthropic organizations that provide grants and operating funds, which for some organizations covers a large portion of the operating budget. When it comes to transitioning your organization into an anytime, everywhere leader, you shouldn't feel that you are at the mercy of a funder, but instead that you have the opportunity to teach them a thing or two!

Start building multichannel techniques and plans into the proposals you present and the processes documented in your applications. Taking a multichannel approach to your work isn't just for your communications department, so highlight the way your engagement plans, information and campaigning, and even program or direct service deliverables are supported across social and mobile channels. On top of your own plans, be sure to include the data that support your case: both data like those in the multichannel technology snapshot (see Figures 1.1 and 1.2) and the data you've put together internally from individual channels and the impact of working across them.

Just as we suggested that you add learning goals into your internal plans, be sure to highlight the learning goals you have for the work to be funded. It may be that you want to test which channels are most appropriate for the specific program or campaign, or even that you want to track service users across all channels from offline to the website to the text message reminder.

And as you learn, invite the funder to join you! Offer your data up for their analysis or your experiences for other grantees to learn from. For foundations and other grantmakers, the bottom line is really the impact and investment of their financial support. If you can accomplish progress on your mission while also learning and advancing your own multichannel strategies, you can report back on their investment on two levels. And offering to share it all, too? Well, now you're just putting icing on the cake.

INVEST IN PEOPLE OR FADE AWAY

At this point, you may be saying to yourself, staffing for social change anytime, everywhere and creating a culture of collaboration is going to take a lot of resources and money. Even if some of the tools you use are free to use, there are real costs associated with using them well. We are not going to lie to you: it's going to take an investment and, to be blunt, you really don't have a choice if your organization is going to survive into the next decade.

While we recognize that nonprofits are on tight budgets and are slowly investing more staff and resources into these channels, they need to ramp up faster to keep up with the channels, which themselves continue to evolve. This means investing in a digital team and adopting a hybrid staff model, as well as fostering an open and collaborative culture.

Think of the hybrid model as a way to better utilize current staff for current and future needs. Meeting the needs of digital and multichannel strategies doesn't have to mean adding new positions or adding more work to already burdened staff. Rather, it may be a matter of changing priorities and making more efficient use of current resources and staff.

We know that this is a lot to digest. You're also probably wondering how you will transition your organization to operate with new staffing structures and a more open culture. What privacy issues will staff face? By having a more public presence on multiple channels, how will your organization respond to community feedback? The next chapter addresses all of these issues and provides suggested safeguards and processes to help you position your staff and community for positive engagement.

DISCUSSION QUESTIONS

Spark a conversation with your team or organization about these core principles with the following questions:

1. Do you have siloes at your organization? What are they defined by (Department? Project? Campaign? Tenure at the organization?)?

2. What kind of regular meeting would work for your staff and how do you want to create the agenda so it reflects participation from across the organization?

3. Do you have a have a social media staff guide? What are some of the topics you and your colleagues would want included in one?

4. Do you plan to hire new staff this year who will have interdepartmental roles?

5. What steps will you take to invest in talented staff who are driven to create social change and are not afraid to experiment?

chapter EIGHT

Transitioning to Anytime Everywhere

S ocial change anytime, everywhere isn't just an idea or an ideal. Using multichannel strategies and integrating your calls to action across online channels and mobile can help your nonprofit connect with your community—wherever they are and however they can contribute—today. When it comes to using a new or unfamiliar tool, following different strategies, or even changing the way you work as a team or organization, it's not unusual for staff to feel anxious, overwhelmed, or even fearful. If you sense that your coworkers are feeling this way, communicating how your organization will operate when you transition to these new strategies and tools can help diminish their anxiety, as will supporting them throughout the process. Remember that success isn't measured just by how much money your organization raised or how many actions your constituents have taken. When it comes to using new technologies and strategies, learning what works and what doesn't is a sign of success too.

It's important to discuss any hesitations your staff may have as an organization at the same time as you talk about the opportunities and benefits of these tools and strategies. As we noted in Chapter Seven, creating a culture in your organization that is open to testing and learning requires that staff can also talk openly about their questions and concerns.

Regardless of the size of your organization, budget, project, or mission, these issues are important to consider and understand. This chapter will equip you with ways to transition effectively to an anytime, everywhere connected organization and move forward without these fears as barriers to your success.

ACCESS

Regardless of the specific services, programs, or other mechanisms for impact that your organization provides, the issue of access has inevitably been discussed among your staff, probably more than once. Access in this sense is focused on the opportunities your staff have for getting training and information about the tools they need to use. How do people find and participate in your services? How do people apply for your programs? How do you make sure that you are really reaching all of the people you intend to in your mission or directives? These are all common questions for organizations and are based on access. How you use anytime, everywhere tools to address these questions is equally important for your staff and board to discuss.

Access to Knowledge and Support

Many organizations support staff with continued growth and education through professional development funds or initiatives. To support your staff with knowledge about an ever changing, expanding, and evolving subject like social and mobile technologies and multichannel strategies, the approach to professional development needs to evolve as well.

First, as we have noted throughout the book, this work is not something for just one staff person. Professional development focused on social and mobile technology use should not be devoted to a single staffer. There are many ways you can provide access to knowledge and support to your entire staff effectively. For example, if you have a choice, elect "organizational" membership options when purchasing memberships to industry-specific or nonprofit support organizations—this will extend benefits, education, and other resources to all your staff.[106]

Second, you can create knowledge sharing opportunities inside the organization. The American Red Cross, National Wildlife Federation, and many others use their regular reporting of social and mobile engagement to also share what they are learning about popular kinds of content or hot topics from the community. Whether it is through daily bulletins sent via email about the stories or conversations of interest on your social channels, a shared listening dashboard pulling in feeds and alerts, or a standing agenda item for staff meetings to discuss what they are hearing and learning from social and mobile channels, there should be clear opportunities for staff to learn from each other and share their experiences across the organization.

Some organizations have used social media tools internally to support continued growth and learning. For example, using Yammer, a Twitter-like tool that connects only those within an organization or team, to post news and updates throughout the day has helped bridge time zones and departments in organizations such as TechSoup Global.

Other organizations support staff connecting with peers and learning outside of the organization through participation in Twitter chats—conversations linked together by a hashtag on Twitter occurring regularly on topics such as community building (#commbuild), nonprofits (#nptalk), social media (#smchat), and more. Creating easy and formal processes for staff to share lessons, examples, or methodologies learned in these chats back to the organization helps in two critical ways: First, your support shows staff that the organization values collaborative learning. Second, staff are able to learn while also exploring the very tools being discussed in context.

Access to the Tools

As we have talked about previously in the book, even though many social media tools are free to use from the service provider, they still cost your organization in staff time and resources to maintain. Whether it is by number of staff or accounts, size limitations on content or storage, the kinds of data you can monitor, or even frequency of access or posting, many tools offer several payment tiers above the free service. For many organizations, using the free version of a tool works at the beginning, but as your usage expands or needs increase, you may have to start paying for higher access. You will need to revisit your goals and budget to determine the value and relevance of the higher-cost options.

If your Facebook fans are also on your email action list, for example, you can more successfully put multichannel strategies into place. Access to contact information and other basic supporter data can be a major hurdle. For example, Facebook has not yet allowed for organizations with a Page or a Group to export fans or member information. But new third-party applications such as Pledgematic are emerging, using Facebook's Open Graph, to allow nonprofits to access the contact information of supporters and participants.

Collecting contact information is possible, it just requires thoughtful and strategic uses of these outside platforms. Be sure that you post information prominently that directs people to where they can sign up for other alerts. This means they are opting-in through your standard processes and can be managed in your database. You may also want to place fields on your sign-up forms or any profiles you may provide your users on your website so they can input their user names or profile URLs to social media platforms. This way you can store user names in your database and pull lists together for outreach when preparing campaigns or cultivating volunteers.

Access to the Infrastructure

It may not seem like a barrier, but access to Internet and mobile infrastructure is still a very tumultuous and important issue in the United States and elsewhere.

At the close of 2011 and the start of 2012, two sister bills, the Stop Online Piracy Act (SOPA) in the House of Representatives and Protect Internet Privacy Act (PIPA) in the Senate, drew the attention of companies, nonprofits, entrepreneurs, and individuals all around the United States. The stated aim of the bills was to make it much harder for websites (especially websites created outside of the United States) to sell or provide pirated copyrighted materials or content. It sounds like a goal worth supporting, but the details of these bills, even as open for negotiation, could fundamentally disrupt the architecture of the Internet itself in an attempt to reign in pirated content.

In addition, the Obama Administration's response to the bills included the position that, "While we believe that online piracy by foreign websites is a serious problem that requires a serious legislative response, we will not support legislation that reduces freedom of expression, increases cybersecurity risk, or undermines the dynamic, innovative global Internet. Any effort to combat online piracy must guard against the risk of online censorship of lawful activity and must not inhibit innovation by our dynamic businesses large and small."[107]

After an incredible day of action, bringing together thousands of websites—from Google and Wikipedia to independent blogs—in various levels of blackout, as well as the millions of Americans signing anti-SOPA/PIPA petitions (over 4.5 million signatures on the petition from Google, over 1.4 million signatures from Avaaz.org, in addition to others),[108] the bills were postponed.

Although these two bills have lost much of their political support by current elected officials at the time of this writing, various politicians and supporters are still working to refine them and find opportunities to resurface the conversations.

Beyond legislation like SOPA and PIPA, countries such as the United States and the United Kingdom are also trying to find the best ways to support broadband access. As Julius Genachowski, Chairman of the FCC, stated in the May 2010 statement of "The Third Way":

> Broadband is increasingly essential to the daily life of every American. It is fast becoming the primary way we as Americans connect with one another, do business, educate ourselves and our children, receive health care information and services, and express our opinions. As a unanimous FCC said a few weeks ago in our Joint Statement on Broadband, "Working to make sure that America has world-leading high-speed broadband networks—both wired and wireless—lies at the very core of the FCC's mission in the 21st Century."[109]

The FCC's position is to support innovation and education online while not directly regulating the Internet itself (including online services, applications, and so on), establish boundaries to prevent overreach by regulatory bodies, and continue moving forward on broadband initiatives to reach all Americans and protect consumers.

What does this mean for your organization? With legislation and other support from bodies such as the FCC, it is important not just to find the tools and access most effective for and aligned with your work, but also to help advocate for a free and open Internet for your community.

Whether the questions of access point to learning more, growing your community, or using the very infrastructure you need to communicate, you can support your staff and your constituents by leading the way. Walk the talk, so to speak: ask questions to your colleagues and share your experiences or concerns you are hearing online with your staff through meetings or shared communications; ensure that you provide opportunities and paths for your community members to find other ways to connect directly with you outside of social media platforms; stand up for the rights of fair access and usage of the Internet for all those in your community.

PRIVACY

Ever (tried to) read the entire privacy policy or terms of service for any of your favorite online applications or platforms? You probably wondered what you were really agreeing to when you checked the box and clicked to join. Whether it is about spam, the privacy of your personal contact information or actual data, or the option to share or even sell your contact information and usage data to other organizations or companies, privacy is incredibly important to supporting your staff and community in using online tools.

Protecting the Privacy of Staff

Part of an internal social media policy or handbook should be guidelines for recommended use of the web in general, as well as more specific examples for individual platforms. The reason is not to create boundaries or barriers to how your staff uses the Internet, in or out of work, but to provide guidelines for being safe and protecting them from those that may disagree with your mission and from general trolls or malicious behavior.

If your organization deals with controversial legislation, services, or topics, you may already have measures in place to support the privacy and safety of staff members in and out of work. In many cases, those same measures can be applied online. For example, if the physical location or meeting schedule of a staff member is secret to avoid confrontations, you should reflect that policy in your social media guidelines so that upcoming meetings or travel plans are not posted online until the event has started or has finished.

Similarly, staff using location-based social services, such as Foursquare or the check-in feature on Facebook, should ensure that their privacy settings match the level of security approved by the organization. We recommend for both individual and organizational use adopting a "check-out" policy. This means instead of identifying your location online when you arrive, you check in when you are leaving. You can still document where you go and share your tips or pictures from events or your favorite coffee shop, but you prevent possible negative repercussions by not identifying locations where you are or will be for any length of time.

Another thing to work toward is building transparency for your organization. Many staff use their personal accounts online to promote or discuss the work of the organization. It is valuable for them to identify their affiliation and actual job title at the organization in their profiles so that it is clear to the public. This way, your community won't mistake them for an avid follower, volunteer, or even someone imitating the organization. To complement this transparency, we also suggest that staff include a disclaimer in their profiles to suggest that the channel is not the official voice of the organization.

Privacy Concerns for Your Community

Just as you provide guidelines to help your staff protect their privacy and safety while using social tools, both in and out of work, you can make public guidelines to support your community.

Many organizations that have a blog or other user-generated content component of their website have posted guidelines or rules of engagement. This is a great start. You should also consider having a community policy that you can post on other social channels, such as Facebook. As we discuss later in this chapter, posting these general rules will give you support if you do need to take action or remove content.

When creating community guidelines, we suggest you consider the following factors:

Youth: Do you serve young people (legal minors) or have youth volunteers? Although many young people are familiar with social platforms and the options for setting customized privacy controls, it is important to post and maintain a

---

Here are a few examples of Twitter bios with personal disclaimers from actual organizations:

From @sarahdmapes:

Director of Communications @CCMUTweets. Health marketing enthusiast, technology fangirl, and proper spelling/grammar tyrant. Opinions expressed are my own.

From @kristinatabor:

I love dogs, sci fi, Doctor Who, sewing & education reform. Director of Communications for @donnellkay but tweets here are entirely my own.

From @jonwerbell:

I work at Bloomberg Philanthropies (www.bloomberg.org). The opinions expressed here are my own.

position that does not encourage minors to post personal, health, or other critical information about themselves directly on your website, Facebook Page, or elsewhere. Someone may be asking for your professional or medical advice, requesting your services, or otherwise trying to engage with your programs by supplying their information directly. Instead, direct them to any official applications or forms, or to the options for contacting you privately.

Social services: Similar to working with minors online, it is important to promote opportunities for your community to contact you directly if and when requesting your services or support. Especially when working with communities new to the web and social media, it is important that you make guidelines and directions for contacting you clear and obvious from all of your platforms, and make sure to post regular reminders to the page, email list, or comment thread.[110]

Terms of use: Regardless of the amount of user data you gather or store, you should be clear and transparent with your community about how you will use their data. This includes their name, email address, and phone number, in addition to their physical address and any other personal information. Do you share email addresses of your supporters with other similar organizations? Many do. Do you sell email addresses to other organizations, to companies, or even to list-building services? Some organizations do. Whatever you do, even if you have never done so but may in the future, it is important that you are clear about the way data are stored or shared through your organization so that supporters can be deliberate in the information they provide.

Reporting: To promote a healthy community exchange, make it clear how your community members can report potentially malicious activity, spam, or even instances where other members may be sharing information that should not be public. On your site, you may enable features such as a "flag" or reporting system. Elsewhere on the social web, you may not have that kind of management functionality. Include directions in your guidelines for users to let you know about any kind of content that requires your attention and action, whether it is a comment or an email.

NAVIGATING TOUGH CONVERSATIONS

Your blog, social networks, and website should all be used to foster discussions with your community in real time. As we discussed in Chapter Five, these conversations also make your community feel like your organization is accessible and that you value their opinions—especially important when building a grassroots movement among passionate people who want to help you activate social change.

Admittedly, this can be a big transition for organizations because they think that they will be overwhelmed with public criticism and do not yet have a good response plan in place. As we saw in Chapter Seven, organizations usually see positive and supportive messages from the community across the web. Sometimes, organizations are shocked with the level of passion and dedication some supporters have for the cause. As such, staff may think it's easier to ignore people saying something negative about their organization or that they have more important work to do than to address the naysayers. Don't make this mistake. People will still talk about your organization and the issues you tackle whether you join the conversation or not, just as they did with Susan G. Komen for the Cure in early 2012.

Komen for the Cure: A Lesson in Listening to the Community

When Planned Parenthood released a statement saying that Susan G. Komen for the Cure would not be renewing grant funding to support 19 local Planned Parenthood affiliates, which provided 170,000 clinical breast exams and 6,400 mammogram referrals to women in low-income communities through the Komen grant, many activists, Facebook fans, and donors of the Komen community revolted.

Once the news began to spread, people expressed their sadness and anger over Komen's decision on Twitter, Komen's Facebook Page, and on their founder Nancy Brinker's Facebook Page. A Komen sponsor, Energizer Battery Company, was caught in the middle of the firestorm as people were posting their heartfelt responses to Komen's news on the nonprofit's last update highlighting the sponsor.

Instead of forming a rapid response and sharing it with their community, Komen went silent for 24 hours. Not even a 140-character tweet acknowledging the thousands of comments, with a note such as, "Thank you. We hear your concerns and are looking into this. Will report back shortly."

You may be asking yourself, how could this have happened? Politics aside, the answer is that they were not prepared to deal with high-volume criticism. To make matters worse, when they finally responded publicly, they issued a statement on their Facebook Page stating that the situation was "regrettable" but Komen had changed its priorities and policies, which impacted grantees such as

Planned Parenthood. Then Brinker released a video that said she was "dismayed and extremely disappointed" by the community's responses. Chastising your community for expressing their opinions, even if you don't agree, is one of the worst things you can do to your supporters. It can also further exacerbate any issues. The criticism escalated so much so that Komen ended up not only restoring the funding to Planned Parenthood but they also hired a reputation consultant to assess how much damage was done to their brand.[111]

Responding to Your Community

If you are going to truly build a community based on openness and transparency, you must be responsive. Every day you should respond to the comments from your community, thank them for sharing your message, answer questions, and even promote the positive work of supporters. When working on real social change, though, you can't escape criticism from time to time. Here are some tips that you can adapt to be responsive across multiple online channels.

Develop a clear and focused commenting policy. These ground rules will help set the tone for the discussions on these channels and help weed out some of the more hostile commentary.

Here's a good example of a commenting policy from the Union of Concerned Scientists.

> UCS welcomes comments that foster civil conversation and debate. To help maintain a healthy, respectful discussion, please focus comments on the issues, topics, and facts at hand, and refrain from personal attacks. Posts that are commercial, obscene, rude or disruptive will be removed.
>
> Please note that comments are open for two weeks following each blog post. When commenting, you must use your real name. Valid email addresses are required. (UCS respects your privacy; we will not display, lend, or sell your email address for any reason.)[112]

Your commenting policy should include a plan for addressing all comments, not just the bad ones. Will you premoderate all comments? Premoderate just new users who want to comment on your blog for the first time? Or is your organization comfortable allowing all comments to be published automatically (with spam filters in place) and with the option of deleting comments that don't follow your commenting policy?

NATIONAL WILDLIFE FEDERATION COMMENTING POLICY ON FACEBOOK

We reserve the right to delete posts containing any of the following elements:

- Profanity

- Personal attacks

- Willful misinformation

- Spam

- Any advertising that's unrelated to wildlife

- Off-topic or irrelevant posts

- Promoting violence

- Anything that infringes on copyrights or trademarks

- Promoting illegal or questionable activities

If you repeatedly violate this policy, you will be removed from our page. If you have any questions, please email friends@nwf.org.

Personally, we feel that to foster discussion, you should allow all non-spam comments that follow your commenting policy to publish automatically so that people can join the conversation in real time. Once you have established your overarching commenting policy, you can then determine the best course of action for handling negative comments.

HOW TO GUIDE: MANAGING THE CRITICS

Whether it is on your blog or on a social network, you need to be prepared to support your community sharing content and to deal with opposing viewpoints. Here's a practical list of tips we have seen work the best in dealing with negative comments.

1. **Respond quickly.** When you see a negative comment on your blog or social media channel, don't delay your response. Many of these channels

are public spaces and you don't want people piling on to the criticism because you are not responding fast enough. Acknowledge people and address their concerns to build community. If you don't have all of the facts or information to respond or help them, acknowledge it and tell them you are checking into it and that you will update them shortly. It is better to say, "Thanks for your feedback. We are investigating and will post more information as soon as we can," than it is to wait hours or days to respond with all the information. If you feel that their criticism is not totally valid, thank them for taking the time to share their feedback with you. Then, cordially address the issue they referenced, debunk myths, and set the record straight. Sometimes commenters will have a valid criticism; it's essential that you acknowledge it and admit when you are wrong.

2. **Be nice.** You are representing your organization so it's important that you respect your community and act professionally when responding to people. This means both on your organization's online channels and when commenting or responding to others' comments on blogs maintained by other organizations or individuals. Remember: everyone is entitled to express their opinion, even if you don't always agree.

3. **Move the discussion offline.** When negative conversations start to go back and forth a lot or you feel the commenter has a challenging personality (hey, all of us do at times, right?), try to take it offline. Sometimes a simple phone call or even a direct email can help defuse the situation.

4. **Debunk misinformation but don't feed the trolls.** Admittedly, this part can get kind of tricky, especially on social networks, which are public, and where anyone (including your opposition) can engage with your organization. This is a great space to debunk misinformation they may be feeding to your community. But sometimes the opposition can act like trolls (relentless instigators) and you will need to pick and choose your battles. Use your commenting policy as support and ignore the relentless trolls.

5. **Don't delete constituents' comments.** Unless people have clearly violated your commenting policy, don't delete their comments. This is one of the quickest ways to cause a firestorm in your community and draw attention to potentially harmful topics, because angry constituents can lash out at

you on multiple channels about it. This can cause the organization great embarrassment (like it did to Komen) and you will be forced to deal with the repercussions of both a negative topic and your treatment of it. There is no hiding on the real-time web.

6. **Let the community come to your defense.** The more you build up your community online, the more they will feel empowered to respond to commenters, particularly the negative or hostile ones.

HOW-TO GUIDE: MANAGING A ROGUE STAFFER

Here's a recent question we received from a participant at a conference:

We don't yet have an organizational account on Facebook but many staff members promote our events or blog posts from their personal profiles and many staff are friends with each other on Facebook. Over the last few weeks we have seen one staff person in particular saying very mean things about coworkers and derogatory things about the organization. We do not have a social media policy because we do not use social media with any organizational branding. How should we deal with this?

The first thing organizations should do is establish a social media policy. Here's a quick list of potential topics to include in a social media policy for your staff to help guide their use of social tools on behalf of the organization or in promoting your work:

- Don't tell secrets—sharing personal or confidential information about other staff, the organization, or even yourself can be dangerous

- Be honest—nothing attracts attention on the web like trust (or, unfortunately, dishonesty)

- Respect copyright—be sure to provide links to sources and only share content that you have permission to share or reuse

- Be respectful—of your coworkers, your partners, your community, and even those who may not agree with you or your organization's work.

- Use disclaimers—be transparent about your investment in a conversation as well as your role with the organization (examples mentioned earlier in this chapter)

Proactive Planning

The best response to a potentially negative situation, especially one that involves your own staff member, is "We already prepared a plan for this." When thinking about staff saying harmful or negative things about the organization as a whole or other staff members, it's best to prepare general guidelines and repercussions. You may be surprised by the situation, if one ever develops, and if your plan assumes that the only people who would do something like this are your most junior staff, you could be essentially without a way to react. Your plans should include both junior and senior staff, as well as your executive director and board.

Just as we discussed earlier with your community, it's important that you define the kinds of comments or topics that are not aligned with your goals or your employee conduct standards. Providing clear context up front for staff is the best way to position them for feeling comfortable and confident using social media inside and outside of work, as well as providing you with an easy way to highlight potential issues with staff directly. Your guidelines should be flexible enough to include social channels and tools in use today and those that may be adopted in the future. Similarly, guidelines should also provide specific examples of comments that are encouraged and those that would either create alarm or elicit disciplinary action.

Reactive Intervention

Despite the best policies, guidelines, or even trainings, some organizations will still find a staff person, board member, or even volunteer that finds something negative to say (and sometimes says it loudly). Hopefully you've done the first step already: providing guidelines and examples.

As soon as a staff person does cross the line, it's important that it is dealt with immediately and professionally. Remember, your organization's name and reputation are on the line with the way you treat these issues, not just what was originally said. Use your employee handbook or staff policies to navigate disciplinary action. Ensure that the offending comments or content are addressed appropriately and removed as necessary.

Take action. Here are the basic steps for responding to staff or other supporters infringing on your social media policy.

- Document any content by the infringing staff person as well as the responses that content receives.

- Take note of any privacy settings that may impact the content (was it shared on a private Facebook group or on a public profile?).

- Bring it to the attention of the staff person immediately as well as a review of the organizational policies or guidelines.

- Be prepared to take action and have next steps for dealing with the content itself, as well as the staff person, ready for discussion as quickly as possible.

The more you invest in planning for and supporting your staff to use these tools safely and in support of all they do, in and out of work, the more you actually create a culture that is open and positive.

TRANSITIONING YOUR ORGANIZATION

As an organization working to create social change anytime, everywhere, you are inspiring people every day—those on your staff and in the community. Even though your supporters are often giving you positive feedback and contributing to your social channels with their ideas and actions, you need to be prepared for all types of feedback. Responding to your community in a timely manner lets them know you're listening, and that you truly value their feedback. It also means that when there is a negative comment in the mix, you can be there right away to deal with it directly.

The process of creating plans, guidelines, and policies provides an opportunity to have meaningful and transparent conversations with your community groups such as your advocates, donors, and stakeholders. For many organizations transitioning to this new way of operating, these topics are often not discussed or given the attention they deserve. In today's multichannel world, it's imperative that your organization start implementing them today. Focus on creating the most positive environment for your staff and community by providing access to training and information, policies that encourage dialogue and interaction, and examples of the kind of engagement and interaction you want to see across the community.

DISCUSSION QUESTIONS

Spark a conversation with your team or organization with the following questions:

1. How do you track positive comments and actions the community takes on your behalf, and how do you share those with your colleagues inside the organization?

2. What do you include in your commenting or community engagement policy that encourages comments?

3. What do you include in your commenting or community engagement policy that supports your staff in taking action to deal directly with trolls or trouble makers?

4. How do you plan to support staff understanding privacy settings on social networks as part of your organizational practices?

5. What kind of training would you and your colleagues like to participate in together to learn more about using a certain tool?

CONCLUSION

Disrupting the Nonprofit Sector

In the last ten years, the nonprofit sector has grown more than 60%[113] in the United States to an estimated 1.5 million organizations.[114] In every vertical, ranging from the environment to public health, there are hundreds if not thousands of organizations with similar names and missions competing for advocacy, donor, and foundation support. No wonder our constituents' in-boxes and mailboxes are stuffed with action alerts, fundraising appeals, and newsletters with similar messaging from several nonprofits vying for attention. You probably recognize this problem too, and find it frustrating that your community has to sift through so much noise to determine which organization's actions to take or where to donate money.

If we are going to truly solve the world's toughest social problems and obtain the necessary resources to do it right, we need to examine how the nonprofit sector can evolve to create more innovative and efficient organizations. This involves disrupting the nonprofit sector as we know it today. Here are some ideas to consider as you think about the future of your organization and of the nonprofit sector.

REDUCE COMPETITION AND CONSOLIDATE RESOURCES

"Nonprofits need a fundamental change in how they collaborate with each other. If the mission is the most important thing, why is there unnecessary competition? I think the industry as a whole needs a more transparent, decentralized way of eliminating resource-waste. Collective energy could go so much further," says Maddie Grant, founder of Social Fish.

One way to address this is to reduce competition within each cause area by combining nonprofits to bring the best talent, resources, and innovation together. Imagine how much more of an impact nonprofits would have if staff could spend more time working on solving issues rather than struggling for funding, resources, or spending time on internal politics and grant reports that offer little value to the foundation or donors.

David Svet, CEO of Spur Communications, says setting up nonprofit venture funds developed for each of the world's problems could help combine nonprofits and make them much more effective in solving social issues. "If we care to address social justice issues, we may want to look at investing in a nonprofit fund that will endeavor to remedy the problem and who can hire and invest in the necessary solutions. So if we were passionate about domestic violence and its many forms, there would be a venture fund for it. The fund would collect investments, distribute the money to the few vetted nonprofits working on domestic violence, and manage the nonprofits' work around the investment. Investments would go 50 cents on the dollar to the cause with the balance going to an endowment to remedy the problem. When the problem is remedied, the endowment would be moved to another issue," said Svet.

Measuring impact and reporting outcomes of the investment would be crucial to the success of the nonprofit venture fund concept. Donors would need to be treated like investors and given clear documentation of needs and outcomes.

What's great about Svet's vision is that people want to feel like they are investing in an issue that they are passionate about instead of trying to figure out which organization they should support. Nonprofits in the fund could then spend even more time on the ground working with the community to solve social issues. Equally important, organizations would have the capacity to build stronger relationships with their community and inspire more people to get involved and contribute their ideas as potential solutions to social issues. All too often nonprofits dictate how some issues should be solved as if social justice issues are nonprofits' problems to face alone. They are everyone's problem to address together.

THINK LIKE A STARTUP

Even though there are 1.5 million nonprofits in the United States alone, social change is not happening fast enough. Yes, you can blame this on partisan politics, the economy, and myriad other things; but nonprofits that also enforce rigid top-town management and don't foster innovation within their organization are to blame, too. We are hopeful that organizations can begin to change that by adapting some strategies from the startup sector.

Test New Ideas Quickly

Startups are often encouraged not to be risk averse and to test new ideas quickly to figure out what aspects of their product do not work so that they can learn from their failure and iterate. Nonprofits can adapt this model too. For example, Save the Children Italy has a testing budget to test new online fundraising and outreach ideas to empower people in Italy to help children in need. Staff are encouraged to test a variety of ideas ranging from online games to apps so that they can learn from their successes and failures fast. All of this knowledge is then shared with the rest of the organization so that they can invest more in the digital strategies that are actually working.

"Testing helped us to create a better digital 'ecosystem' which is linking digital engagement and digital fundraising, while offering our supporters different experiences according to their interests," said Daniela Fatarella, head of marketing and communications at Save the Children Italy. "When we failed, we analyzed reasons for failing: wrong content, language, timing of [campaigns], activities, type of request and level of engagement, and sometimes also the willingness to innovate much more than to consolidate. All this has leveraged our knowledge of digital fundraising and helped us to build on our experience and get better in acquiring and retaining our digital donors."

Save the Children Italy has learned that recycling the same old solutions to solve social issues clearly isn't working. Can you imagine how much more they would learn if they increased their budget to have an incubator inside the organization solely focused on dreaming up and testing new ideas to address the ongoing struggles children in poverty face every day in Italy? Since Save the Children has affiliates in 120 countries, the incubator could share the results and resources with the rest of the affiliates, benefitting the entire network of organizations.

"I'd love for everyone to wake up working for organizations that demand endless experimentation and creativity from their employees, and whose donors and supporters are 100% aware and on-board with exactly how the organization works and what it's working toward," said Porter Mason, deputy director of Social Media at UNICEF USA. We agree! And while some organizations are trying to operate in this way now, there will need to be many more moving in this direction soon. As our community members continue to expect more from your communications, your campaigns, and impact, so too do your staff.

charity: water's Fundraising Experiment

Towards the end of 2011, charity: water launched an innovative social fundraising experiment that they thought had potential to raise hundreds of millions of

Figure C.1
Screen Shot of charity: water's Microsite WaterForward:
Suggesting Friends to Pay It Forward to You

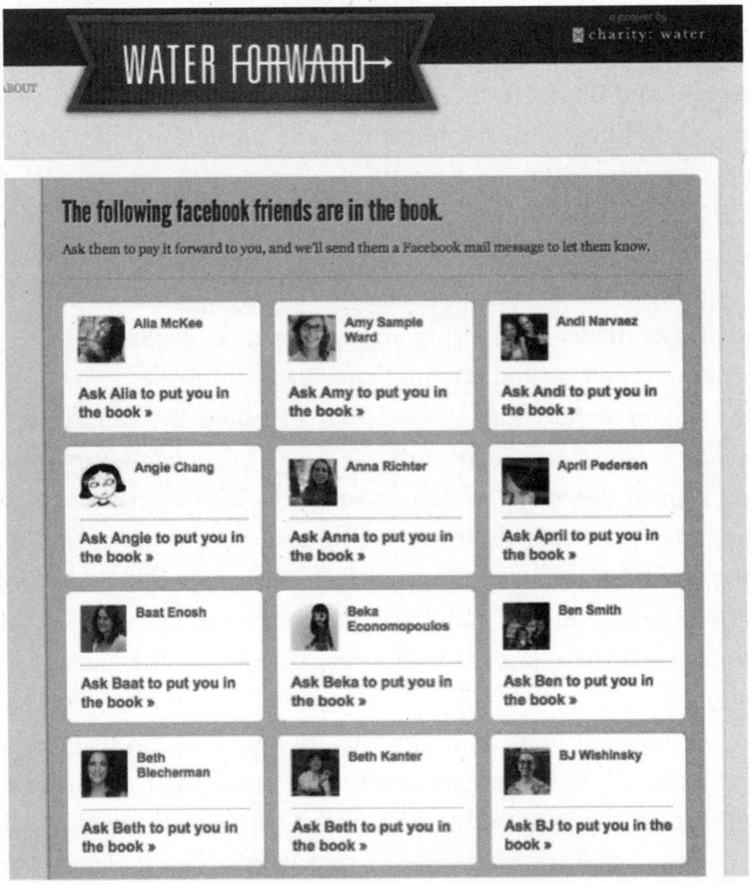

WATER FORWARD→

a project by
charity: water

ABOUT

The following facebook friends are in the book.

Ask them to pay it forward to you, and we'll send them a Facebook mail message to let them know.

Alia McKee

Ask Alia to put you in the book »

Amy Sample Ward

Ask Amy to put you in the book »

Andi Narvaez

Ask Andi to put you in the book »

Angie Chang

Ask Angie to put you in the book »

Anna Richter

Ask Anna to put you in the book »

April Pedersen

Ask April to put you in the book »

Baat Enosh

Ask Baat to put you in the book »

Beka Economopoulos

Ask Beka to put you in the book »

Ben Smith

Ask Ben to put you in the book »

Beth Blecherman

Ask Beth to put you in the book »

Beth Kanter

Ask Beth to put you in the book »

BJ Wishinsky

Ask BJ to put you in the book »

dollars. They created an online book called WaterForward[115] filled with faces of people helping to end the water crisis (see Figure C.1).

charity: water started the fundraising campaign by posing the question to their community, "What if the billion people around the world using social media could help the billion people without clean water?"

How WaterForward Works

You can't put yourself in the WaterForward online book. Someone else, who is already in the online book, such as a friend or family member, has to sponsor you with a $10 donation. Since you can sign in to the WaterForward website using your Facebook or Twitter account, you can ask your friends on these networks to make a donation on your behalf and "pay it forward" for you. Alternatively, you can pledge $10 to put someone else in the online book and rely on karma that someone will see your pledge and sponsor you as well. The site also tracks everyone you pay it forward to so you can see the impact your donations have.

As of this writing, there were over 30,000 people in the online book and over $300,000 raised. While the experimental campaign has not generated millions of dollars yet, despite iterating and testing three different ways to engage people on the website, charity: water is not giving up. The organization plans to continue testing because they are determined to find out what triggers people to give, and to apply what they learn to future campaigns.

BE SELF-SUSTAINABLE: HAVE A HEART AND A HEAD FOR BUSINESS

Similar to nonprofits, entrepreneurs in startups are driven by their ambition to change the world, but through products. To build products and iterate they need resources and capital to self-sustain. Part of the founding team is often someone who has strong business skills and can help the startup scale. While nonprofits have finance departments and some even have chief financial officers, they are often narrowly focused on accounting, budgets, reporting, and meeting payroll. This is a problem for the nonprofit sector because charitable giving only grew by 0.9% in 2011 and about 40% of the wealth of foundation endowments that many organizations depended on has been eliminated.[116] Nonprofits now need to be focused on developing models that are more self-sustainable.

"As a social enterprise [or nonprofit], it's easy to get swept up in the feel-good, I'm-a-world-changing-ninja feeling. Be wary of over-investing in your social mission and under-investing in your revenue strategy and sustainability. You can't impact the world if your own revenue strategy doesn't work," says Amanda Steinberg, founder of the startup DailyWorth and who founded Soapbxx, a web firm that worked with the nonprofit community from 2006 to 2011.

DC Central Kitchen, whose mission is to use food as a tool to strengthen bodies, empower minds, and build communities, has been successful operating their nonprofit more like a business. Since 1989, the organization has prepared 25 million meals for low-income residents in Washington, D.C. To support their mission they run a culinary job-training program that trains unemployed people who have been homeless, addicted to drugs, or incarcerated. The trainees receive job experience through the organization's catering company, called Fresh Start Catering. For several years DC Central Kitchen has also partnered with farmers in Virginia's Shenandoah Valley, who offer discounts on produce. This enables DC Central Kitchen to not only provide a lot of fresh and local ingredients in the 4,500 daily meals they provide to local shelters and soup kitchens, but it also saves the organization money. In addition to the produce being used in the daily meals they serve, the produce is also used in their wholesale food business, which sells fruits and vegetables to local grocery stores and restaurants.

DC Central Kitchen also partners with the D.C. Public School System. Since August of 2010, they have prepared over 4,000 healthy, home-style cooked meals each day for low-income children at eight public and private schools in Washington, D.C. And the organization's school contracts have employed at least 35 people who completed the organization's culinary job training program.

"Arrangements like these give local businesses an opportunity to express their philanthropy as part of everyday commerce, rather than digging into their pockets to make a donation," said blogger Ed Bruske who wrote about DC Central Kitchen's innovative business model at Grist.org.[117]

We think that all nonprofits bring their own unique set of expertise to the table that they can market and generate revenue from. Perhaps your nonprofit is an expert in conducting trainings, or has spent years developing and refining a human resources program for global affiliates focused on recruitment, training, and professional development. Why not offer paid consulting services to peer organizations that can benefit from this expertise?

RECLAIM REPORTING

It's an open secret that traditional philanthropic reporting is broken. As currently structured, conventional reporting fails to meet its potential and creates an enormous drain on time, energy, and resources across the board. "We've become too focused on a labor-intensive validation process in which nonprofits produce 60-page reports, that few read, in an effort not only to justify the use of funds received from individual grants, but also to ensure that money keeps flowing," said Ned Breslin, CEO of Water For People. Our misplaced reporting priorities are now an obstacle to learning.

Reporting matters, of course, but it can only serve missions when it's actually focused on the impact funding has on people over time by advancing and refining programming, rather than being focused solely on where money is spent. In the drive for protection and "aid transparency," we've missed reporting's full potential as a unique moment and learning opportunity to reflect on how an organization is really doing and what it can do to improve.

With these challenges in mind, Water For People's Re-Imagine Reporting offers a heartening effort to rebalance our reporting efforts. Re-Imagine Reporting's web platform builds on new technologies for data management and visualization to bring information to life visually in ways that are consistent with how people learn across cultures, continents, and languages. Photography, video, infographics, and financial data are highlighted, with donors having the ability to see their contribution to the overall pie, as far down as receipts.

"The platform aims to facilitate a constant dialogue that allows staff, partners, communities, donors, and the broader development community to reflect on the full picture of what the organization is doing, programmatic outcomes, challenges, and future direction in light of progress toward clear and ambitious goals," said Breslin.

Reporting should no longer be an obstacle to learning. Water For People's commitment to reclaim the reporting process offers a glimpse of how reporting can drive an organization to ask hard questions on the impact of its work with an eye on constant improvement. We see this as just one example of advanced reporting, and we hope organizations look not just at using multichannel strategies to create impact, but also to document it.

PREPARE FOR A MORE SOCIAL AND MOBILE WORLD

We've also talked about mobile technology throughout this book, and the power of mobile tools and applications is only going to grow. Another arena where change is happening is in the mobility and responsiveness of the information we push out to our supporters.

Today, knowing where a supporter lives helps us segment our messages so that we can send geographically relevant messages to suggest, for example, that they attend an upcoming event we are planning in that area. Already, we can leave the segmenting up to the supporter, or, rather, his or her phone's GPS. When supporters open our advocacy alert and the mobile GPS indicates they are in Austin, Texas, the details of your nearest event can be recommended automatically—even if their billing address in the database is in another state. In addition, supporters can forward the message to friends and family, allowing them to see the geographically relevant events near them whenever they open the message. The mobility of our messages, calls to action, and information will provide more opportunities to create richer relationships with our supporters and donors and help them decide how and when to take action.

When it comes to tracking engagement, participation, and communication with your supporters, one of the biggest hurdles is actually getting the data. In many instances, there's an intermediary platform like Facebook or an application in the way. The web is getting more social in a way that means our data and actions are tracked everywhere we go. In the future we hope to see people in charge of maintaining and sharing their own data directly with the organizations they want to support.

Michelle Murrain, a technologist, and Beth Kanter, an author and trainer in the nonprofit space, have talked about the importance of having a portable social graph. "The 'social graph' is, basically, your data about who you are, and who is connected to you—who your friends are. A portable social graph would be one that you can take with you, wherever you are—so the friends that are connected with you on one network are also connected with you on another. It's the holy grail of social network connectivity—you are connected to who you are connected to, no matter what site you are on," said Murrain.[118]

Not only will we see our supporters bringing their friends and colleagues with them into our channels, but we will also see our tracking, analytics, and database technologies evolve to help capture and manage these new social data.

PREPARE FOR THE FUTURE TODAY

These are just a few of the advances and changes we see on the horizon. Whatever your focus, mission, or goals, you can start preparing your organization and your community for a new way of working together and creating social impact today. Use the tips throughout the book to start creating organizational plans, policies, and structures to support your staff in using multichannel strategies. Start with small tests and learn as you ramp up to full-blown campaigns. Use the lessons from all the organizations and individuals who shared stories in the previous chapters to identify options for your next email series and corresponding social media updates. The discussion questions are designed to get you talking with your colleagues, but the ideas you come up with from those conversations are your real invitation to dive in and get started right now.

JOIN US!

Have questions? Examples from your organization to share? We look forward to connecting with you on our website, http://www.socialchangeanytime.com, to support you in implementing multichannel strategies for real social impact anytime, everywhere! In addition to discussion topics on the website, there are also additional worksheets and handouts to help you lead your staff in succeeding in an anytime, everywhere world. We know it may sound cliché, but we really hope this is just the beginning of our working together to change the world: come join us!

NOTES

PREFACE

1. philanthropy.com/article/Response-to-Japan-Disaster/126760/

2. articles.cnn.com/2010-01-18/tech/redcross.texts_1_red-cross-haiti-relief-facebook-and-twitter?_s=PM:TECH

3. www.huffingtonpost.com/2012/01/11/haiti-earthquake-recovery_n_1197730.html

4. www.charitynavigator.org/index.cfm?bay=content.view&cpid=1194

CHAPTER 1—WHY ARE ONLINE AND MOBILE CHANNELS SO IMPORTANT TO NONPROFITS TODAY?

5. www.internetworldstats.com/stats14.htm

6. communities-dominate.blogs.com/brands/2012/02/the-state-of-the-union-blog-for-mobile-industry-all-the-stats-and-facts-for-2012.html

7. blog.nielsen.com/nielsenwire/social/

8. en.wikipedia.org/wiki/Blog

9. pewinternet.org/Reports/2010/Cell-Phones-and-American-Adults/Overview.aspx

10. www.dmnews.com/study-20-of-emails-opened-on-mobile-devices/article/217905/

CHAPTER 2—GUIDING PRINCIPLES FOR ANYTIME EVERYWHERE

11. Additional Tumblr statistics and information from 2011 available at: www.businessinsider.com/tumblr-blows-past-15-billion-pageviews-per-month-2012-1

12. The "Rise Above Plastics" campaign images can be found at: www.surfrider .org/coastal-blog/entry/new-rise-above-plastics-print-psas-from-pollinate and the Campaign information at surfrider.org/rap

13. Komen Sues Over Use of Cure and Pink: www.huffingtonpost.com/2010/12/07/ komen-foundation-charities-cure_n_793176.html

CHAPTER 3—ADVOCACY ANYTIME EVERYWHERE

14. www.mobilisationlab.org/top-ten-tips-in-email-writing-from-organisations-changing-the-world/

15. www.womenwhotech.com

16. www.pewinternet.org/Reports/2012/Older-adults-and-internet-use.aspx

17. digitalteams.org/

18. www.comscoredatamine.com/2012/01/u-s-mobile-email-audience-grows-by-nearly-20-million-users-in-the-past-year/

19. www.comscore.com/Insights/Press_Releases/2011/1/Web-based_Email_ Shows_Signs_of_Decline_in_the_U.S._While_Mobile_Email_Usage_on_ the_Rise

20. www.radicati.com/wp/wp-content/uploads/2011/05/Email-Statistics-Report-2011–2015-Executive-Summary.pdf

21. www.npaction.org/article/articleview/607/1/222

22. themobilenonprofit.org/2011/12/19/mobile-growth-strategy/

23. www.mobilisationlab.org/missed-calls-help-in-campaign-to-protect-indian-forests/

24. jdrfpromise.org/

25. www.aqua.org/

26. www.epolitics.com/download-online-politics-101/

27. www.mobilemarketer.com/cms/opinion/columns/10465.html

28. www.wired.co.uk/magazine/archive/2011/04/features/how-rovio-made-angry-birds-a-winner?page=all

29. stateofthemedia.org/2011/overview-2/

30. Learn more about ShareThis at: sharethis.com/

31. www.pbs.org/idealab/2012/06/how-upworthy-makes-important-content-sharable163.html

32. Meetup.com's Meetup Everywhere feature is available at: www.meetup.com/everywhere/

33. Access the list of participating Occupy Together events at: www.meetup.com/occupytogether/

34. www.congressfoundation.org/projects/communicating-with-congress/perceptions-of-citizen-advocacy-on-capitol-hill and www.frogloop.com/storage/CWC-Perceptions-of-Citizen-Advocacy-1.pdf

35. www.e-benchmarksstudy.com/

36. nonprofitsocialnetworksurvey.com/

37. Learn more about 350.org and their campaigns at 350.org

38. www.climateaccess.org/blog/what-occupy-means-climate-movement

CHAPTER 4—FUNDRAISING ANYTIME EVERYWHERE

39. www.convio.com/our-products/luminate/teamraiser.html

40. spring2action.razoo.com/giving_events/spring2action2012/home

41. www.nonprofitquarterly.org/philanthropy/20153-boston-marathon-a-test-of-runners-fundraising-endurance.html

42. m.npr.org/news/front/142780599?page=0

43. invisiblepeople.tv/blog/

44. www.razoo.com/story/Punishgeoff

45. www.afpnet.org/Audiences/ReportsResearchDetail.cfm?itemnumber=4620

46. www.frogloop.com/care2blog/2009/5/31/is-direct-mail-dying-or-dead-hogwash.html

47. www.blackbaud.com/nonprofit-resources/online-giving-report.aspx

48. Source: 2011 Online Giving Report

49. www.flickr.com/photos/13159483@N00/6355681921/in/photostream

50. www.flickr.com/photos/13159483@N00/6355681921/in/photostream

51. www.guardian.co.uk/voluntary-sector-network/2011/sep/26/seven-tips-mobile-fundraising

52. www.nptrends.com/nonprofit-trends/how-much-money-is-raised-through-online-giving.htm

53. resources.convio.com/BenchmarkReport.html

54. www.afpnet.org/Audiences/ReportsResearchDetail.cfm?itemnumber=4620

55. nonprofitsocialnetworksurvey.com/

56. www.frogloop.com/care2blog/2011/12/27/is-facebook-good-for-fundraising.html

57. mobileactive.org/fundraising-and-mobile-phones-update

58. www.pewinternet.org/Reports/2012/MobileGiving/Key-Findings.aspx

59. www.mgive.com/Studies/DonorSurveyReport.aspx

60. www.raise-funds.com/2003/nonprofit-fund-raising-demystified/

61. www.npengage.com/advocacy/advocates-more-likely-give/

62. www.event360.com/blog/nonprofit-fundraising-strategies-a-b-testing-to-optimize-online-conversions/

63. support.google.com/analytics/bin/answer.py?hl=en&topic=1745207&answer=1745147#utm_source=gablog&utm_medium=blog&utm_content=content&utm_campaign=content_experiments_launch

64. philanthropy.com/article/tech-guide/131007

65. www.slideshare.net/farra/secrets-of-integrated-fundraising

66. www.slideshare.net/farra/secrets-of-integrated-fundraising

67. This section was adapted from www.frogloop.com/care2blog/2010/2/6/five-online-fundraising-tips-to-raise-more-money.html

68. https://care2.webex.com/care2/lsr.php?AT=pb&SP=EC&rID=2551692&rKey=b44710ac91058749

69. seachangestrategies.com/blog/2010/08/17/webinar-reprise-the-overachievers-guide-to-year-end-fundraising/

70. https://care2.webex.com/care2/lsr.php?AT=pb&SP=EC&rID=2551692&rKey=b44710ac91058749

71. www.npengage.com/online-fundraising/7-online-fundraising-tips-learned-from-participating-movember/

72. www.frogloop.com/care2blog/2011/8/18/qr-codes-in-action-five-nonprofits-share-their-experiences.html

73. www.npengage.com/social-media/the-power-social-fundraising-and-friends-asking-friends-infographic/

74. www.bigducknyc.com/blog/fundraising-advice-and-predictions-2010

75. resources.convio.com/COP_Benchmark2012.html

CHAPTER 5—COMMUNITY BUILDING ANYTIME EVERYWHERE

76. Based on the essay Amy contributed to Thrivability: A Collective Sketch—thrivable.wagn.org/Book+listening

77. Charity Navigator: www.charitynavigator.org/

78. Guidestar: www2.guidestar.org/

79. GreatNonprofits: greatnonprofits.org/

80. To see CARE's donation form and financial information, visit: https://my.care.org/site/Donation2?df_id=9140&9140.donation=form1

81. AJWS financial information and downloads are available at: ajws.org/who_we_are/financial.html

82. Screen shot from: ajws.org

83. Diabetes Hands Foundation maintains tudiabetes.org and estudiabetes.org on Ning.com platforms. Learn more about Diabetes Hands Foundation at diabeteshandsfoundation.org

84. Learn more about this case study from Mobile Commons CEO, Jed Alpert, on the Nonprofit Technology Network's blog: www.nten.org/blog/2011/05/05/listen-your-data-lessons-multi-lingual-text-message-campaign

85. View up-to-date data on the number of participating students and explore the DOT actions at www.acespace.org/dot

86. Visitor data and other information about The American Museum of Natural History from Wikipedia: en.wikipedia.org/wiki/American_museum_of_natural_history

87. Information about the downloads and usage of these apps is available from Xyologic: xyologic.com/search/iphone/

88. Learn more about Do Something and review campaigns and actions at: www.dosomething.org/

89. Waiting on updated stats from George Weiner at DoSomething

90. Learn more about the Freedom Connect online social network from Survivors Connect at: www.survivorsconnect.org/get-involved/freedomconnect

91. List churn and unsubscribe information can be found in the eNonprofit Benchmarks Report conducted by NTEN and M+R Strategic Services, available at nten.org/research

CHAPTER 6—MULTICHANNEL STRATEGIES IN ACTION

92. Deepwater Horizon information on Wikipedia: en.wikipedia.org/wiki/Deepwater_Horizon

93. www.nwf.org/oilspill

94. www.nwf.org/Kids/Ranger-Rick/Parents-and-Educators/How-To-Talk-With-Kids-Gulf-Oil-Spill.aspx

CHAPTER 7—EQUIPPING YOUR ORGANIZATION FOR ANYTIME EVERYWHERE

95. digitalteams.org/

96. www.organizing20.org/2011/04/25/strategic-plannery/

97. www.ssireview.org/blog/entry/four_models_for_organizing_digital_work_part_two

98. digitalteams.org/

99. Need some help determining the right social media policies for your organization? Check out this social media policy generator: socialmedia.policytool.net.

100. www.slideshare.net/ayeletb/social-media-for-social-good-1599758

101. foundationcenter.org/getstarted/faqs/html/howmany.html

102. yourlife.usatoday.com/mind-soul/doing-good/kindness/post/2011/02/haiti-earthquake-taught-world-the-power-of-mobile-giving/142536/1

103. www.mgive.com/Studies/Default.aspx

104. Here are step by step instructions from Amy about creating a content map: amysampleward.org/2010/09/01/diy-content-mapping/

105. To learn more about North York Community House's process for adopting social media, visit the Appendix to see a detailed timeline.

CHAPTER 8—TRANSITIONING TO ANYTIME EVERYWHERE

106. Membership organizations and associations like NTEN (nten.org/) or State Associations (listed at: www.councilofnonprofits.org/salocator/) provide membership options for your entire organization.

107. Read the full position and response from the Obama Administration to the SOPA/PIPA bills: www.whitehouse.gov/blog/2012/01/14/obama-administration-responds-we-people-petitions-sopa-and-online-piracy

108. Read more about the impact of the petitions and SOPA/PIPA strike participation from Forbes: www.forbes.com/sites/erikkain/2012/01/19/4–5-million-people-signed-googles-anti-sopa-petition/

109. Read Genachowski's full statement, titled "The Third Way: A Narrowly Tailored Broadband Framework" on the FCC website: www.broadband.gov/the-third-way-narrowly-tailored-broadband-framework-chairman-julius-genachowski.html

110. For more information and resources about HIPAA compliance for organizations managing, storing, or otherwise receiving health information, visit: www.hipaasurvivalguide.com/

111. www.huffingtonpost.com/2012/02/23/susan-g-komen-planned-parenthood_n_1297483.html

112. blog.ucsusa.org

CONCLUSION: DISRUPTING THE NONPROFIT SECTOR

113. www.nytimes.com/2009/12/06/us/06charity.html?_r=2&scp=1&sq=charities&st=cse

114. www.grantspace.org/Tools/Knowledge-Base/Funding-Research/Statistics/Number-of-nonprofits-in-the-U.S

115. www.waterforward.org/

116. www.frogloop.com/care2blog/2009/5/20/nonprofit-mergers-and-alliances-dont-try-this-at-home.html

117. grist.org/article/food-dc-public-schools-partners-with-ex-con-agency/

118. Footnote quote from frogloop—www.frogloop.com/care2blog/2009/11/9/is-your-nonprofit-too-social-media-dependent.html

INDEX

Page references followed by *fig* indicate an illustrated figure; followed by *t* indicate a table.

B

Baldacious Campaign calendar (Leukemia and Lymphoma Society), 93*fig*

Ban the Bag campaign (Surfrider Foundation), 149–150

Barely Political (YouTube channel), 60

Barry, Frank, 95, 110

"Being a Woman is Not a Pre-Existing Condition" campaign (NWLC), 41–42*fig*

Benston, Katie, 180

Berkman Center for Internet and Society (Harvard University), 89

Better Business Bureau, 106

Big Duck, 92

Blackbaud, 64, 86, 107, 110

BlogHer, 47

Blogs: building trust through series of, 121; dealing with trolls, 57, 59; description and use of, 57; MMT's "Two Way Street Tour," 121; MobileActive.org, 88; online sharing of, 59; Shepherds Secondary School (Epic Change), 40*fig*–41*fig*; tips for writing, 58–59. *See also* Commenting

BlueGreen Alliance (BGA), 31–32*fig*

Boing Boing blog, 60

Boston Marathon, 81

Branding, 24–25

Breslin, Ned, 209

Brigida, Danielle, 167, 168

Brinker, Nancy, 193, 194

Brown, Ian, 83

Bruske, Ed, 208

C

Calendars: Baldacious Campaign by the Leukemia and Lymphoma Society, 93*fig*; building an engagement ladder, 92

California State Parks Foundation, 119–120

CARE, 88

CARE: Cooperative for Assistance and Relief Everywhere, Inc., 118

Care2, 46

Catholic Relief Services, 88–89

Causes.org, 145, 147

Center for Social Impact Communication (Georgetown University), 6

Change.org, 47

charity: water: commitment to culture change by, 169–170; multiple channels used to engage supporters by, 47–48; origins and strategic plan for developing, 37–38; strategy of showing donors the impact of donations, 83; WaterForward online book fundraising by, 206*fig*–207

Charity Navigator, 106, 118

"Check-out" policy, 190

Churn rates: across the nonprofit sector, 69*fig*–70; buying and selling contact lists and, 138; description of, 69; plan for handling, 137

Cisco Systems, 176

Click through rates, 67, 68

Clicktivism, 28–29

Clinton Bush Haiti Fund, 97–98*fig*

CNN "Disaster in the Gulf Telethon," 147

Co-creating social change: cycle of, 27*fig*–28; keeping organizational metrics to assess, 29–31; listen for action element of, 118; process of, 25–26; slacktivism or micro-action form of, 28, 29–31; YouthNet's website redesign by volunteers example of, 26–27

Coleman, Lauren DeLisa, 55

Collaboration: DC Central Kitchen's partnership with DC Public School System, 208; 1Sky and 350.org, 31–32*fig*; partnerships to increase impact, 31–33; reduce competition and consolidate resources through, 203–204

Commenting: creating policy for responding to community, 194–195; National Wildlife Federation Facebook policy on, 195; strategies for managing critical, 195–197; by trolls, 57, 59, 196; Union of Concerned Scientists, 194. *See also* Blogs

"Communicating with Congress: Perception of Citizen Advocacy on Capital Hill" study (Congressional Management Foundation Study), 64

Communication: empowering and supporting subgroup, 130; experiment with tools for staff, 168–169; frequency of posts and, 135; keep shared goals prominent in, 127; language used for, 122–125; listen for action, 116–118, 193–194. *See also* Multichannel communication; Online communication

Community: building trust into the, 120–122; community mapping of your, 15; connect impact across platforms and campaigns, 132–133; designing engagement overview for the, 12*t*; empowering and supporting subgroups in your, 130; exercise your value in the, 133–139; focus on the needs of the, 122; frequency of posts to your, 135; identifying groups within your, 15; identifying shared goals (sweet spot) with your, 13*fig*–16; identifying your, 8–9*fig*; identifying your supporters in the, 44; managing the critics within your, 195–197; navigating tough conversations with your, 192–195; privacy concerns for your, 191–192; responding to concerns of your, 194–195; segmenting your, 96; staffing to support your, 133–134; time, action, and people elements of relationships with, 11–12

Community building: connecting the community across platforms, 127–133; customer service role in, 136–137; engaging in immediate conversations via text, 126–127; exercise your value in the community for, 133–139; four essential elements of multichannel strategy for, 115; keep shared goals prominent in communications, 127; legal concerns related to, 137; speak the same language for, 122–125; trust required for, 116–122

Community mapping: description and purpose of, 15; identifying the groups prior to, 15

Competition. *See* Nonprofit competition

Completion rates, 67

comScore study (2012), 48

Congress. *See* U.S. Congress

Congressional Management Foundation Study "Communicating with Congress," 64

Conservation International, 175

Contact lists, 138

Conversations, 116

Conversion rates, 66

Convio, 64, 172

Convio's Online Marketing Benchmark Study, 111–112

craigconnects, 83, 137

craigslist, 83, 137

Critic management strategies: be nice, 196; debunk misinformation but don't feed the trolls, 196; don't delete constituents' comments, 196–197; let the community come to your defense, 197; move the discussion offline, 196; respond quickly, 195–196. *See also* Trolls

CRM (constituent relationship management system): segmenting emails using, 49, 64; to send personalized thank email to donors, 106; Small Act's Thrive and SpotRight, 67; submitting emails to members of Congress using, 64

The crowd: defining, 9*fig*, 10–11; designing engagement overview for, 12*t*; time, action, and people elements of relationships with, 11–12

Culture change: commit to improved, 169–170; convincing funders on the benefits of, 182–183; convincing your senior staff and board on benefits of, 178–179; engaging leaders in, 177–183; getting rid of organizational silos through, 162–164; investing in people to continue positive, 183; preparing for the future through, 211. *See also* Nonprofit organizations; Organizational culture

Curation tools, 23

CurrentTV, 60

Customer service, 136–137

D

DailyKos, 47

DailyWorth, 208

Data sharing, 118

Database manager, 172

Days of Action campaign (350.org), 73

DC Central Kitchen, 208

DC Public School System, 208

Deepwater Horizon oil spill (2010): events leading to the, 141; National Wildlife Foundnation's campaign response to, 141–148

Delany, Colin, 61

Diabetes Hands Foundation, 123

Dickert, Stephan, 79

Digital Engagement (American Red Cross), 89

Din, Rabia, 181–182

Direct mail: capturing donor email addresses through, 100; description of, 85; promote your website and social media channels through, 100; strategies for raising money through, 99–100

"Disaster in the Gulf Telethon" (CNN), 147

Do Something, 131, 132–133

Donate callout boxes, 105

Donor Digital, 100

Donor motivations: connection between feeling and, 81–83; donors are influenced by their peers, 80–81; people are ruled by their emotions, 79–80; people want to save one person as, 79; people want to see their impact, 83

donorCentrics Internet, 85, 86

Donors: examining what motivates, 78–85; identifying your target, 91; the more suffering the more money will be raised by, 81–83; segmenting your, 95, 96; sending personalized thank you emails to, 106; Thank You Note from NOI to Donor Craig Newmark, 83, 84*fig*; treating them with respect, 95. *See also* Prospects; Supporters; Target audience

DoSomething.org website, 131

DOT ("Do One Thing") text pledges, 125, 126–127

E

Eberhard, James, 88

Email addresses: capturing through direct mail, 100; CRM for segmenting, 49, 64, 67

Emails: CRM (constituent relationship management system) to segment your, 49, 64, 67; delivery considerations for, 64; description and widespread of, 48; example of NWF action fund email alert, 50*fig*; fundraising appeals, 111–112; IAVA's #GoSilent, 153, 155*fig*, 156*fig*; NWF disaster response campaign use of, 145; petition drives through, 62; response rate to advocacy, 68–69; sending personalized thank you to donors via, 106; tips for raising more money with appeals via, 101–103; tips for successful, 48–49

Emotions: connection between donating and, 81–83; donors ruled by their, 79–80

Employee Free Choice Act, 55

Energizer Battery Company, 193

Engagement ladder, 92

Engaging Networks, 64

eNonprofit Benchmark Study, 68, 69, 70

Epic Change: Epic thanks campaign of, 174; multiple online channels used to communicate their goals, 40; Shepherds Secondary School photos and blog posted by, 40*fig*–41*fig*; staffing annual campaigns and events, 174; To Mama With Love projects of, 33–34, 174

Epic thanks campaign, 174

Epolitics.com, 61

Estrada, Joseph, 51

Event 360, 97

F

Facebook: Days of Action campaign (350.org) shared on, 73; fundraising using platform of, 87*fig*; Generations X and Y's attitude toward, 6; Greenpeace Brazil use of, 61; inherent fundraising value of, 88; "It Gets Better" campaign active on, 60; "like" as slacktivism or micro-action, 28, 29–31; nonprofit leveraging of, 2; NWF disaster response campaign use of, 144, 147; online traffic of, 1, 61; Open Graph tool of, 187; petition drives through, 62; sharing blogs on, 59; Surfrider Foundation's Ban the Bag campaign reposted on, 150

Facebook Causes, 109

Facebook Extra report, 69

Facebook Groups, 168–169

Facebook pages: California State Parks Foundation, 119–120; churn rates measuring interest in your, 69*fig*–70; Fan page, 29; fans of nonprofit sector, 70; frequency of postings to your, 135; IAVA's #GoSilent, 157*fig*, 159*fig*; include your website link on your, 119; "like" button widget of, 62; metrics of "like" on, 29; 1 Million Strong Against Offshore Drilling, 24, 25*fig*; posting central message on wall of, 65; Susan G. Komen for the Cure, 193–194

Fatarella, Daniela, 205

Faxing, 65

FCC, 189

Feelings: connection between donating and, 81–83; donors ruled by their, 79–80

Fickes, Ted, 53, 94

Flexibility in action, 134, 136

Flickr: Days of Action campaign (350.org) shared on, 73; fundraising using platform of, 87*fig*; NWF disaster response campaign use of, 142, 144

Focus on shared goals principle: community mapping of your community, 15; description of, 13; find the sweet spot with your community, 14; identifying what your community wants to do, 13*fig*–15

Four Models for Managing Digital (Silberman, Mogus, and Roy), 170

Frauzel, Tracy, 43

Freedom Connect, 132

Freedom of Information Act, 143

Fresh Start Catering, 208

Fundraising: baking bread metaphor for, 77–78; channels used for, 85–89; understanding the psychology of giving, 78–85. *See also* Multichannel fundraising campaign

Fundraising channels: mobile, 88–89; offline and direct mail, 85; online, 85–87; social media, 87*fig*–88

G

Gallagher, Tara, 149

Genachowski, Julius, 189

Generations X and Y, online use by, 6

Georgetown University's Center for Social Impact Communication, 6

Global advocacy reach: description of, 71; measurement challenges for, 73–74; seed the channels to extend your, 71–72; 350.org's, 72–73

Glynn, Charlie, 167

Goals: communicating shared, 127; creating multichannel advocacy plan by identifying, 39–42; focusing on your community's shared, 13*fig*–15; identifying your community, 15–16

Google Adwords, 67

Google Analytics, 18

Google docs, 168

Google Earth, 45

Google Insights, 67

Google tools: Adwords, 67; Google Analytics, 18; Google Earth, 45; Google Insights, 67; Google+, 59, 66–68

Google+: button widget of, 62; Google's "Search Plus Your World" integration with, 66–67; include your website link on, 119; sharing blogs on, 59

#GOSilent campaign. *See* IAVA's #GoSilent campaign

GOTV (Get Out the Vote), 51

GPS (Global Positioning System), 55

Movement building: challenge of mobilizing base for, 37; charity: water's use of storytelling for, 37–38; how photos and videos document, 74; KPIs measuring impact on the ground for, 67; listening for action as trigger for, 117; strategies for, 24–34. *See also* Advocacy campaigns

Movement building strategies: branding, 24–25; co-creation efforts, 25–28; organizational metrics used as, 29–31; partnerships to increase impact, 31–33; slacktivism or micro-action as, 28, 29–31; 350.org and 1Sky approach to, 31–33; To Mama With Love projects as example of, 33–34

Movements: characteristics of, 23–24; photos for documenting, 74; strategies and tools for building, 24–34, 67, 117. *See also* Social change

MoveOn.org, 63, 64

Multichannel advocacy campaigns: global reach of, 71–74; IAVA's #GoSilent, 150–160; metrics of your, 66–74; NWF's response to oil spill crisis, 141–148; planning your, 38–74; summary of how to put together your, 74–75; Surfrider Foundation's advocacy, 149–150

Multichannel advocacy planning: craft your core message, 43; engaging people by using multiple channels, 38; find out what makes your supporters tick, 45–46; identify advocacy targets, 42–43; identify realistic short-term and long-term goals and objectives, 39–42; know who your supporters are, 44; using multiple channels to engage supporters, 47–65; outline what actions you want people to take, 43; reaching your people in online communities, 46–47; understand how your supporters think, 44–45

Multichannel communication: blogs, 57–59; connect impact across, 132–133; delivering messages to advocacy targets across, 63–65; designing for distribution, 61–63; email, 48–50*fig*; fundraising, 85–89; identifying audience preference, 46; make it easy to find all your chapters and, 128–130; measuring impact across, 65–71; "missed calls" used as campaign tool, 53; mobile advertising using, 55; mobile applications, 55–57; mobile texting (SMS), 51–54*fig*, 62; online petition drive, 62; social networks, 61; spam laws covering, 52; Surfrider Foundation's advocacy campaign using, 149–150; tailoring messages and calls to action using, 48; video, 59–60; widgets and share buttons as, 62–63. *See also* Communication; Online communication

Multichannel fundraising campaign: be realistic, 113; email fundraising appeals, 111–112; evaluate your, 111; how to raise $100,000 through social media, 110–113; mobile channel used for, 107–109; planning a, 90–94; rolling out your,

94–99; showing results in real time, 107; strategies to increase donations, 99–109. *See also* Fundraising

Multichannel fundraising campaign implementation: conduct A/B testing, 95–99, 108; segment your donors and prospects, 95, 96; write series of fundraising appeals, 94–95

Multichannel fundraising campaign planning: define the messaging hook, 91; develop campaign goals and messaging, 90–91; establish goals, 90; establish staffing and resources, 92, 94; identify your target donors and their channels, 91; set up a fundraising calendar, 91–92, 93*fig*

Multichannel fundraising strategies: intro to direct mail channel, 99–100; intro to email channel, 101–103; intro to mobile channel, 107–109; intro to social networks channel, 109; intro to website channel, 103–107; tailor pitches to multiple channels, 111. *See also specific channel*

Multichannel Giving Benchmarking Report, 85, 86

Murrian, Michelle, 210

N

National Aquarium (Baltimore), 54

National Wildlife Federation (NWF): Action Fund Email Alert, 50*fig*; benefits of monthly staff meetings by, 167; creating knowledge sharing opportunities, 186; multichannel campaign response to oil spill crisis, 141–148

National Wildlife Federation (NWF) disaster response campaign: CNN "Disaster in the Gulf Telethon" donated ads to the, 147; for Deepwater Horizon oil drilling explosion, 141; example of fundraising appeal during, 146*fig*; Facebook, Twitter, Flickr, email, and Causes. org used for, 142, 144–145, 147; to fix the damage, 142–143; get resources to where they are needed, 142; getting information about the spill out to people, 142; help people cope work of, 143; lessons learned from the, 148; long-term goal of the, 143; online and offline channels used during, 143; results and metrics of, 147–148; text-to-give used during, 145–147; two goals of the, 141–142; website information on the, 144

National Women's Law Center (NWLC): "Being a Woman is Not a Pre-Existing Condition" campaign by, 41–42*fig*; goals set by, 41

Netvibes, 168

Network for Good, 85

Network identification, 9*fig*–10

New Organizing Institute (NOI), 83, 84*fig*

Newmark, Craig, 83, 137

NGP VAN, 172

Social change guiding principles: build a movement, 23–34; choose tools for discovery and distribution, 16–19; focus on shared goals, 13*fig*–16; highlight personal stories, 19–23; identify your community from the crowd, 8–12*t*; overview of, 7–8; putting principles into action, 34

Social change transition: access required for, 186–189; how-to guide for managing a rogue staffer, 197–199; managing the critics during, 195–197; navigating tough conversations during, 192–195; preparing your organization for, 185; privacy concerns during the, 190–192; your organization's process through the, 199

"Social graph," 210

Social media: "check-out" policy to track use of, 190; creating access through tools of, 187–188; using direct mail to promote your channels, 100; fundraising across channels of, 87*fig*–88; fundraising metrics on, 112; guide for staff use of, 175–176; how to raise $100,000 through, 110–111; mobile use statistics (2012), 5*fig*; Nonprofit Social Network Benchmark Report on nonprofit use of, 70; petition drives using, 62; preparing for a more social and mobile world of, 210; public forum of, 64–65; racial demographics and U.S. traffic rankings (2012) of, 4*fig*; year-to-year growth (2011 to 2012) of, 3*fig*

Social Media for Social Good (Baron presentation), 176

Social Network Benchmark Report, 68

Social network channel: Humane Society of the United States (USUS) use of, 109; leveraging the, 61

Social networks: using direct mail to promote your, 100; growth of, 2; how nonprofits can leverage, 61; identifying your, 9*fig*–10; "social graph" of your, 210

Social publishing tools: sharing personal stories using, 20–21; Tumblr blogging platform, 2, 18–19

Social sharing donations, 106–107

socialchangeanytime.com, 211

Spam laws, 52

Spring2Action, 81

Spur Communications, 204

Staff: break out of your comfort zone and take risks with your, 165–166*fig*; "check-out" policy for your, 190; commit to culture change by, 169–170; culture change support by broadbase, 179–182; culture change support by senior, 178–179; experiment with tools for communicating and collaborating with, 168–169; host weekly interdepartmental meetings with

your, 167; how-to guide for managing a rogue, 197–199; invest and believe in your, 164–170; private Facebook Groups used to communicate with, 168–169; seize opportunities offered by, 169; social media guide for, 175–176; welcome all ideas from your, 165. *See also* Nonprofit organizations

Staffing: annual campaigns and events, 174; establishing your fundraising campaign, 92, 94; hybrid model of, 170–171, 183; mobile programs, 176–177; social media and mobile, 173; to support your community, 133–134; website and online communications, 171

Staffing positions: database manager, 172; Internet director, 171; online campaigner, 172; shared social media, 173–174; web producer, 172

Startup thinking: charity: water's fundraising experiment as, 206*fig*–207; nonprofit adoption of, 204–205; test new ideas quickly, 205–206

State of News Media 2011 report (Pew Research Center), 57

"State of the Media: The Social Media Report" (Nielsen report), 2

Steinberg, Amanda, 208

Stop Online Piracy Act (SOPA), 188, 189

Storytelling/stories: charity: water's use of, 37–38; framing your email as, 49; highlighting personal, 19–23; how PPFA facilities the sharing of, 22; moving people into action using, 38–39; organizational storytelling and, 21–23; social publishing tools for sharing individual, 20–21; video used for, 59–60

Strahilevitz, Michal Ann, 80

"Suffering" motivation for donating, 81–83

Sunlight Foundation, 57

Sunlight Labs, 57

Supporters: finding out what makes them tick, 45–46; identifying your, 44; using multiple channels to engage, 47–65; reaching them through online communities, 46–47; understanding how they think, 44–45. *See also* Donors; Target audience

Surfrider Foundation: Ban the Bag campaign by, 149–150; "Rise Above Plastics" campaign by, 19

Survivors Connect, 132

Susan G. Komen for the Cure, 22, 24, 193–194

Susan G. Komen Race for the Cure, 80

Svet, David, 204

The sweet spot: finding your community, 14; focus on shared goals, 13*fig*–15

Swenson, Mwosi, 100

Sybrant, Milo, 106